IN AND OUT

OF THE

OLD MISSIONS OF CALIFORNIA

SAN CARLOS MISSION AND BAY OF MONTEREY — *Frontispiece.*

IN AND OUT

OF

THE OLD MISSIONS
OF CALIFORNIA

AN HISTORICAL AND PICTORIAL
ACCOUNT OF

THE FRANCISCAN MISSIONS

BY

GEORGE WHARTON JAMES

AUTHOR OF

"IN AND AROUND THE GRAND CANYON," "INDIANS
OF THE PAINTED DESERT REGION"
"INDIAN BASKETRY," ETC.

WITH 142 ILLUSTRATIONS FROM PHOTOGRAPHS

BOSTON
LITTLE, BROWN, AND COMPANY
1905

THE UNIVERSITY PRESS, CAMBRIDGE, U. S. A.

TO SCRAGGLES,

MY PET SPARROW AND COMPANION

---

*S*AINT FRANCIS, *the founder of the Franciscan order, without whom there would probably have been no missions in California, regarded the birds as his "little brothers and sisters." Just as I began the actual writing of this book I picked up in the streets a tiny song sparrow, wounded, unable to fly, and that undoubtedly had been thrust out of its nest. In a short time we became close friends and inseparable companions. Hour after hour she sat on my foot, or, better still, perched, with head under her wing, on my left hand, while I wrote with the other. Nothing I did, such as the movement of books, turning of leaves, etc., made her afraid. When I left the room she hopped and fluttered along after me. She died just as the book was receiving its finishing pages. On account of her ragged and unkempt appearance I called her Scraggles; and to her, a tiny morsel of animation, but who had a keen appreciation and reciprocation of a large affection, I dedicate this book.*

TABLE OF CONTENTS

LIST OF ILLUSTRATIONS

LIST OF ILLUSTRATIONS xiii

LIST OF ILLUSTRATIONS

FOREWORD

THE following pages are not offered as an original contribution to the subject of the Franciscan Missions in California. I am not a Spanish scholar, hence I have consulted no " original Spanish records," nor have I " brought to light important matters hitherto unknown." I am but one of the great mass of laymen who love the Old Missions for their own sake, for their history, for the noble deeds they have enshrined, for the good their builders did — and more than what they actually did, what they sought to do — for the Indians, whom the later comers, my own race, have treated so abominably. For nearly twenty-five years I have venerated them; I have made pilgrimages to them; and several times sent both artists and photographers to bring me their impressions of them. My own camera, with me, has peered into every kind of nook and cranny, and thousands of photographs and many mental impressions are the result. So now I put some of these on paper for others to share with me.

Experts have studied the history and digested it, and in my own readings I have browsed and culled wherever I could find anything that I thought would help make this story more complete and interesting. The fields from which I have reaped are many, and if, for any reason, save in the case of Bancroft, I have quoted and failed to give credit, I tender my apologies in advance, make confession, and ask for the absolution that I am sure, were I dealing with one of the old padres, would generously be given.

There are a few chapters upon which I have bestowed especial care, and in the presentation of which I have had nothing to guide me. These are the original portions of the book. The features that I believe have not been presented before, or at least so fully, are as follows: 1. An analysis of the Details of the Mission Style of Architecture. 2. The Condition of the Indians prior to, during, and immediately after the Mission Epoch, with a Brief Account of their Present State. 3. A Careful Survey of the Mural Decorations of the Missions. 4. A Pictorial Account of the Furniture, Pulpits, Doors, and Other Woodwork of the Missions. 5. A Pictorial Account of the Crosses, Candlesticks, and Other Silver and Brass Ware of the Missions. 6. A Pictorial Account of the Various Figures of the Saints at the Missions.

If any one objects that many of these details are trivial and unnecessary, I can only say that I regret that time and opportunity were not afforded me to make them more complete. Every year is bringing these Mission memorials nearer to their end, and it is important that even all the fragments, however trivial and unsatisfactory, be not lost.

While making acknowledgments of my general indebtedness to Bancroft, Shea, Salpointe, Zephyrin, Lummis, Palou, Clinch, I desire to note my especial gratitude to Bancroft and Zephyrin. The former, in spite of all the opprobrium and censure that have been visited upon him, is still the well of knowledge from which even his traducers draw most of their stock in trade. His wonderful work has never been surpassed in any history of any people yet written, and, in spite of his errors and failures, common decency at least should lead those whose hands are seldom away from his books to an honest acknowledgment of what they owe to him. For myself, I confess that most of the historic part of these pages is taken almost bodily from Bancroft. I have not even sought to disguise from my readers, by paraphrasing the matter, the source of its origin. All that I have done is to select and arrange it, and bring it together for convenient use.

To Father Zephyrin, the zealous historian of the Arizona and California Franciscans, my thanks are due for information cheerfully given.

I am also grateful to Messrs. C. C. Pierce & Co., of Los Angeles, Cal., whose artistic and copyrighted photographs they have freely allowed me to use; to Gustav Stickley, editor and proprietor of *The Craftsman*, for permission to use from the pages of that magazine certain articles and illustrations which he aided me to procure; to Mrs. A. S. C. Forbes for needed information; to Mr. Samuel Howe, of New York, for critical estimates of the silverware of the Missions, and to Father O'Sullivan, of Santa Clara, for many kind helps and suggestions.

I am also indebted for many courtesies to His Grace, Archbishop Montgomery, Bishop Conaty, and all the clergy (with but two exceptions) who now officiate at the respective Missions, and to these I tender my sincere and cordial thanks.

It will be well for the reader to gain a clear idea of the meaning of certain Spanish words, which Americans use with too great laxity of meaning, before reading further. In establishing their settlements the civil, religious, and military forces of the Spanish government were involved. A civic settlement was called the *pueblo*.

"This term, in its most extended meaning, may embrace towns of every description, from a hamlet to a city; and consequently might apply equally well to the missions, with their adjacent Indian villages (called by the Spaniards, *rancherías*), to the small villages springing up around the presidios, or to the regularly settled colony. However, in its special significance, a pueblo means a corporate town, with certain rights of jurisdiction and administration. . . . When complete it had a town council (ayuntamiento), composed of councilmen (regidores), judges (alcaldes), and a mayor."[1]

[1] Blackmar's Spanish Institutions of the Southwest.

The *mission* was the religious establishment, under the control of the laws, but especially directed by the Padre Presidente (father president), who at the beginning was Junipero Serra. The ultimate expectation of the king in establishing the Missions was that, as soon as the Indians were Christianized, civilized, and self-supporting, they (the Missions) were to be converted into civil pueblos, the Mission churches become parish churches, and the missionary give way to the regular parish priest.

The *presidio* was the fortress, the military establishment, which guarded the pueblo and the mission. As settlers made their homes around it, it gradually grew into the military town.

The *asistencia*, or chapel, was a branch station of one of the Missions, generally located where there was a large *ranchería* (or several of them) too far away from the regular Missions. These chapels afforded places for the services of the church, and were often most valuable adjuncts to the Mission proper. In effect they were the same as the outside stations of the later circuit rider of early Methodist days. The asistencia was sometimes called a *visita*, which one authority thus describes:

" A *visita* was a clerical outpost visited or to be visited by a padre residing elsewhere, having no resident minister of its own. There were usually several such in the vicinity of the principal missions where resided the padre, and all were under his administration; all also were considered as one 'mission' — the main one with its *pueblos de visita*."

Padre is Spanish for " father," and is the term commonly used by the people of that language, of the Catholic Church, to designate their " father confessors." The word has come to have a wider meaning to Americans, inasmuch as all Catholic priests of Spanish-American days are indiscriminately termed padres. In order, however, that there might be no possibility of misunderstanding, I wrote to Father Zephyrin asking him to explain their use of the word *padre* and its abbreviation, P., also why the Spanish writers invariably designate the Franciscan priests as *Fr.* this or that. Here is his lucid reply in full:

"In reply to your question as to why we use *Fr.* before our names, I have to say, the *Fr.* stands for *Fray*, which is Spanish for the Italian *Fra* and the Latin *Frater*, and indicates that the person so designated or designating himself belongs to a Religious Brotherhood, notably some one of the Mendicant Orders, as the Dominicans, Franciscans, and Capuchins, also Augustinians, which latter Martin Luther had entered. The term is not applicable to all Religious Orders; for instance, the Jesuit Fathers are never so designated. All the members of the Mendicant Orders are *Frailes* (plural form of *Fray*), or Brothers; therefore each one uses *Fr.* in writing his name.

"Some of the members, however, are priests, and some are not, nor do they aspire to the priesthood. These latter are termed *laicos*, or lay-brothers, to distinguish them from the priests, who in addition place *P.*, Padre,=Father, before the *Fr.* or *Fray*, in order to indicate their standing in the Brotherhood; but they both follow the same Rule. A priest, however, only uses *Fr.*, like the others, unless a distinction is called for, or when he is addressed by another person, or when spoken of by a third person. Thus in all the California records the 144 or 146 missionaries that labored in the twenty-one Missions always sign themselves *Fr.* or *Fray* this or that; whereas when they write of another they as a rule use the letters *P. Fr.* Hence it is impossible for any one not conversant with the standing of the missionaries to say that any particular one was either a priest or a simple Brother, because all have the *Fr.* Only those thus designated have been either Franciscans or Dominicans. It is so even now. However, for your information I will add that in the whole California history down to 1854 not one lay-brother appears. Every one was a priest, and consequently made the usual studies of a priest more or less thoroughly, just as is done now. Some were brilliant, some less so, just as is the case now with students of every branch of learning and of every calling; but all were animated, more or less zealously so, with the same motive: the Christianization and the civilization of the natives."

During the early years and, indeed, throughout the whole of the last century, especially after American occupation, there was much confusion in the use of the name *California*. During the time of the founding of the Missions on the Peninsula, California meant that region alone, practically speaking. Then, when Serra began his work in Alta California, the two were distinguished by the prefixes Baja (Lower) or Antiqua (Old), and Alta (Higher) or Nueva (New). But now to all United States Americans California means *alone* the State of that name. And so it will be used throughout this book. When Lower California, the peninsula belonging to Mexico, is meant, it will be distinguished, so that there can be no misapprehension. The term *California* will apply solely to the Golden State of the United States of North America.

In describing the Mission buildings I have used the Spanish *fachada* instead of the French *façade*. The former is as good American as the latter, and I see no reason for not using the word regularly. It is pronounced *fah-tchah-dah*.

I had originally intended to give in this volume the history of the Missions in New Mexico, Arizona (once an integral part of N. M.), Texas, and Lower California; but as this book grew it was found impossible without condensing to such an extent as to cripple the whole narrative. So, with the kind acquiescence of my obliging publishers, I have written nearly all I wished to say in these pages, and shortly they will publish a companion volume which will fully treat, with beautiful illustrations, of the missions of those equally historic and fascinating regions.

GEORGE WHARTON JAMES

August, 1905.

IN AND OUT OF THE OLD MISSIONS

CHAPTER I

THE FOUNDING OF THE CALIFORNIA MISSIONS

PERHAPS nowhere in the history of the world is there to be found a clearer example of the nothingness of Time and Place when man is absent than is presented in the history of California. It was the same California that it is now long centuries before Cabrillo first discovered it. It was still the same in the ages that it remained practically undisturbed after Cabrillo, until the time of Serra. And that was little over a century and a quarter ago. But see the change in that hundred and thirty years! The seed of man's enterprise once sown, how its fruits sprang forth!

Not the wildest conceptions of the Mission founders could have foreseen the results of their California enterprises. To see the land that they found in the possession of thousands of rude savages converted in one short century into the home of tens of thousands of happy, contented, progressive people would have been a wild vision indeed. God surely does work mysteriously, marvellously, His wonders to perform, and nothing is more wonderful than the rapid settlement of California with the choicest elements of America's Eastern civilization.

It seems almost as if the coming of Serra and his coadjutors — the best the Spaniards had to offer of earnestness, power, ability, and sympathetic brotherhood — was

1

prophetic of what the future had in store for California. America was to give of its best, — East, North, South, in its Starr King, Joseph and John LeConte, Frémont, and a host of others for its physical, mental, and spiritual development.

The East has not yet taken the full measure of the West, — not even as well as did Serra, Crespí, Palou, and Lasuen. The spirit of those men is still in the air, and the results are beyond the ken of all except the few whose vision is prophetic. The Pacific Coast States are yet in their swaddling-clothes. The world has yet to be astounded at their youth and matured manhood.

Many and diverse are the elements which have gone into the making of that " State of the Golden Gate " of which Americans generally are so proud. It has been the stage upon which strangely different actors have played their part — important or insignificant — and left their impress where they played. It has been a composite canvas upon which painters of every school have practised their art: a vivid mass of color here, a touch there, a single stroke of the brush yonder. Then, too, look at it as you will, stage or canvas, it had a marvellous natural setting. Curtains, side-wings, drops, scenes, accessories, suitable for every play, adequate for every requirement. Tragedy? Great mountains, awful snow storms, trackless sand-wastes, fearful deserts, limitless canyons, more ocean line than any other of the North American States, and the densest forests. Comedy? Semi-tropical verdure, orange blossoms, carpets of flowers, delicate waterfalls, the singing of a thousand varieties of birds, the gentlest zephyrs, the bluest of blue skies. What wonder, then, as its history is studied, as a whole or in parts, that it is unusually fascinating, and that it presents features of unique interest?

It has long been the belief of the English-speaking peoples that England is the one great colonizing power of all history; and, possibly, if extent of achievement be con-

PLATE II

SANTA INÉS MISSION

sidered this popular conception is true. Yet, considering
the time and conditions under which it took place, the student may be pardoned if he is inclined to give to Spain the
honor and credit of the larger achievement, — larger in
the difficulties to be overcome; larger in the spirit in which
it was undertaken; larger in its ultimate results; larger
in the wisdom by which its operators were directed; larger
in the marvellous manhood it developed. The discoveries
of Columbus had fired the imagination of the bold and
adventurous spirits throughout Europe. They believed
that the nether coast of India had been discovered by sailing westward instead of eastward as hitherto. For it must
not be overlooked that this was the popular belief for many
decades after Columbus; there was no knowledge that a
new continent had been discovered.

Four hundred years! How much may transpire in that
time. Columbus had sailed from Palos, Aug. 3, 1492, in
Spanish ships and backed by Spanish faith and money.
Fifty years previously the Byzantine Empire had sunk
under the weight of Turkish arms, and thus Europe was
opened up to vivifying influences from both East and West.
The dark ages were coming to an end. A flood of literature
and learning, science and art was released from the East,
and the discoveries in the West so fired men's imagination
that the mental and spiritual results bid fair to outrival
the material benefits.

The activity to which Spain was aroused was marvellous.
Fifty years saw expedition after expedition equipped with
fiery zeal and fervent enthusiasm. Ponce de Leon had
sailed from Puerto Rico and discovered Florida in 1512.
The following year Balboa discovered the Pacific. In 1517
and 1518 Córdoba and Grijalva sailed down the coast of
Yucatan, and the following year Cortés set forth from
Cuba to conquer the countries discovered by his two prede-
cessors. Born at Estremadura, Spain, seven years before
Columbus sailed, he was now, at 33 years of age, the alcalde

of Santiago, strong, crafty, brave, unscrupulous, am-
bitious, fearless, determined. The story of the conquest
of Mexico is more exciting and thrilling than any romance.
And let it not be forgotten that one of the *avowed* objects
his superior, Velasquez, had in sending him forth was the
conversion of the natives to Christianity. In all such expeditions a padre accompanied the explorers, and whatever
may have been the character, the motives, the religious or
irreligious life of the promoter or commander of the expedition, there can be no doubt as to the genuine piety, the
single-heartedness, the devotion and purity of the major
part of the priests who went along to undertake the conversion of the natives. Indeed, as Padre Salmeron truly
says of New Mexico:

" It is worth consideration that there has been no corner discovered in this New Spain in which the first Columbus was not
a fraile of St. Francis. They have ever been first to shed their
blood, that with such good mortar the edifice should be lasting
and eternal."

Mexico conquered, the Pacific Coast was reached, vessels
built upon its shores, and expeditions equipped for the
discovery of other lands, and the subjugation of their
peoples. Guzman, Becerra, Jimenez, Ulloa, Alarcon, and
Cabrillo were all important names on the Pacific Coast in
the first half of the sixteenth century.

And on the Atlantic events were transpiring that were
to lead to the ultimate colonization of our American Southwest, in what are now Arizona and New Mexico. For it
is indirectly to one of the Spanish explorations to the
Atlantic Coast that we owe their discovery.

How thrilling are the accounts of the adventures of
these early explorers. What direful risks men have
always taken to satisfy their lust for conquest, gold,
and power. How different results have been from what
they expected or anticipated. How short the distance the

most keen-sighted could peer into the dim obscurity of the future.

Think for a few moments of the proud and haughty Spanish don, with the high-sounding and potent name, Alvar Nuñez Cabeza de Vaca, treasurer of the expedition of Panfilo de Narvaez. In June, 1527, this adventurous and ill-fated leader started from Spain with a fleet of five ships and six hundred men, to conquer and colonize a province north of Panuco on the Gulf of Mexico. Storms, hurricanes, and general disaster followed him and his party as they neared the Gulf shores. In April, 1528, they anchored in Tampa Bay, and tired of buffetings by sea, the headstrong and wilful Narvaez resolved to march ashore and let the vessels follow along the coast. He and three hundred men and forty horses went inland. After incredible hardships they grew as weary of the land as before they had been of the sea, and, making five rude craft, those who were still alive embarked, intending to skirt the coast to Panuco. Six weeks of storm, thirst, hunger, exposure, and attack by Indians found the fleet divided. The boat commanded by Vaca, with one other, remained together. Their complete force numbered eighty men. These landed only to be taken captive by the Indians. Slavery was their lot until famine and pestilence swept away all but fifteen. Of this fifteen, four ultimately escaped, and after nine long years of wandering on foot, nakedness, starvation, adventures with wild beasts, to-day in slavery, to-morrow almost worshipped because of supposed supernatural powers, they found their way across the continent to the Spanish settlements in northwestern Mexico, — San Miguel in New Galicia, — April 1, 1536.

Vaca's stories, when, again clothed and in his right mind, he came in contact with the Spanish officers, made a wonderful impression. The hot blood of the *conquistadores* was aroused to go forth and take possession of the land, and it required great effort on the part of the viceroy to restrain them. He refused to allow any exploring expeditions to start until he had sent out a scouting party. Who should go? This was no pleasure trip. It was not to be a going forth " of an army with banners." It was to be a surveying of a country peopled with savages, where trackless deserts might be encountered, and frightful hardships anticipated with tolerable certainty. Priests — no matter of what church — have always made brave, adventurous, and successful explorers. " To seek and to save," — was not that their commission, given by Christ Himself? What, then, was danger, what suffering, torture, death itself? No greater reward could come to them than the crown of martyrdom. Hence their fearlessness, their persistency, their eagerness, their energy. Knowing this, the viceroy, Mendoza, asked Marcos de Niza, the chief of the band of Franciscan missionaries, to adventure forth, accompanied only by a fellow friar, and Stephen, a negro who had been one of Cabeza de Vaca's comrades, to spy out the land and report upon Vaca's stories. Marcos, accompanied by Fray Onorato, left Culiacan, March 7, 1539, penetrated into New Mexico, and from a hillside secretly surveyed one of the villages of Cibola, now known to us as the pueblos of Zuni. This was as far as he deemed it necessary to go. He therefore returned to Mexico and made his report.

It was Marcos's favorable report that led Coronado to start out on his great expedition, — the expedition that led to the subjugation of Zuni, the pueblos of the Hopi (or Moki), the Tiguas — Teewahs — of the Rio Grande Valley, and the discovery of the Grand Canyon of the Colorado River, Acoma, &c. Accompanying Coronado were three Franciscan friars, Marcos aforesaid, Fray Antonio Victoria, and Fray Juan de Padilla and Luis de Escalona, a lay brother. Marcos soon returned, and Antonio Victoria was compelled to do so by a broken leg; so Juan de Padilla and the lay brother were the first missionaries to enter the great field, now Arizona and New Mexico.

But Mexico proper, and all the newly established Central American provinces were being flooded with missionaries. The whole Church in Spain was alive with zeal to convert the vast populations of the new world. Jesuits, Dominicans, Jeromites, and Franciscans were alike active and zealous. Each order had its own work, and there was considerable rivalry, if not jealousy, between them.

Churches by the score, nay by the hundreds, were built, and missions established on every hand in what are now the Mexican provinces. But it was not until Russian aggression in the North rendered Spain fearful, that a real and determined effort was made to establish missions and promote colonization in Alta California; and this was two hundred and thirty years after Juan de Padilla had begun work in New Mexico.

In that two hundred and thirty years much had transpired in the Mission field of what is now New Mexico, Arizona, Texas, and Lower California. In another volume I shall present the results of the missionary labors of these years in the four districts named.

It had always been the intention of Spain to colonize Alta California, but the pressure of events elsewhere had prevented. The Church earnestly desired it in order to extend its dominion over the souls of the aborigines. These, according to the stern theology of the time, were eternally damned unless the saving offices of Holy Church were given to them, and full of earnestness and zeal the priests never ceased to urge the establishment of colonies and missions that they might accomplish that highly desirable end. But not until political events crowded the Spanish monarch into action was it effected.

Spain was already conducting a large and profitable trade with its possessions, the Philippines. It was a long sail across the Pacific Ocean to Mexican ports, and the

English free-booters often played sad havoc with the galleons laden with merchandise and other wealth on their passage. England had just gone to war with Spain (this was in 1760), and her naval activities were especially pernicious; Russia was crowding down from the North, having already established herself in Alaska, and Charles and his ministry began to feel the urgent necessity of doing something quickly if it were to be done at all.

It is not always a safe policy to conjecture results if certain events had happened, yet in this case it seems probable that the whole history of California would have been materially different, indeed that to-day California would not be ranged under the flag of the United States, had not King Charles sent out his colonizers and missionaries just at the time he did. Whether one believes or disbelieves in " the hand of God in history," it was at least exceedingly fortunate that the Missions were established by Spain, for in the course of time, she lost her hold in Mexico, and California became a province of the new Republic of Mexico. Now, had California at this time, or earlier, been under control of the Russians, who, it must not be forgotten, were slowly reaching down toward San Francisco from Alaska, and who later reached Mt. St. Helena and Fort Ross, — the latter but sixty-five miles north, — the United States would have had Russia to deal with instead of Mexico. California was seized because the United States was at war with Mexico. Two years after the seizure, gold was discovered, and California became a Mecca for the adventurers and the gold-lustful of the world.

Let us here briefly review the facts as they occurred, and then note what they would have been had Russia, instead of Spain, colonized California.

First: Spain assumes political control of California, and at the same time establishes the Missions.

Second: Mexico severs her relations with Spain, and California becomes a province of the Republic of Mexico.

Third: The United States and Mexico go to war; California is seized by the United States as a war measure, and finally becomes an integral part of United States territory.

Had the Russians gained a foothold in California prior to the Spanish Franciscans, it is scarcely possible that they would have relinquished the natural advantages afforded by so remarkable a base of supplies for their Alaskan colonies.

Had Russia owned or controlled California when gold was discovered, the territory would never have been relinquished; for, as yet, the United States has had no occasion to go to war with Russia. So it is apparent that California owes its place in the North American Union of States to Spain and the Franciscan Mission Fathers. Owing to this fact, the steps of the founders of these Missions assume new interest and greater importance.

Now to return after this brief digression which forestalls the actual events. Just at this particular juncture King Charles decided to banish the order of Jesuits completely from his dominions. To carry out this order in Mexico and the peninsula of Lower California (then, as now, a province of Mexico), he appointed Don José Galvez, a tried and trusted crown official, as *Visitador General* with almost plenary authority.

The Jesuits had long been growing in power. Their Missions were planted wherever the name of Spain was known. While many of the members of the Order were simple-hearted, honest toilers for God, others, and these the leaders, were fired with lust for political as well as ecclesiastical power. Possibly it was their success in gaining this power that led to their banishment. Writing in 1793, Gigedo unconsciously shows what influence they had in government circles. In his report upon Loreto, the capital of Lower California, he says:—

" It had as garrison a troop of cavalry, mounted and armed in accordance with the customs of the country ; its pay (including that of the crew of the vessel carrying supplies) amounted to $32,515, which was paid out of the royal treasury.   The Jesuits really collected and distributed this money, and also took care of the discipline and service of said troop, placed in commission for the sole purpose of defending and preserving the fifteen missions established and administered by the Society of Jesus."

It would be interesting could a full recital of the history of Jesuit expulsion from Spanish dominions be given. It is too long a story. It was the most extensive proscription known in European history.   Henry the Eighth's cruel treatment of the Carthusians and Bene- dictines affected a far less number than the action of Charles, this " Most Catholic King," in thus banishing, without open accusation or public trial, over six thousand men, many of them of the best families and the highest edu- cation. Ever since his accession to the throne he had seem- ingly been friendly to the Jesuits, indeed, had chosen one, Father Wendlingen, as tutor for his eldest son.   Suddenly, and without any reason which he was willing to give to the world, — it never was given and to this day is unknown, — he completely turned against them. A secret council was called, the proceedings of which were never recorded fully in the archives, and with a care and thoroughness that reveal a relentless purpose, arrangements were perfected for the arrest and deportation of every professed Jesuit in the Spanish dominions. In order that there might be no failure, the maps were studied, and a date fixed upon, so that the secret orders of the King might be carried out simultaneously in every part of his domain. This was not possible in the far-away colonies, but even there a later date was fixed, and the royal commissioners were required to see the decree enforced with exactitude at the time set. Galvez was the appointed officer for Mexico and Lower California.   Those who were arrested in Spain were de- ported to Italy, and those from Mexico were sent to the remote Island of Corsica. On landing, each man received a letter saying that so long as he remained there, refrained from criticising the act which had banished him, refrained from any communication, even with relatives in Spain or Mexico, he should receive a yearly allowance of one hundred dollars.   And then, to make the secrecy more effective, it added that if any one of them violated any of these conditions the yearly contribution would be withdrawn from all.

Thus it was that Lower California lost its Jesuit missionaries.

They were sixteen in number, officiating at fourteen Missions, which extended from Cape San Lucas, on the south, to Santa Maria, not far from the mouth of the Colorado River, on the north.   The story of the founding of these Missions by the Jesuits forms an interesting part of the companion volume to this, and their banishment from their arduous labors, in which many of them were expending the tireless energy of devoted lives, is pathetic in the extreme.

By the same royal order that banished the Jesuits the charge was laid upon the Franciscan College of San Fernando, in the City of Mexico, to send priests to take their place.   In casting about for a man to direct this important work, the unanimous choice fell upon Fray Junipero Serra. The fifteen others, hurriedly gathered together, were sent over to direct the affairs of the peninsula Missions.

Here Galvez found them when he arrived three months later.   Of his work in the peninsula the companion volume to this will fully treat.   What now concerns us is his action towards the colonization and missionizing of Alta California.   His orders upon the subject were clear and imperative: " Occupy and fortify San Diego and Monterey for God and the King of Spain." Galvez was a good son of the Church, full of enthusiasm, having good sense, great executive ability, considerable foresight, untiring energy, and decided contempt for all routine formalities.   He began his work with a truly Western vigor. Being invested with almost absolute power, there were none above him to interpose vexatious formalities to hinder the immediate execution of his plans.

In order that the spiritual part of the work might be as carefully planned as the political, Galvez summoned Serra. What a fine combination! Desire and power hand in hand! What nights were spent by the two in planning! What arguments, what discussions, what final agreements the old adobe rooms occupied by them must have heard! But it is by just such men that great enterprises are successfully begun and executed. For fervor and enthusiasm, power and sense, when combined, produce results. Plans were formulated with a completeness and rapidity that equalled the best days of the *conquistadores*. Four expeditions were to go: two by land and two by sea. So would the risk of failure be lessened, and practical knowledge of both routes be gained. Galvez had two available vessels: the " San Carlos " and the " San Antonio."

For money the visitor-general called upon the Pious Fund, which, on the expulsion of the Jesuits, he had placed in the hands of a governmental administrator. He had also determined that the Missions of the peninsula should do their share to help in the founding of the new Missions, and Serra approved and helped in the work.

When Galvez arrived he found Gaspar de Portolá acting as civil and military governor, and Fernando Javier Rivera y Moncada, the former governor, commanding the garrison at Loreto. Both were captains, Rivera having been long in the country. He determined to avail himself of the services of these two men, each of them to command one of the land expeditions. Consequently with great rapidity, for those days, operations were set in motion. Rivera in August or September, 1768, was sent on a commission to visit in succession all the Missions, gathering from each one all the provisions, live-stock, and implements

PLATE III

a. SAN DIEGO MISSION

b. SAN CARLOS MISSION

that could be spared. He was also to prevail upon all the
available families he could find to go along as colonists.
In the meantime others sent out by Galvez gathered in
church furniture, ornaments, and vestments for the Missions, and later Serra made a tour for the same purpose.
San José was named the patron saint of the expedition,
and in December the " San Carlos " arrived at La Paz
partially laden with supplies.

The vessel was in bad condition, so it had to be unloaded,
careened, cleaned, and repaired, and then reloaded, and in
this latter work both Galvez and Serra helped, the former
packing the supplies for the Mission of San Buenaventura
in which he was particularly interested, and Serra attending to those for San Carlos. They joked each other as they
worked, and when Galvez completed his task ahead of
Serra he had considerable fun at the Padre presidente's
expense. In addition to the two Missions named, one other,
dedicated to San Diego, was first to be established. By the
9th of January, 1769, the " San Carlos " was ready.
Confessions were heard, masses said, the communion administered, and Galvez made a rousing speech. Then
Serra formally blessed the undertaking, cordially embraced
Fray Parron, to whom the spiritual care of the vessel
was intrusted, the sails were lowered, and off started
the first division of the party that meant so much to
the future California. In another vessel Galvez went
along until the " San Carlos " doubled the point and
started northward, when, with gladness in his heart and
songs on his lips, he returned to still further prosecute
his work.

On the 15th of February the " San Antonio," under the
command of Perez, was ready and started. Now the land
expeditions must be moved. Rivera had gathered his
stock, etc., at Santa Maria, the most northern of the Missions, but finding scant pasturage there he had moved
eight or ten leagues farther north to a place called by the

Indians Velicatá. Fray Juan Crespí was sent to join Rivera, and Fray Lasuen met him at Santa Maria in order to bestow the apostolic blessing ere the journey began, and on the 24th of March Lasuen stood at Velicatá and saw the little band of pilgrims start northward for the land of the gentiles, driving their herds before them. What a procession it must have been! The animals, driven by Indians under the direction of soldiers and priests, straggling along or dashing wildly forward as such creatures are wont to do! Here, as well as in the starting of the " San Carlos " and " San Antonio," is a great scene for an artist, and some day canvases worthy the subjects should be placed in the California State Capitol at Sacramento.

Governor Portolá was already on his way north, but Serra was delayed by an ulcerated foot and leg, and, besides, he had not yet gathered together all the Mission supplies he needed, so it was May 15 before this division finally left Velicatá. The day before leaving, Serra established the Mission of San Fernando at the place of their departure, and left Padre Campa in charge.

Now blow, ye favoring winds, and, ye baffling storms, be restrained; the sea has upon its bosom two vessels that are to begin the history of the Golden State, and near by, comparatively speaking, on the land two divisions of weary pilgrims are marching along, in one of which is a man who is to leave his powerful impress upon the new country to which he journeys with so much fiery zeal and religious enthusiasm.

Padre Serra's diary, kept in his own handwriting during this trip from Loreto to San Diego, is now in the Edward E. Ayer Library in Chicago. Some of his expressions are most striking. In one place, speaking of Captain Rivera's going from Mission to Mission to take from them " whatever he might choose of what was in them for the founding of the new Missions," he says: " Thus he did;

and altho' it was with a somewhat heavy hand, it was
undergone for God and the king."

The work of Galvez for Alta California was by no means
yet accomplished. Another vessel, the " San José," built
at his new shipyard, appeared two days before the " San
Antonio " set sail, and soon afterward Galvez went across
the gulf in it to secure a load of fresh supplies. On
the 16th of June the " San José " sailed for San Diego
as a relief boat to the " San Carlos " and " San Antonio,"
but evidently met with misfortune, for three months later
it returned to the Loreto harbor with a broken mast and
in general bad condition. It was unloaded and repaired
at San Blas, and in the following June again started out,
laden with supplies, but never reached its destination, disappearing forever without leaving a trace behind.

The " San Antonio " first arrived at San Diego. About
April 11, 1769, it anchored in the bay, and awakened in
the minds of the natives strange feelings of astonishment
and awe. Its presence recalled to them the " stories of the
old," when a similar apparition startled their ancestors.
That other white-winged creature had come long generations ago, and had gone away, never to be seen again. Was
this not to do likewise? Ah, no! in this vessel was contained the beginning of the end of the primitive man.
The solitude of the centuries was now to be disturbed and
its peace invaded; aboriginal life was to be destroyed forever. The advent of this vessel was the death knell of the
Indian tribes. Now was to begin the actual change in the
life of the California Indians, such a change as they had
never before known, perhaps, in the whole of their history.
As we look back upon it, the picture is a fascinating one.
A handful of priests, hampered by long gowns, in a far-
away, strange land, surrounded by a vast population of
aborigines, neither as wild and ferocious nor as dull and
stupid as various writers have described them, yet brave,
courageous, liberty-loving, and self-willed enough to render

their subjugation a difficult matter. With a courage that was sublime in its very boldness, and which, better than ten thousand verbal eulogies, shows the self-centered confidence and mental poise of the men, this handful of priests grappled with their task, brought the vast horde of un-tamed Indians under subjection, trained them to systematic work, and in a few short years so thoroughly accomplished what they had determined, that the Mission buildings were erected by these former savages, who were made useful workers in a large diversity of fields.

Little, however, did either the company on board the " San Antonio " or the Indians themselves conceive such thoughts as these on that memorable April day.

But where was the " San Carlos," which sailed almost a month earlier than the " San Antonio "? She was strug-gling with difficulties, — leaking water-casks, bad water, scurvy, cold weather. Therefore it was not until April 29 that she appeared. In vain the captain of the " San Antonio " waited for the " San Carlos " to launch a boat and to send him word as to the cause of the late arrival of the flagship; so he visited her to discover for himself the cause. He found a sorry state of affairs. All on board were ill from scurvy. Hastily erecting canvas houses on the beach, the men of his own crew went to the relief of their suffering comrades of the other vessel. Then the crew of the relieving ship took the sickness, and soon there were so few well men left that they could scarcely attend the sick and bury the dead. Those first two weeks in the new land, in the month of May, 1769, were never to be for-gotten. Of about ninety sailors, soldiers, and mechanics, less than thirty survived; over sixty were buried by the wash of the waves of the Bay of Saint James.

Then came Rivera and Crespí, with Lieutenant Fages and twenty-five soldiers.

Immediately a permanent camp was sought and found at what is now known as Old San Diego, where the two

PLATE IV

FIGURE OF CHRIST, MISSION SAN JOSÉ ORPHANAGE

old palms still remain, with the ruins of the *presidio* on the hill behind. Six weeks were busily occupied in caring for the sick and in unloading the " San Antonio." Then the fourth and last party of the explorers arrived, — Governor Portolá on June 29, and Serra on July 1. What a journey that had been for Serra! He had walked all the way, and when but two days out his badly ulcerated leg began to trouble him. Portolá wished to send him back, but Serra would not consent. He called to one of the muleteers and asked him to make a salve for his wound just such as he would put upon the saddle galls of one of his animals. It was done, and in a single night the ointment and the Father's prayers worked the miracle of healing.

After a general thanksgiving, in which exploding gunpowder was used to give effect, a consultation was held, at which it was decided to send back the " San Antonio " to San Blas for supplies, and for new crews for herself and the " San Carlos." A land expedition under Portolá was to go to Monterey, while Serra and others remained at San Diego to found the Mission. The vessel sailed, Portolá and his band started north, and on July 16, 1769, Serra raised the Cross, blessed it, said mass, preached, and formally established the Mission of San Diego de Alcalá.

It mattered not that the Indians held aloof; that only the people who came on the expedition were present to hear. From the hills beyond, doubtless, peered and peeped the curious natives. All was mysterious to them. Later, however, they became troublesome, stealing from the sick and pillaging from the " San Carlos." At last, they made a determined raid for plunder, which the Spanish soldiers resisted. A flight of arrows was the result. A boy was killed and three of the new-comers wounded. A volley of musket-balls killed three Indians, wounded several more, and cleared the settlement. After such an introduction, there is no wonder that conversions were slow.

2

Not a neophyte gladdened the Father's heart for more than a year.

In the meantime, Portolá, Crespí, Rivera, and Fages were on their way north. They reached the Bay of Monterey and, failing to recognize it, passed farther north, where they saw the Bay of San Francisco. This was not the great inland sea we now know by that name, but the water under Point Reyes, which for years had been thus known. It was on this expedition, however, that Ortega discovered the present-known Bay of San Francisco, although it was not until several years later that it received that name.

Disheartened and weary, the party returned to San Diego; only to bring sorrow and sadness to the sick and waiting ones at that place. Portolá announced his decision to return to Mexico and to abandon the enterprise. But this was not to be. When hope seemed to have gone, and waiting had become despair, the " San Antonio " returned with abundant supplies. Oh, what a blessed vision was that of the long-looked-for vessel on the very day the abandonment had been decided! Captain Perez had started from La Paz with instructions to proceed directly to Monterey. Of course, he knew nothing of the return of the party from that point, and although the natives of the Santa Barbara channel informed him of such return, he would have gone on, had not the loss of an anchor compelled him to return to San Diego to replace it from the " San Carlos." Thus, the small matter of losing an anchor perhaps led to the saving of the enterprise and to the founding of the Missions as planned.

With new energy, vigor, and hope, Portolá set out again for the search of Monterey, this time accompanied by Serra as well as Crespí. This time the attempt was successful. They recognized the bay, and on June 3, 1770, a shelter of branches was erected on the beach, a cross made ready near an old oak, the bells were hung and blessed, and the

services of founding began. Padre Serra preached with
his usual fervor; he exhorted the natives to come and be
saved, and put to rout all infernal foes by an abundant
sprinkling of holy water. The Mission was dedicated to
San Carlos Borromeo.

Mrs. Leland Stanford recently erected at Monterey a
marble statue of Serra standing in a boat, about to land
at that point. On the pedestal is a tablet which recounts
his heroic deeds.

Thus two of the long desired Missions were established,
and the passion of Serra's longings, instead of being as-
suaged, raged now all the fiercer. It was not long, however, before he found it to be bad policy to have the Missions for the Indian neophytes too near the *presidio*, or barracks for the soldiers. These latter could not always be
controlled, and they early began a course which was utterly
demoralizing to both sexes, for the women of a people
cannot be debauched without exciting the men to fierce
anger, or making them as bad as their women. Hence
Serra removed the Missions: that of San Diego six miles
up the valley to a point where the ruins now stand, while
that of San Carlos he re-established in the Carmelo valley.

The Mission next to be established should have been
San Buenaventura, but events stood in the way; so, on
July 14, 1771, Serra (who had been zealously laboring
with the heathen near Monterey), with eight soldiers, three
sailors, and a few Indians, passed down the Salinas River
and established the mission of San Antonio de Padua.
The site was a beautiful one, in an oak-studded glen, near
a fair-sized stream. The passionate enthusiasm of Serra
can be understood from the fact that after the bells were
hung from a tree, he loudly tolled them, crying the while
like one possessed: " Come, gentiles, come to the Holy
Church, come and receive the faith of Jesus Christ! "
Padre Pieras could not help reminding his superior that
not an Indian was within sight or hearing, and that it

would be more practical to proceed with the ritual. One
native, however, did witness the ceremony, and he soon
brought a large number of his companions, who became
tractable enough to help in erecting the rude church, barracks, and houses with which the priests and soldiers were
compelled to be content in those early days.

On September 8, Padres Somera and Cambon founded
the Mission of San Gabriel Arcángel, originally about
six miles from the present site. Here, at first, the natives
were inclined to be hostile; a large force under two chieftains appearing, in order to prevent the priests from holding their service. But at the elevation of a painting of
the Virgin, the opposition ceased, and the two chieftains
threw their necklaces at the feet of the Beautiful Queen.
Still, a few wicked men can undo in a short time the work
of many good ones. Padre Palou says that outrages by
soldiers upon the Indian women precipitated an attack
upon the Spaniards, especially upon two, at one of whom
the chieftain (whose wife had been outraged by the man)
fired an arrow. Stopping it with his shield, the soldier
levelled his musket and shot the injured husband dead.
Ah! sadness of it! The unbridled passions of men of
the new race already foreshadowed the death of the old
race, even while the good priests were seeking to ele-
vate and to christianize it. This attack and consequent
disturbance delayed still longer the founding of San
Buenaventura.

On his way south (for he had now decided to go to
Mexico), Serra founded, on September 1, 1772, the Mission of San Luis Obispo de Tolosa. The natives called the
location Tixlini, and half a league away was a famous
canyada in which Fages, some time previously, had killed
a number of bears to provide meat for the starving people
at Monterey. This act made the natives well disposed towards the priests in charge of the new Mission, and they
helped to erect buildings, offered their children for baptism,

and brought of their supply of food to the priests, whose stores were by no means abundant.

While these events were transpiring Governor Portolá had returned to Lower California, and Lieutenant Fages was appointed commandant in his stead. This, it soon turned out, was a great mistake. Fages and Serra did not work well together, and, at the time of the founding of San Luis Obispo, relations between them were strained almost to breaking. Serra appears to have had just cause for complaint. The enthusiastic, impulsive missionary, desirous of furthering his important religious work, believed himself to be restrained by a cold-blooded, official-minded soldier, to whom routine was more important than the salvation of the Indians. Serra complained that Fages opened his letters and those of his fellow missionaries; that he supported his soldiers when their evil conduct rendered the work of the missionaries unavailing; that he interfered with the management of the stations and the punishment of neophytes, and devoted to his own uses the property and facilities of the Missions.

In the main, this complaint received attention from the Junta in Mexico. Fages was ultimately removed, and Rivera appointed governor in his place. More missionaries, money, and supplies were placed at Serra's disposal, and he was authorized to proceed to the establishment of the additional Missions which he had planned. He also obtained authority from the highest powers of the Church to administer the important sacrament of confirmation. This is a right generally conferred only upon a bishop and his superiors, but as California was so remote and the visits of a bishop impossible, it was deemed appropriate to grant this privilege to Serra.

Rejoicing and grateful, the earnest president sent Padres Fermin Francisco de Lasuen and Gregorio Amurrio, with six soldiers, to begin work at San Juan Capistrano. This occurred in August, 1775. On the thirtieth of the following October, work was begun, and everything seemed auspicious, when suddenly, as if God had ceased to smile upon them, terrible news came from San Diego. There, apparently, things had been going well. Sixty converts were baptized on October 3, and the priests rejoiced at the success of their efforts. But the Indians back in the mountains were alarmed and hostile. Who were these white-faced strangers causing their brother aborigines to kneel before a strange God? What was the meaning of that mystic ceremony of sprinkling with water? The demon of priestly jealousy was awakened in the breasts of the *tingaivashes* — the medicine men — of the tribes about San Diego, who arranged a fierce midnight attack which should rid them forever of these foreign conjurers, the men of the " bad medicine."

Exactly a month and a day after the baptism of the sixty converts, at the dead of night, the mission buildings were fired and the eleven persons of Spanish blood were awakened by flames and the yells of a horde of excited savages. A fierce conflict ensued. Arrows were fired on the one side, gun-shots on the other, while the flames roared in accompaniment and lighted the scene. Both Indians and Spaniards fell. The following morning, when hostilities had ceased and the enemy had withdrawn, the body of Padre Jayme was discovered in the dry bed of a neighboring creek, bruised from head to foot with blows from stones and clubs, naked, and bearing eighteen arrow-wounds.

The sad news was sent to Serra, and his words at hearing it, show the invincible missionary spirit of the man: " God be thanked! Now the soil is watered; now will the reduction of the Dieguinos be complete! "

At San Juan Capistrano, however, the news caused serious alarm. Work ceased, the bells were buried, and the priests returned.

The reader's attention is directed now to another part

PLATE V

a. SAN GABRIEL MISSION

b. SAN LUIS OBISPO BEFORE RESTORATION

of the King of Spain's dominions, soon to be closely connected at this stage of affairs with the California Missions. In Western New Mexico (in that portion now called Arizona) there were several Missions not far from the presidio of Tubac, which is now a small village some forty miles south of Tucson. It was deemed desirable that a road should be established between these New Mexico (Arizona) points and the California Missions, and, as a midway stopping place, it was decided to establish Mission settlements on the Colorado River.

For many years, — indeed ever since the days of the Jesuits, — when the revered Padre Kino was at work among the Pimas, it had been purposed to establish Missions among the Yuma Indians on the Colorado River. Accordingly, in 1774, Don Juan Bautista de Anza, captain of the presidio of Tubac, left that post on the 8th of January with a body of thirty-four men, sixty-five cattle, and 140 horses, and accompanied by Padres Garcés and Diaz. Anza was to find a means of communication between Sonora (his post of Tubac was in Northern Sonora, which reached up as far as the Gila River), and the Missions of California. He arrived at San Gabriel May 22, and then went to Monterey with Padre Serra, who reached San Gabriel from San Diego at the time of his arrival.

As they passed through the Colorado River region the priests investigated conditions as carefully as possible in regard to the foundation of Missions, and on the return trip, Garcés made a prolonged visit in order that he might add to his knowledge. Some three years previously he had made a survey of the country and its inhabitants. He was fired with the same untiring zeal that dominated Serra, and he never rested until the desire of his heart in the establishment of Missions for the conversion of the Yumas was accomplished. These Missions will be referred to elsewhere.

This journey of Anza's was the first exploration across

the vast waste of country stretching from Western Arizona, over the Colorado Desert, to the California Missions, though Garcés had already been as far as the Colorado River.

The first trip thus successfully accomplished, the new viceroy, Bucareli, instructed Anza to proceed to Sonora and Sinoloa to recruit soldiers and settlers for a new presidio which he had decided to establish at San Francisco. The party was made up in the presidio of San Miguel de Orcasitas, and marched up to Tubac, where a complete roster was made by Padre Font, who accompanied the expedition, and whose diary of the trip is still in existence in the Library of Brown University, Providence, R. I.

On their arrival at San Gabriel, January 4, 1776 (memorable year on the other side of the continent), they found Rivera had arrived the day before, on his way south to quell the Indian disturbances at San Diego, and Anza on hearing the news, deemed the matter of sufficient importance to justify his turning aside from his direct purpose and going south with Rivera. Taking seventeen of his soldiers along, he left the others to recruit their energies at San Gabriel, but the inactivity of Rivera did not please him, and, as things were not going well at San Gabriel he soon returned and started northward. It was a weary journey, the rains having made some parts of the road well-nigh impassable, and even the women had to walk. Yet on the 10th of March they all arrived safely and happily at Monterey, where Serra himself came to congratulate them.

After an illness which confined him to his bed, Anza, against the advice of his physician, started to investigate the San Francisco region, as upon his decision rested the selection of the site. The bay was pretty well explored, and the site chosen, near a spring and creek, which was named from the day, — the last Friday in Lent, — *Arroyo de los Dolores*. Hence the name so often applied

PLATE VI

b. CURVED ARCH OVER CHAPEL DOORWAY, SAN LUIS REY

a. SACRISTY SIDE OF DOORWAY, SAN JUAN BAUTISTA

shall build their houses as best they may, and dwell in them; shall open the proper ditches for the irrigation of their lands, placing on their boundary lines, instead of landmarks, useful fruit or forest trees, at the rate of ten to the Field; and equally that they shall open the *acequia* or *zanja madre* (mother ditch), build a reservoir and other public works necessary to benefit the crops."

Settlers are explicitly instructed in such matters even as the breeding of their stock, and distinctly forbidden to kill one of the original head given to him within the term of five years.

Matters outside their immediate California jurisdiction also gave considerable worry to the authorities. Russia and England were constantly buzzing about, like troublesome flies, and Spain was irritated and disturbed. One has but to read the report of Viceroy Gigedo to see how the Spanish felt about English and Russian aggressions. Explorations were pushed far to the north, and landings were made at Nutka and elsewhere, and formal possession taken. April 14, 1789, in an order to Gigedo, the King informed him of the protest he had lodged with Russia " stating therein that the subjects of that power should not found establishments on our northern coasts of the Californias."

Trouble was made with the English for landing at Nutka, two vessels being seized and taken as prisoners to San Blas. These were ultimately set at liberty, and after considerable negotiations between the courts of Spain and England, the King of Spain by royal letter, dated May 12, 1791, ordered that Nutka should be transferred to the English. It was at this transfer that Vancouver, the English captain, insisted that the boundary between Spanish and English possessions on the California coast should be the port of San Francisco. On reference of the matter, however, to higher authority, the bounds were settled more in accord with the claims of the Spanish. In spite of this dogged insistence of Vancouver he was well treated by the officials at Monterey, and Gigedo reports:

"He expressed to me in writing heartfelt thanks, and in proof of his gratitude, made a gift, of the value of two thousand dollars, more or less, to the 'presidio' and mission of Monterey in implements useful for agriculture and timber cutting, beads and other small articles."

One other matter of geographical importance it is as well to understand at this point. Knowledge of the Northwest was still so imperfect that therein lay one great secret of the fears of the Spanish. They deemed it possible that a *strait or passage between the Atlantic and Pacific* might yet be found, and that if this were to be discovered by some foreign and hostile power it would place the New Mexico Colonies and Missions as well as those of California in jeopardy. In 1793, Viceroy Gigedo, in making his most useful, interesting, and exhaustive report, fully discusses this matter.

When the Columbia River's mouth was discovered it was thought that it was possibly the entrance to the channel which connected the two oceans. He urged the necessity for exploring it; for, said he:

"If this river should be the passage between the two oceans, then we would have acquired all necessary information about the volume of water it carries, the rapidity or slowness of the current, the Indian tribes either nomadic or stable which live on its banks, and the place more or less accessible, where the river empties into the Atlantic."

But with practical common sense Gigedo discountenanced the further extension of territory without reason, and, in summing up the results of what the various explorations had accomplished, says that "during the period of twenty-five years many millions of dollars have been expended in establishing and maintaining the new

PLATE VII

b. FACHADA OF SAN BUENAVENTURA MISSION

a. FACHADA OF SAN FRANCISCO MISSION

settlements of Upper California; in repeated explorations of its northern coasts; and in the occupation of Nutka."

The same month in which Palou dedicated the Northern Mission, found Serra, with Padre Gregorio Amurrio and ten soldiers, wending their way from San Diego to San Juan Capistrano, the foundation of which had been delayed the year previous by the San Diego massacre. They disinterred the bells and other buried materials and without delay founded the Mission. With his customary zeal, Serra caused the bells to be hung and sounded, and said the dedicatory mass on November 1, 1776. The original location of this Mission, named by the Indians *Sajirit*, was approximately the site of the present church, whose pathetic ruins speak eloquently of the frightful earthquake which later destroyed it.

Aroused by a letter from Viceroy Bucareli, Rivera hastened the establishment of the eighth Mission. A place was found near the Guadalupe River, where the Indians named *Tares* had four *rancherías*, which they called *Thamien*. Here Padre Tomás de la Peña planted the cross, erected an *enramada*, or brush shelter, and on January 12, 1777, said mass, dedicating the new Mission to the Virgin, Santa Clara, one of the early converts of Francis of Assisi.

On February 3, 1777, the new Governor of Alta California, Felipe de Neve, arrived at Monterey and superseded Rivera. He quickly established the *pueblo* of San José, and, a year or two later, Los Angeles, the latter under the long title of the *pueblo* of " Nuestra Señora, reina de los Angeles," — Our Lady, Queen of the Angels.

For many years, — indeed ever since the days of the Jesuits, — when the revered Padre Kino was at work among the Pimas, it had been purposed to establish Missions among the Yuma Indians on the Colorado River. But not until 1775-6 was anything definite accomplished. Then, Francisco Garcés and Tomás Eixarch visited the

Yumas, on the site of what is now the United States Indian School, and were well received by a local chief named Palma. The order for the establishment of Missions at this point was ultimately given by General Croix, on March 20, 1780. With fateful stubbornness this man, unfamiliar with the dangerous conditions, ordered the introduction of a system of management altogether different from that which obtained elsewhere. Indians and Spaniards were to live promiscuously in the *pueblo*. There was to be no distinct mission for the former, and the priests were given no temporal control over their converts. Indeed, it was to be a modern town, where colonists and natives should live in proximity, with the priests as pastors and teachers, under a kind of semi-military government. The *pueblo* was named " La Purísima Concepción," and was situated on the California side, where the Indian school now stands. Garcés and Barreneche were its missionaries. A little later, San Pedro y San Pablo de Bicuñer was established, some eight or ten miles farther down the river, on the California side. These were ill-fated establishments, unfortunate experiments in colonization, destined to offer sad proofs of the determination of the Yumas, shown even to-day, not to yield anything of their belief to others. They were the scenes of pathetic preparations for martyrdom, and finally rude and terrible butcheries. Priests, settlers, soldiers, and Governor Rivera himself perished in the terrific attack. Forty-six men met an awful fate, and the women were left to a slavery more frightful than death. This was the last attempt made by the Spaniards to missionize the Yumas.

With these sad events in mind the Fathers founded San Buenaventura on March 31, 1782. Serra himself preached the dedicatory sermon. The Indians came from their picturesque conical huts of tule and straw, to watch the raising of the Cross, and the gathering at this dedication was larger than at any previous ceremony in California;

more than seventy Spaniards with their families, together with large numbers of Indians, being there assembled.

The next month, the *presidio* of Santa Barbara was established, and later the Mission of the same name.

In the end of 1783, Serra visited all the southern Missions to administer confirmation to the neophytes, and in January, 1784, he returned to San Carlos at Monterey. Then he visited the two northern Missions of Santa Clara and San Francisco, returning home in June. His last days were saddened by the death of his beloved friend and brother, Crespí, and embittered by contests with the military authorities for what he deemed the right. His last act was to walk to the door, in order that he might look out upon the beautiful face of Nature. The ocean, the sky, the trees, the valley with its wealth of verdure, the birds, the flowers — all gave joy to his weary eyes. Returning to his bed, he " fell asleep," and his work on earth ended. He was buried by his friend Palou at his beloved Mission in the Carmelo Valley, and there his dust now rests.

His successor as the president of the Missions was Fermin Francisco Lasuen, who, at the time of his appointment, was the priest in charge at San Diego. He was elected by the directorate of the Franciscan College of San Fernando, in the City of Mexico, February 6, 1785, and on March 13, 1787, the Sacred Congregation at Rome confirmed his appointment, according to him the same right of confirmation which Serra had exercised. In five years this Father confirmed no less than ten thousand, one hundred thirty-nine persons.

Santa Barbara was the next Mission to be founded. For awhile it seemed that it would be located at Montecito, now the beautiful and picturesque suburb of its larger sister; but President Lasuen doubtless chose the site the Mission now occupies. Well up on the foothills of the Sierra Santa Inés, it has a commanding view of valley, ocean, and islands beyond. Indeed, for outlook, it is doubtful if any other Mission equals it. It was formally dedicated on December 4, 1786.

Various obstacles to the establishment of Santa Barbara had been placed in the way of the priests. Governor Fages wished to curtail their authority, and sought to make innovations which the Padres regarded as detrimental in the highest degree to the Indians, as well as annoying and humiliating to themselves. This was the reason of the long delay in founding Santa Barbara. It was the same with the following Mission. It had long been decided upon. Its site was selected. The natives called it *Algsacupi*. It was to be dedicated "to the most pure and sacred mystery of the Immaculate Conception of the most Holy Virgin Mary, Mother of God, Queen of Heaven, Queen of Angels, and Our Lady" : a name usually, however, shortened in common parlance to "La Purísima Concepción." On December 8, 1787, Lasuen blessed the site, raised the Cross, said mass and preached a sermon; but it was not until March, 1788, that work on the buildings was begun. An adobe structure, roofed with tiles, was completed in 1802, and, ten years later, destroyed by earthquake.

The next Mission founded by Lasuen was that of Santa Cruz. On crossing the coast range from Santa Clara, he thus wrote: "I found in the site the most excellent fitness which had been reported to me. I found, beside, a stream of water, very near, copious, and important. On August 28, the day of Saint Augustine, I said mass, and raised a cross on the spot where the establishment is to be. Many gentiles came, old and young, of both sexes, and showed that they would gladly enlist under the Sacred Standard. Thanks be to God!"

On Sunday, September 25, Sugert, an Indian chief of the neighborhood, assured by the priests and soldiers that no harm should come to him or his people by the noise of

PLATE VIII

Copyright, 1899, by G. P. Thresher

b. MISSION BELL AT SANTA BARBARA

a. TILED PYRAMIDAL ROOF TO BELL TOWER, MONTEREY

exploding gunpowder, came to the formal founding. Mass was said, a *Te Deum* chanted, and Don Hermenegildo Sol, Commandant of San Francisco, took possession of the place, thus completing the foundation. To-day nothing but a memory remains of the Mission of the Holy Cross.

Lasuen's third Mission was founded in this same year, 1791. He had chosen a site, called by the Indians *Chuttusgelis*, and always known to the Spaniards as Soledad, since their first occupation of the country. Here, on October 9, Lasuen, accompanied by Padres Sijar and Garcia, in the presence of Lieutenant José Argüello, the guard, and a few natives, raised the Cross, blessed the site, said mass, and formally established the Mission of " Nuestra Señora de la Soledad."

One interesting entry in the Mission books is worthy of mention. In September, 1787, two vessels belonging to the newly founded United States sailed from Boston. The smaller of these was the " Lady Washington," under command of Captain Gray. In the Soledad Mission register of baptisms, it is written that on May 19, 1793, there was baptised a Nootka Indian, twenty years of age, " Inquina, son of a gentile father, named Taguasmiki, who in the year 1789 was killed by the American Gret (undoubtedly Gray), Captain of the vessel called *Washington*, belonging to the Congress of Boston."

For six years no new Missions were founded: then, in 1797, four were established, and one in 1798. These, long contemplated, were delayed for a variety of reasons. It was the purpose of the Fathers to have the new Missions farther inland than those already established, that they might reach more of the natives: those who lived in the valleys and on the slopes of the foothills. Besides this, it had always been the intent of the Spanish government that further explorations of the interior country should take place, that, as the Missions became strong enough to support themselves, the Indians there might be brought under the influence of the Church. Neve's Regulations say:

" It is made imperative to increase the number of Reductions (stations for converting the Indians) in proportion to the vastness of the country occupied, and although this must be carried out in the succession and order aforesaid, as fast as the older establishments shall be fully secure, etc.," and earlier, " while the breadth of the country is unknown (it) is presumed to be as great as the length, or greater (200 leagues), since its greatest breadth is counted by thousands of leagues."

On this subject Von Langsdorff in his " Voyages," published in London in 1814, says:

" Every year military expeditions are sent out to obtain a more exact knowledge of the interior of the country, with a view, if possible, of establishing, by degrees, a land communication between Santa Fé and the northwest coast of America. While I was at the Mission of St. Joseph, thirteen soldiers, with a serjeant and corporal, arrived there on their return from one of these expeditions. These people asserted that they had penetrated between eighty and ninety leagues into the country, and had arrived in the neighborhood of a high and widely extended chain of hills, covered with eternal snow; this chain is known to the Spaniards under the name of the Sierra Nevada, or Snowy Mountains. The river, or rivers of St. Francisco and another stream which flows into the sea near St. Michael, must have their sources in these mountains.

Individuals, inhabitants of the Sierra Nevada, affirm, that three or four days journey eastward of this chain, they have seen men with blue and red clothing, who entirely resembled the Spaniards of California; they were very probably soldiers of Santa Fé, who had been sent on a similar expedition from the Eastern coast, to examine the interior of the country westwards.

According to this information, the Spaniards, between the thirty-fifth and thirty-eighth degrees of latitude on the different sides of the continent, must have come pretty near to each other; a probability is thus afforded, that, in time, a regular inland communication may be established between Santa Fé and St. Francisco."

Further on he states that one of these expeditions was fitted out for travel to the Sierra Nevada during their stay. The Padre, José Uria, went " partly in the hope of engaging fresh converts, partly for the purpose of gaining a more extensive knowledge of the interior, with a view to establish a new Mission, from which he expected great advantages to be derived."

In spite of the fact recorded by Langsdorff, however, I think it must generally be conceded that the priests in California were more active as local pastors than as explorers. They were not possessed of the spirit that animated Kino and Garcés. Had the latter been in charge in California, it is hard to believe that he would not have known more of the interior country, even had he been forced to make the explorations alone.

Various investigations were made by the nearest priests in order to select the best locations for the proposed Missions, and, in 1796, Lasuen reported the results to the new Governor, Borica, who in turn communicated them to the Viceroy in Mexico. Approval was given and orders issued for the establishment of the five new Missions.

On June 9, 1797, Lasuen left San Francisco for the founding of the Mission San José, then called the Alameda. The following day, a brush church was erected, and, on the morrow, the usual foundation ceremonies occurred. The natives named the site *Oroysom*. Beautifully situated on the foothills, with a prominent peak near by, it offers an extensive view over the southern portion of the San Francisco bay region. At first, a wooden structure with a grass roof served as a church; but later a brick structure was erected, which Von Langsdorff visited in 1806.

It seems singular to us at this date that although the easiest means of communication between the Missions of Santa Clara, San José and San Francisco, was by water on the Bay of San Francisco, the Padre and soldiers at San Francisco had no boat or vessel of any kind. Langsdorff says of this: "Perhaps the missionaries are afraid lest if there were boats, they might facilitate the escape of the Indians, who never wholly lose their love of freedom and their attachment to their native habits; they therefore consider it better to confine their communication with one another to the means afforded by the land. The Spaniards, as well as their nurslings, the Indians, are very seldom under the necessity of trusting themselves to the waves, and if such a necessity occur, they make a kind of boat for the occasion, of straw, reeds, and rushes, bound together so closely as to be watertight. In this way they contrive to go very easily from one shore to the other. Boats of this kind are called *walza* by the Spanish. The oars consist of a thin, long pole somewhat broader at each end, with which the occupants row sometimes on one side, sometimes on the other."

For the next Mission two sites were suggested; but, as early as June 17, Corporal Ballesteros erected a church, missionary-house, granary, and guard-house at the point called by the natives *Popeloutchom*, and by the Spaniards, San Benito. Eight days later, Lasuen, aided by Padre Catalá and Martiarena, founded the Mission dedicated to the saint of that day, San Juan Bautista.

Next in order, between the two Missions of San Antonio de Padua and San Luis Obispo, was that of "the most glorious prince of the heavenly militia," San Miguel. Lasuen, aided by Sitjar, in the presence of a large number of Indians, performed the ceremony in the usual form, on July 25, 1797. This Mission eventually grew to large proportions. In a subsequent chapter, dealing with the interiors of the Mission churches, a detailed description of the interior of San Miguel will be given; since it remains to-day almost exactly as decorated by the hands of the original artists.

San Fernando Rey was next established, on September 8, by Lasuen, aided by Padre Dumetz.

PLATE IX

ALTAR IN MORTUARY CHAPEL, SAN LUIS REY

After extended correspondence between Lasuen and Governor Borica, a site, called by the natives *Tacayme*, was finally chosen for locating the next Mission, which was to bear the name of San Luis, Rey de Francia. Thus it became necessary to distinguish between the two saints of the same name: San Luis, Bishop (Obispo), and San Luis, King; but modern American parlance has eliminated the comma, and they are respectively San Luis Obispo and San Luis Rey. Lasuen, with the honored Padre Peyri and Padre Santiago, conducted the ceremonies on June 13, and the hearts of all concerned were made glad by the subsequent baptism of fifty-four children.

It was as an adjunct to this Mission that Padre Peyri, in 1816, founded the chapel of San Antonio de Pala, twenty miles east from San Luis Rey: to which place were removed the Palatingwas, or Agua Calientes, recently evicted from Warner's Ranch. This chapel has the picturesque *campanile*, or small detached belfry, the pictures of which are known throughout the world.

With the founding of San Luis Rey this branch of the work of President Lasuen terminated. Bancroft regards him as a greater man than Serra, and one whose life and work entitle him to the highest praise. He died at San Carlos on June 26, 1803, and was buried by the side of Serra.

Estevan Tapis now became president of the Missions, and under his direction was founded the nineteenth Mission, that of Santa Inés, virgin and martyr. Tapis himself conducted the ceremonies, preaching a sermon to a large congregation, including Commandant Carrillo, on September 17, 1804.

With Lasuen, the Mission work of California reached its maximum power. Under his immediate successors it began to decline. Doubtless the fact that the original chain was completed, was an influence in the decrease of activity. For thirteen years there was no extension. A few minor at-

tempts were made to explore the interior country, and many
of the names now used for rivers and locations in the San
Joaquin Valley were given at this time. Nothing further,
however, was done, until in 1817, when such a wide-spread
mortality affected the Indians at the San Francisco Mission, that Governor Sola suggested that the afflicted neophytes be removed to a new and healthful location on the
north shore of the San Francisco bay. A few were taken
to what is now San Rafael, and while some recovered,
many died. These latter, not having received the last rites
of their religion, were subjects of great solicitude on the
part of some of the priests, and, at last, Father Taboada,
who had formerly been the priest at La Purísima Concepción, consented to take charge of this branch Mission.
The native name of the site was *Nanaguani*. On December 14, Padre Sarría, assisted by several other priests,
conducted the ceremony of dedication to San Rafael Arcángel. It was originally intended to be an *asistencia* of
San Francisco, but although there is no record that it was
ever *formally* raised to the dignity of an independent Mission, it is called and enumerated as such from the year
1823 in all the reports of the Fathers. To-day, not a brick
of its walls remains; the only evidence of its existence
being the few old pear trees planted early in its history.

There are those who contend that San Rafael was
founded as a direct check to the southward aggressions of
the Russians, who in 1812 had established Fort Ross but
sixty-five miles north of San Francisco. There seems,
however, to be no recorded authority for this belief, although it may easily be understood how anxious this close
proximity of the Russians made the Spanish authorities.

They had further causes of anxiety. The complications between Mexico and Spain, which culminated in the
independence of the former, and then the establishment
of the Empire, gave the leaders enough to occupy their
minds.

The final establishment took place in 1823, without any idea of founding a new Mission. The change to San Rafael had been so beneficial to the sick Indians that Canon Fernandez, Prefect Payeras, and Governor Argüello decided to transfer bodily the Mission of San Francisco from the peninsula to the mainland north of the bay, and make San Rafael dependent upon it. An exploring expedition was sent out which somewhat carefully examined the whole neighborhood and finally reported in favor of the Sonoma Valley. The report being accepted, on July 4, 1823, a cross was set up and blessed on the site, which was named New San Francisco.

Padre Altimira, one of the explorers, now wrote to the *padre presidente* — Señan — explaining what he had done, and his reasons for so doing; stating that San Francisco could no longer exist, and that San Rafael was unable to subsist alone. Discussion followed, and Sarría, the successor of Señan, who had died, refused to authorize the change; expressing himself astonished at the audacity of those who had dared to take so important a step without consulting the supreme government. Then Altimira, infuriated, wrote to the Governor, who had been a party to the proposed removal, concluding his tirade by saying: " I came to convert gentiles and to establish new missions, and if I cannot do it here, which, as we all agree, is the best spot in California for the purpose, I will leave the country."

Governor Argüello assisted his priestly friend as far as he was able, and apprised Sarría that he would sustain the new establishment; although he would withdraw the order for the suppression of San Rafael. A compromise was then effected by which New San Francisco was to remain a Mission in regular standing, but neither San Rafael nor old San Francisco were to be disturbed.

Is it not an inspiring subject for speculation? Where would the modern city of San Francisco be, if the irate

Father and plotting politicians of those early days had been successful in their schemes?

The new Mission, all controversy being settled, was formally dedicated on Passion Sunday, April 4, 1824, by Altimira, to San Francisco Solano, " the great apostle to the Indies." There were now two San Franciscos, de Asis and Solano, and because of the inconvenience arising from this confusion, the popular names, Dolores and Solano, and later, Sonoma, came into use.

From the point now reached, the history of the Missions is one of distress, anxiety, and final disaster. Their great work was practically ended.

Before entering upon the history of each Mission in detail it is well to recapitulate the list of Missions established and the *jurisdiction* to which each one belonged. As has been shown, a presidio was established for the military guardianship of the Missions. Each presidio was responsible for all the Missions and pueblos under its jurisdiction as follows:

Jurisdiction of San Diego.

Presidio of San Diego; Mission of San Gabriel; Mission of San Juan Capistrano; Mission of San Diego; Mission of San Luis Rey.

Jurisdiction of Santa Barbara.

Presidio of Santa Barbara; Mission of La Purísima; Mission of Santa Inés; Mission of Santa Barbara; Mission of Buenaventura; Mission of San Fernando; Pueblo of La Reyna de Los Angeles.

Jurisdiction of Monterey.

Presidio of Monterey; Village of Branciforte; Mission of San Juan Bautista; Mission of San Carlos; Mission of Nuestra Señora de Soledad; Mission of San Antonio; Mission of San Miguel; Mission of San Luis Obispo.

PLATE X

a. SANTA BARBARA MISSION

b. SANTA CLARA MISSION IN 1849

JURISDICTION OF SAN FRANCISCO.

Presidio of San Francisco; Pueblo of San José de Guadalupe; Mission of San Francisco Solano; Mission of San Rafael; Mission of San Francisco; Mission of Santa Clara; Mission of San José; Mission of Santa Cruz.

CHAPTER II

JUNIPERO SERRA AND HIS COADJUTORS

TO the indomitable energy of Galvez, the California
Missions owed much, but his work was largely
initial. It required the steady, patient, constant
labors of men on the ground, to see that the plans so carefully formulated were carried out. From St. Francis
down, the chief aim of the members of his order has been
to help mankind. Other men might work for honor or
glory or fame or riches or power, but their highest endeavor was to " go about doing good." Self-renunciation,
a prodigality of giving of one's self for others, were the
chief means of salvation to them. Not alone by praying in
a cell, doing penance, and reciting prayers were their souls
to be saved, but by yielding to the Spirit of the Divine One
of whom one of His persecutors cried: " He saved others,
Himself he cannot save." Oh! for more of this divine un-
selfishness in those who stand as the ambassadors of God.
What the world needs is men who will spend themselves
freely to benefit others. Life, example, unselfish work are
more effective than preaching, and many more hearts have
been reached by the devotion of a sister of charity to the
needy sick than by the eloquence of a cardinal.

Francis of Assisi believed this with all his soul. The
order that bears his name has always been more or less
full of the same spirit. In Junipero Serra St. Francis
had a worthy son and follower. All through life he was
simple, single-hearted, enthusiastic, a firm believer in Holy
Church, with never a doubt as to its mission, and with a
practical turn to his mind that was bound to make a suc-

cess of everything he undertook. A firm believer in miracles, yet he knew how to plan for a long campaign of hard work with little result; like a child in dealing with Indians, yet hard-headed enough to circumvent the plottings of indifferent and selfish politicians. This was the man chosen by his college of San Fernando, in the City of Mexico, to carry out the plans of Galvez for the christianizing of the aborigines of the new country of California.

He was born on the 24th of November, 1713, at Petra, in the Island of Majorca. His parents were devout catholics, and the boy being of the gentle, obedient, naturally good kind, it was borne in upon them that he was especially fitted to be a priest; therefore they early sent him to Palma, the capital, there to be under the wise and benign influences of a priest of the cathedral. This devout man so led the impressionable mind of the lad that when he was seventeen years old he applied to the Franciscan Convent to be allowed to enter, and on the 14th of September, 1730, he made his profession as a novitiate. During the year of his probation he was peculiarly attracted to the lives of the missionaries to the Indians. Something in the abandon of enthusiasm with which these men gave up all the world holds dear for the salvation of the souls of these poor savages so appealed to the large-eyed, gentle-hearted, earnest-souled youth that, then and there, his vocation for life was settled. It is a remarkable proof of the power of the printed word over the very inmost soul of an ardent and impressionable youth.

On the 15th of September, 1731, he took his final vows and assumed the name of Junipero, out of love for the jovial and pure-hearted companion of St. Francis; he of whom the saint once said, " O that I had a forest of such junipers." Here was another sapling just growing in one of the nurseries he had established that was to lead other fervent souls to a like remark.

Before his profession Junipero writes that he was small

and somewhat puny, but now he immediately sprang up, broadened out, and became well and strong. Sent to another college to study philosophy and theology, he worked so diligently that he was soon made a professor, and received the degree of Doctor of Divinity. He began to preach also, and the simple-minded fervor of such an implicit believer, who was yet so learned, combined with the clear-headed way he had of looking at things, soon brought him great fame as a pulpit orator. As a teacher he was equally successful. Indeed the pathway of fame and honor was clearly before him. He had but to open the door himself, and enter it. The Church of Rome has never been niggardly in its gifts to its able sons, and here was one who soon could have had pretty nearly all he might have asked. Yet he wilfully and willingly turned away from the shining pathway, and begged to be sent away to a dark and unknown road, where trials, difficulties, dangers, and possible death awaited him. He longed to be a missionary to the heathen. The theology of Dante was a real, terrible, absorbing truth to him. Only to such a belief was such work as his possible. Hell, with its dire circles of horror and terror for those who were unbelievers in the Christ he worshipped, yawned before the feet of these untamed and rude natives. If they should be trained into a knowledge of the Church and its saving ordinances by an apostolic guide, they could attain a new hereafter. Purgatory was open, and from thence, duly purged from their sin and ignorance, they might climb into the blessed regions of Paradise. Felicity untold, then, to that man who would brave their savagery, dare their treachery, love them even in their unlovableness, and thus lead them into the fold of the Church.

Who should do it? Should he, Serra, with his soul athirst for great deeds, full of bravery and heroism, stand by, in order to listen to the applause of the civilized world as his words of burning eloquence pleased cultured ears,

and let some half-hearted, half-in-earnest priest go out
to these degraded savages? No! The greater their need
and danger, the greater the necessity for speed, power,
and earnestness in the one who should go to them. So,
begging to be allowed to leave the world and its vain
applause, society and its caresses, civilization and its lux-
urious comforts, casting all these things behind him, he
gladly, joyfully, and yet seriously requested his superiors
to allow him to go as a missionary.

" Narrow," some may say he was! " His theological
conceptions crude and bigoted! " So were Dante's, but
that did not prevent him from giving the Divine Comedy
to the world. And Milton, too, cannot be designated as
" broad," yet Paradise Lost will live when many of the
valueless expressions of these days have sunken into the
" backward of time " and been forgotten.

During his college days his close companions were Palou,
Verges, Crespí, and Vincens, who were all more or less
dominated by the spirit of Serra, and when, finally, the
authorities allowed him to join a band of missionaries that
was gathering at Cadiz, ready to go to Mexico, Palou,
without hesitation, set out with him. And when, at Cadiz,
he learned that three of those who were there desired to
withdraw he blessed God for the opportunity and immediately begged for his other three companions to be sent
in their place. This was granted, and the five, after a
fearfully hard voyage of ninety-nine days, in which they
were reduced to great straits for want of water, arrived
at Vera Cruz. On the voyage Serra's boundless devotion
and enthusiasm would not let him rest. He recited the
mass daily and spent long hours in the night hearing
confessions. He took the scarcity of water as a training
for the future, and naïvely remarked when asked if he did
not suffer with thirst: " Not specially, since I have found
out the secret of not feeling thirsty, which is, to eat little
and talk less, so as not to waste the saliva."

Another proof of his determination to harden himself for his chosen work is given in the fact that he refused to avail himself of the transportation provided from Vera Cruz to the City of Mexico, but asked to be allowed to walk. When permission was given, he and a companion, without provisions or guide, started forth on that tramp of a hundred leagues, relying solely upon Providence and the goodness of the people whom they should meet. It was such simple devotion combined with practical good sense that developed the man. I say practical good sense — not common-sense, for this and that are quite different. Here was a man preparing himself for hardships that he might have to undergo *in*voluntarily, by *voluntarily* entering into them. He was putting himself into training, just as an athlete does for a test of strength, and therein lay his practical good sense. He was educating himself, by overcoming obstacles now, to bravely and fearlessly meet the obstacles he knew he might expect in later life.

It was on the last day of 1749 that he gratefully rendered thanks for his safe journey at the altar of Our Lady of Guadalupe, and the next morning, New Year's Day, 1750, he entered the portals of the College of San Fernando, of which he was ultimately to become the most famous and honored son.

To recount his life for the next seventeen years is to tell of work well and devoutly performed, a Mission successfully conducted for several years among the Indians of the Sierra Gorda, and others elsewhere, in places difficult of access; a veritable apostle wherever he went. He was appointed to the Missions then being founded on the San Saba, in Texas, but for some reason could not go, and those who were sent in his stead were brutally murdered. The coincidence seems like a special providence. God had important work for him to do and was just " saving his light to spend."

And when the expulsion of the Jesuits occurred, then

PLATE XI

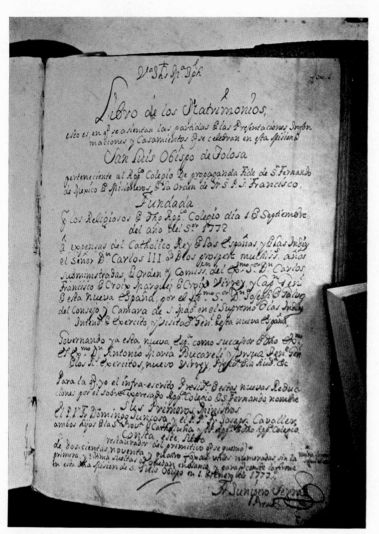

TITLE–PAGE OF MARRIAGE REGISTER OF SAN LUIS OBISPO,
IN PRESIDENT SERRA'S HANDWRITING

was the time. God unclasped His hand and let his " glow-worm " out to give light to those who needed it. Serra was at once chosen by the college authorities to take charge of the Lower California Missions, and, as we have seen, he and Galvez got along so well together, that Serra started for the new California with his good wishes and promises of material assistance. It is not to be wondered at that, when his superior handed him his commission, tears prevented any reply. Here was a larger fulfilment of his hopes than he had ever dared to expect. To minister was to be blessed; but to minister himself and to be able to call upon others to minister where he could not go, — this was to multiply himself many times, and it was bliss indeed.

Serra's life in California is largely the record of its early history, and this has been set forth, with as large degree of fulness as space allowed, in the pages of this book. He died at San Carlos, August 28, 1784, and was buried in the Mission he loved so well, in the beautiful Carmelo Valley.

Palou now became the president, *pro tempore*, in obedience to the expressed wish of his brother friars, and yet in the records not a single act of his as president can be found. He was a fellow student with Serra and Crespí, and they remained warm friends through life. When Serra left the peninsula to take charge of the organization of the Missions of Alta California, Palou was given the official care of the Missions, and he it was who handed them over finally to the Dominicans when the partition was made. This was in May, 1773. By the end of August he was in San Diego and a little later in Monterey, and when Serra went to Mexico, Palou was acting president in his absence. At the time of Serra's death Palou was contemplating retiring to the seclusion of his convent of San Fernando in the City of Mexico. He remained, however, mainly engaged in writing his " Life of Serra," until Lasuen

4

received his appointment in September, 1785. In February, 1786, he reached Mexico, and July 18 he was elected its guardian. It is supposed that he died before 1790, though there is some uncertainty in the matter, which later research will doubtless clear up.

Undoubtedly the worthy successor to Serra's mantle was Padre Fermin Francisco de Lasuen, born in Vitoria, Spain, and who, as one of Serra's co-workers in the peninsula went up to Velicatá in March, 1769, to bless Rivera's expedition as it started for the founding of San Diego. His first work in Alta California was at San Gabriel, where he served from December, 1773, to September, 1775. The next year he served at San Juan Capistrano, and then at San Diego until 1785, when he was elected president. When he died, June 16, 1803, he had been thirty years a missionary in California, and for eighteen years president of the Missions. Of an entirely different type of man from the stern, ascetic Serra, he was yet as full of piety, zeal, earnestness, and purity of life, and the Missions prospered under his guidance.

On account of the long distance, both in miles and time, from Mexico, the College of San Fernando deemed it wise to elect a provisional president, whose duty it should be to assume the office in case of the absence, incapacitation, or death of the incumbent. In 1798 Esteván Tapis was furnished with the necessary document as provisional president, and at Lasuen's death he immediately assumed the office. Three times he was appointed, though he did not deem himself fitted for the office, and finally, in 1812, when relieved, he retired to Santa Inés, where he performed the ordinary duties of a missionary. In 1815 he was sent to San Juan Bautista, where he died and was buried in 1825.

At Tapis's retirement in 1812 José Señan was elected to the office. He resided at San Buenaventura, where he had been the missionary. In 1815 he resigned, and in

1823 died at his old Mission. At the same time that he was appointed, however, a new and superior office was created, that of *comisario prefecto*. He was the prelate, as it were, of the Franciscans in California, and had supreme control of all temporal affairs. Sarría was elected to this office, and he and Señan worked harmoniously together. At the end of six years Sarría resigned.

In 1815 Mariano Payeras was elected president, and he exercised the office in conjunction with Sarría, as prefect, until the resignation of the latter, when, on advices from his college, he assumed the duties of president as they were exercised by Serra and Lasuen. In 1819 the position was changed again, and Payeras was raised to the position of prefect, while Señan was again elected president.

Payeras died April 28, 1823, at his Mission of Purísima, and Señan, who had been appointed by Payeras to succeed him in the higher office, also died August 24 of the same year at San Buenaventura.

Sarría was named prefect by Señan, and held both offices, on account of the refusal of the duly elected president to accept the office.

In 1825, as Sarría refused to take the oath of allegiance to the newly constituted republic of Mexico, Narcisco Duran was required to assume the duties of the presidency, though he also refused the oath. But Sarría continued to perform his official duties, his arrest being merely nominal.

In 1827 José Bernardo Sanchez was elected president and served until 1831, when Duran again assumed the office.

In 1833 ten new friars of the Zacatecas College of Franciscans came to take the places of the old missionaries, and it was decided to give them charge of all the Missions north of San Carlos. The College of San Fernando being composed entirely of Spaniards, and they having been banished from Mexico, the friars of a Mexican college were thus called upon to supply the Missions of California with the needed padres. They brought their own prefect with them, in the person of Francisco García Diego, who, later, became the first bishop of California. Duran's authority was confined, after the coming of Diego, to the Missions south of San Antonio.

With secularization practically came the abolishment of both offices, prefect and president, and since that time the Church has been governed in the usual way.

One thing is seldom remembered by the generality of writers upon the Missions, and that is that all the Padre presidentes were functionaries of the Spanish Inquisition. Serra, Lasuen, Tapis, Sarría, and Payeras were all inquisitors. But in this, as in everything else, it is personality that shows, when men are not urged on by the cries of a mob. As there was no hue and cry in California, and the hearts of the padres were humane, we have the record of but one case that ever came to trial. That was of a Spanish settler in Los Angeles, named Ramon Sotilo, who was accused of "having expressed views on religion that not even a Protestant would dare hold." The prosecutor asked that as a punishment "he be kept in jail some weeks and receive daily instruction from the Mission priest." This sentence was passed upon the culprit, but in a few days he escaped from jail, and no more was ever heard of either him or his case.

PLATE XII

b. FIGURE OF CHRIST, SAN DIEGO MISSION

a. FIGURE OF CHRIST'S AGONY IN THE GARDEN.
SAN DIEGO MISSION

CHAPTER III

THE INDIANS AT THE COMING OF THE PADRES

IT is generally believed that the California Indian in his original condition was one of the most miserable and wretched of the world's aborigines. As one writer puts it:

" When discovered by the padres he was almost naked, half starved, living in filthy little hovels built of tule, speaking a meagre language broken up into as many different and independent dialects as there were tribes, having no laws and few definite customs, cruel, simple, lazy, and — in one word which best describes such a condition of existence — wretched. There are some forms of savage life that we can admire; there are others that can only excite our disgust; of the latter were the California Indians."

This is the general attitude taken by most writers of this later day, as well as of the padres themselves, yet I think I shall be able to show that in some regards it is a mistaken one. I do not believe the Indians were the degraded and brutal creatures the padres and others have endeavored to make out. This is no charge of bad faith against these writers. It is merely a criticism of their judgment. Twenty-five years of acquaintance and frequent association with the Indians of Nevada, California, and the Southwest have demonstrated several important things. Indians, like other people, are not to be judged by the clothes they wear, or do not wear. Exterior appearances are by no means to be relied upon any more than when Thomas Carlyle wrote his " Sartor Resartus."

It is the instinctive habit of the missionary to record, as of chief importance, the evil, degrading, and hideous things that strike him in the character of those to whom he comes to minister. Who has not recognized this in listening to the stories of returned missionaries from India and Africa?

" Where every prospect pleases,
And only man is vile."

It has ever been the same. To the conquered Britons the Vikings were hideous sea-rovers. To the Latins the Goths and Vandals were void of all human traits. Yet history has revealed many wonderfully excellent things alike in Viking, Goth, and Vandal. The Moors overran Spain, and were terrible creatures to those whom they subjugated, yet they left an architecture and an influence which have come down to us and are now coloring the lives of our citizens on the shores of the Sun-down Sea. Everything depends upon the angle of vision at which things are seen. In the case of the subjugated European peoples the angle was oblique; and equally so was it, I believe, in the case of those who have judged the Indians of California.

The fact that in a few years the Indians became remarkably competent in so many fields of skilled labor is the best answer to the unfounded charges of abject savagery. Peoples are not civilized nor educated in a day. Brains cannot be put into a monkey, no matter how well educated his teacher is. There must have been the mental quality, the ability to learn; or even the miraculous patience, perseverance, and love of the missionaries would not have availed to teach them, in several hundred years, much less, then, in the half-century they had them under their control, the many things we know they learned.

The Indians, prior to the coming of the padres, were skilled in some arts, as the making of pottery, basketry, canoes, stone axes, arrow heads, spear heads, stone knives, and the like. Holder says of the inhabitants of Santa

Catalina that although their implements were of stone, wood, or shell " the skill with which they modelled and made their weapons, mortars, and steatite *ollas,* their rude mosaics of abalone shells, and their manufacture of pipes, medicine-tubes, and flutes give them high rank among savages." The mortars found throughout California, some of which are now to be seen in the museums of Santa Barbara, Los Angeles, San Diego, etc., are models in shape and finish. As for their basketry, I have else-where [1] shown that it alone stamps them as an artistic, mechanically skilful, and mathematically inclined people, and the study of their designs and their meanings reveals a love of nature, poetry, sentiment, and religion that put them upon a superior plane. Because people live on food that we do not eat, that is no evidence of barbarism. To the Englishman the frog-eating of the Frenchman was long a source of offence — the stupid insularity of the one deeming it a sign of inferiority in the other. Now he imitates his brother across the channel in this very particular, and glories in his epicurean taste. So with China. The rudest and most ignorant sailor that ever left the shores of a pride-besotted people can sneer at the civilization of thousands of years in Hindoo, Buddhist, or Chinaman because of some racial difference in diet, totally incompetent to see that his own habits are immeasurably more disgusting and revolting than the ones he criticises.

Cabrillo was the first white man whom we know visited the Indians of the coast of California. He made his memorable journey in 1542–3. In 1539, Ulloa sailed up the Gulf of California, and, a year later, Alarcon and Diaz explored the Colorado River, possibly to the point where Yuma now stands. These three men came in contact with the Cocopahs and the Yumas, and possibly with other tribes.

[1] Indian Basketry, especially the chapters on Form, Poetry, and Symbolism.

Cabrillo tells of the Indians with whom he held communication. They were timid, and somewhat hostile at first, but easily appeased. Some of them, especially those living on the islands (now known as San Clemente, Santa Catalina, Anacapa, Santa Barbara, Santa Rosa, San Miguel, and Santa Cruz), were superior to those found inland. They rowed in pine canoes having a seating capacity of twelve or thirteen men, and were expert fishermen. They dressed in the skins of animals, were rude agriculturists, and built for themselves shelters or huts of willows, tules, and mud.

Vizcaino, who "rediscovered" the country in 1602, wrote a letter to the King of Spain, dated May 23, 1603, in which he thus speaks of the Indians:

"This land has a genial climate, its waters are good, and it is very fertile, to judge from the varied and luxuriant growth of trees and plants; for I saw some of the fruits, particularly chestnuts and acorns, which are larger than those of Spain. And it is thickly settled with people whom I found to be of gentle disposition, peaceable and docile, and who can be brought readily within the fold of the Holy Gospel and into subjection to the crown of Your Majesty. Their food consists of seeds, which they have in abundance and variety, and of the flesh of game : such as bears, bisons, and deer, which are larger than cows, and of neat cattle, and many other animals. The Indians are of good stature and fair complexion, the women being somewhat smaller in size than the men, and of pleasing countenance. The clothing of the people of the coast-lands consists of the skins of the sea-wolves abounding there, which they tan and dress better than is done in Castile ; they possess, also, in great quantity, flax like that of Castile, hemp and cotton, from which they make fishing-lines and nets for rabbits and hares. They have vessels of pine wood very well made, which, having fourteen paddlemen at a side, they navigate with great dexterity, even in very stormy weather. I was informed by them and many others whom I met in great numbers along more than eight hundred leagues of a thickly settled coast, that inland there are great communities, which they invited me to visit with them."

Padre Salmeron says of the aboriginal inhabitants of Santa Catalina:

"They are fishermen, using boats of boards; the prows and poops high, and the middle very low. Some will hold more than twenty persons. There are many sea-lions, the which these Indians hunt for food; and with the tanned skins they all cover themselves, men and women, and it is their usual protection. The women are very handsome and decent. The children are white and ruddy and very smiling. Of these Indians, many wished to come with the Spaniards; they are so loving as all this."

In 1770 Don Miguel Costanso tells of the craftsmen of the California Indians in their aboriginal condition. He says:

"The men work handsome trays of wood, with firm inlays of coral or of bone; and some vases of much capacity, closing at the mouth, which appear to be made with a lathe — and with this machine they would not come out better hollowed nor of more perfect form. They give the whole a lustre which appears the finished handiwork of a skilled Artisan."

He says further:

"The dexterity and skill of these Indians is surpassing in the construction of their Launches made of Pine planking (tublazon). They are from eight to ten varas (22 to $27\frac{1}{2}$ feet) in length, including their rake, and of a vara and half (4 feet $1\frac{1}{2}$ inches) beam. Into their fabric enters no iron whatever, of the use of which they know little. But they fasten the boards with firmness, one to another, working their drills just so far apart and at a distance of an inch from the edge, the (holes) in the upper boards corresponding with those in the lower, and thro' these holes they pass strong lashings of Deer sinews. They pitch and calk the seams, and paint the whole in sightly colors. They handle the (boats) with equal cleverness, and three or four men go out to the open sea to fish in them, as they have capacity to carry eight or ten. They use long oars with two blades, and ròw with unspeakable lightness and velocity. They know all the arts of fishing, and Fish abound along their Coasts, as has been said of San Diego. They have communication and Commerce with the Natives of the Islands, whence they get the beads of coral which are current in place of money thro' all these Lands; altho' they hold in more esteem the glass beads which the Spaniards gave them — and offered in exchange for these whatever they had, like trays, Otter skins, baskets, and wooden plates. More than anything they appreciate whatsoever clasp-knife (navaja) or cutting instrument; whose advantages over the (implements) of flint they admire; it causing them much satisfaction to see use made of the axes and machetes, and the facility with which the soldiers, to make firewood, felled a Tree with the said Instruments."

Padre Crespí's testimony is also useful. In telling of the land expedition which led to the discovery of the Bay of San Francisco he thus writes of the Indians:

" It was observed that the Indians along that coast had larger tents than common among the natives, and that each family lived in a separate hut. From Santa Barbara the explorers passed through Santa Clara canyon, where there are now so many splendid farm-homes. The dwellings of the then inhabitants were made of a few poles stuck in the ground, forming a semicircle, brought together in a conical shape, with bundles of sage brush thrown over, leaving an opening at the top which served to permit the escape of smoke and to let in the air and light. Near San Buenaventura they found the Indians more industrious and athletic, and the women better clad. They cleverly made well shaped canoes of pine, and all their work was well finished. Some of their fishing boats would hold ten men; they would go out to sea some distance, and showed great dexterity in managing very long oars. To work out the timber and stone they used only tools made of flint, being ignorant of the use of iron and steel. They readily exchanged highly polished wooden plates for a few trinkets."

The principal written source of authority for our knowledge of the Indians at the time of the arrival of the Fathers is Fray Geronimo Boscana's "Chinigchinich: A Historical Account, etc., of the Indians of San Juan Capistrano." There are many interesting things in this account, some of importance, and others of very slight value. He insists that there was a great difference in the intelligence of the natives north of Santa Barbara and those to the south in favor of the former. Of these he says they "are much more industrious, and appear an entirely distinct race. They formed, from shells, a kind of money, which passed current among them, and they constructed out of logs very swift and excellent canoes for fishing."

Of the character of his Indians he had a very poor idea. He compares them to monkeys who imitate, and especially in their copying the ways of the white men, "whom they respect as beings much superior to themselves; but in so doing, they are careful to select vice in preference to virtue. This is the result, undoubtedly, of their corrupt and natural disposition."

Of the language of the California Indians Boscana says there was great diversity, finding a new dialect almost every fifteen to twenty leagues.

They were not remarkably industrious, yet the men made their home utensils, bows and arrows, the several instruments used in making baskets, and also constructed nets, spinning the thread from yucca fibres, which they beat and prepared for that purpose. They also built the houses.

The women gathered seeds, prepared them, and did the cooking, as well as all the household duties. They made the baskets, all other utensils being made by the men.

The dress of the men, when they dressed at all, was with the skin of animals thrown over the shoulders, leaving the rest of the body exposed, but the women wore a cloak and dress of twisted rabbit-skins. I have found these same rabbit-skin dresses in use by Mohaves and Yumas within the past three or four years.

It has often been said that the men could not grow beards. The truth is that they plucked out the hairs one by one, using a bivalve shell as pincers. To-day many of the men allow the beard to grow. Some have a thinner beard, a condition which is doubtless owing, the Indians believe, to the long-continued practice of plucking out the hairs.

Men and women alike used various colored pigments on their faces. Red, yellow, and blue were the principal colors chosen, and to-day, at their festivals, one may see these Indians decorated in exactly the same fashion that their ancestors have followed for centuries.

The youths were required to keep away from the fire, in order that they might learn to suffer with bravery and courage. They were forbidden also to eat certain kinds of foods, to teach them to bear deprivation and to learn to control their appetites. In addition to this there were certain ceremonies which included fasting, abstinence from drinking, and the production of hallucinations by means of a vegetable drug, called pivat (still used, by the way, by some of the Indians of Southern California), and the final branding of the neophyte, which Boscana describes as follows: " A kind of herb was pounded until it became sponge-like; this they placed, according to the figure required, upon the spot intended to be burnt, which was generally upon the right arm, and sometimes upon the thick part of the leg also. They then set fire to it, and let it remain until all that was combustible was consumed. Consequently, a large blister immediately formed, and although painful, they used no remedy to cure it, but left it to heal itself; and thus, a large and perpetual scar remained. The reason alleged for this ceremony was that it added greater strength to the nerves, and gave a better pulse for the management of the bow." This ceremony was called *potense*.

Another infliction was required of them that recalls the

descriptions Frank H. Cushing gave of the initiation ceremonies of the Zunis:

"They were whipped with nettles, and covered with ants,
that they might become robust, and the infliction was always
performed in summer, during the months of July and August,
when the nettle was in its most fiery state. They gathered
small bunches, which they fastened together, and the poor de-
luded Indian was chastised, by inflicting blows with them upon
his naked limbs, until unable to walk; and then he was carried
to the nest of the nearest and most furious species of ants, and
laid down among them, while some of his friends, with sticks,
kept annoying the insects to make them still more violent."

The education of the girls was by no means neglected.

" They were taught to remain at home, and not to roam about
in idleness; to be always employed in some domestic duty, so
that, when they were older, they might know how to work, and
attend to their household duties; such as procuring seeds, and
cleaning them — making "atole" and "pinole," which are kinds
of gruel, and their daily food. When quite young, they have
a small, shallow basket, called by the natives "tucmel," with
which they learn the way to clean the seeds, and they are also instructed in grinding, and preparing the same for consumption."

When a girl was married her father gave her good
advice as to her conduct. She must be faithful to her
wifely duties and do nothing to disgrace either her husband or her parents. Children of tender years were sometimes betrothed by their parents. Padre Boscana says he
married a couple, the girl having been but eight or nine
months old, and the boy two years when they were contracted for by their parents.

Childbirth was natural and easy with them, as it generally is with all primitive peoples. I have known an
Indian woman to give birth to a child, walk half a mile to
a stream, step into it and wash both herself and the new-
born babe, then return to her camp, put her child in a

yakia, or basket cradle-carrier, sling it over her back, and start on a four or five mile journey, on foot, up the rocky and steep sides of a canyon.

A singular custom prevailed among these people, not uncommon elsewhere. The men, when their wives were suffering their accouchement, would abstain from all flesh and fish, refrain from smoking and all diversions, and stay within the *Kish,* or hut, from fifteen to twenty days.

The god of the San Juan Indians was Chinigchinich, and it is possible, from similarity in the ways of appearing and disappearing, that he is the monster Tauquitch of the Sabobas and Cahuillas described in The Legend of Tauquitch and Algoot.[1] This god was a queer compound of goodness and evil, who taught them all the rites and ceremonies that they afterwards observed.

Many of the men and a few women posed as possessing supernatural powers — witches, in fact, and such was the belief in their power that, "without resistance, all immediately acquiesced in their demands." They also had physicians who used cold water, plasters of herbs, whipping with nettles (doubtless the principle of the counter irritant), the smoke of certain plants, and incantations, with a great deal of general, all-around humbug to produce their cures. I have found the same things to-day among the Cahuillas, these people calling their medicine men "ting'-i-vash." Boscana thus tells of methods of treatment, all of which I have seen pursued:

"They placed feathers upon his head, and encircled him entirely with these, and other articles, such as horse-hair, grass, beads, and hairs of the head; blowing at the same time with their mouths towards the four cardinal points, and muttering to themselves certain low sounds — certain mysterious words — accompanied with antic gesticulations, of which no one knew the meaning. After this, one of them applied his lips to the

---

[1] See Folk Lore Journal, October 1903.

PLATE XIII

b. INDIAN WASHING IN CREEK ABOVE PALA

a. AGED INDIAN NEOPHYTE, SAN LUIS REY MISSION

part affected, and pretended to draw from it, by suction, the particles, which they had stated as being within, and exposed them to all present. The spectators, as well as the patient, placed strict confidence in the fact, and were satisfied whether he recovered or died.

There were many of these impostors spread about the country, who, after being well fed and paid for their services, made all manner of ridicule of their too credulous companions. Wonderful as it may appear, oftentimes they performed cures, when the patients were apparently fast verging into eternity, and in the space of twenty-four hours, by their extravagances and witchcraft, they have enabled them to rise from a bed of sickness, and unite with their companions in their domestic employments."

If this were the only testimony upon the subject of the medicine of the Indians we could do no other than form a very poor idea of their methods, but, fortunately, we have expert testimony from an entirely impartial authority, who, besides extolling their temescals, or sweat-baths, their surgical abilities, as displayed in the operations that were performed upon skulls that have since been exhumed, their hygienic customs, which he declares " are not only commendable, but worthy of the consideration of an advanced civilization," states further:

"It has been reserved for the California Indian to furnish three of the most valuable vegetable additions which have been made to the Pharmacopœia during the last twenty years. One, the Eriodyction Glutinosum, growing profusely in our foothills, was used by them in affections of the respiratory tract, and its worth was so appreciated by the Missionaries as to be named Yerba Santa, or Holy Plant. The second, the Rhamnus purshiana, gathered now for the market in the upper portions of the State, is found scattered through the timbered mountains of Southern California. It was used as a laxative, and on account of the constipating effect of an acorn diet, was doubtless in active demand. So highly was it esteemed by the followers of the Cross that it was christened Casyara Sagrada, or Sacred Bark. The third, Grindelia robusta, was used in the treatment of pulmonary troubles, and externally in poisoning from Rhus toxicodendron, or Poison Oak, and in various skin diseases."

Their food was of the crudest and simplest character. Whatever they could catch they ate, from deer or bear to grasshoppers, lizards, rats, and snakes. In baskets of their own manufacture, they gathered all kinds of wild seeds, and after using a rude process of threshing, they winnowed them. They also gathered mesquite beans in large quantities; burying them in pits for a month or two, in order to extract from them certain disagreeable flavors, and then storing them in large and rudely made willow granaries. But, as Dr. Cephas L. Bard well says:

" Of the Vegetable articles of diet the acorn was the principal one. It was deprived of its bitter taste by grinding, running through sieves made of interwoven grasses, and frequent washings. Another one was Chia, the seeds of Salvia Columbariae which in appearance are somewhat similar to birdseed. They were roasted, ground, and used as a food by being mixed with water. Thus prepared, it soon develops into a mucilaginous mass, larger than its original bulk. Its taste is somewhat like that of linseed meal. It is exceedingly nutritious, and was readily borne by the stomach when that organ refused to tolerate other aliment. An atole, or gruel, of this was one of the peace offerings to the first visiting sailors. One tablespoonful of these seeds was sufficient to sustain for twenty-four hours an Indian on a forced march. Chia was no less prized by the Native Californian, and at this late date it frequently commands $6 or $8 a pound.

" The pinion, the fruit of the pine, was largely used, and until now annual expeditions are made by the few surviving members of the coast tribes to the mountains for a supply. That they cultivated maize in certain localities, there can be but little doubt. They intimated to Cabrillo by signs that such was the case, and the supposition is confirmed by the presence at various points of vestiges of irrigating ditches. Yslay, the fruit of the wild cherry, was used as a food, and prepared by fermentation as an intoxicant. The seeds ground and made into balls were esteemed highly. The fruit of the manzanita, the seeds of burr clover, malva, and alfileri, were also used. Tunas, the fruit of the cactus, and wild blackberries, existed in abundance, and were much relished. A sugar was extracted from a certain reed of the tulares."

Acorns, seeds, mesquite beans, and dried meat were all pounded up in a well made granite mortar, on the top of which, oftentimes, a basket hopper was fixed by means of pine gum. Some of these mortars were hewn from steatite, or soapstone, others from a rough basic rock, and many of them were exceedingly well made and finely shaped; results requiring much patience and no small artistic skill. Oftentimes these mortars were made from the solid granite rocks or boulders, found near the harvesting and winnowing places, and I have photographed many such during late years.

Birds were caught in a most ingenious manner. One method was shown to me by an Indian on the Tule River reservation a few years ago. With semicircular arches of willow, a hiding-place was made, the hoops being covered with leafy brush or weeds. In this the Indian hid himself, after having prepared a bare spot outside his shelter, and upon which he sprinkled a liberal supply of seeds. In his hand he held a long pole, at the upper end of which was affixed a strong but small string; the other end being threaded through loops affixed to the pole. The pole was then thrust out among the seeds, the string being formed into a loop. Then, imitating the call of the birds, it was not long before doves, quail, or other game were attracted to the place, and, seeing the seeds, alighted. In their hopping to and fro, some of them invariably stepped into the noose. Quickly the watching Indian pulled the string tight, and, as quietly as possible, drew back the snared bird into his shelter. Wringing its neck, the Indian thrust forth the pole, and again continued the operation, until sufficient game was secured.

At times there were special foods for men and special foods for women. For instance, a hunter ate the legs of a rabbit or a deer, with the idea that thereby he would gain the speed displayed by these animals. He ate the heart of the mountain lion, that he might be as fearless as the wild beast itself. In eating snakes, the Indian desired and expected the gliding and noiseless quality of the reptile to become a part of himself. Women refused to eat salt lest it turn their hair gray; and a nursing mother took a decoction of the root of milk-weed, in order to promote lacteal secretions.

Most effective testimony to the healthfulness and moderation of their habits is given by Dr. Bard when he thus refers to their longevity:

"That they possessed as a race greater longevity than their successors, there remains no doubt. The great majority of skulls examined are indicative of very advanced age, the cranial sutures being entirely consolidated, with no vestiges of their existence. The records of the Missions furnish many instances of death at extreme old age. Those of San Buenaventura give the ages of three Indian women buried there as, respectively, 100, 105, and 114 years. Father Martinez, in charge of the Mission of San Miguel, shortly after its foundation, wrote that it possessed three Indian women each of whom was more than 100 years old. The records of the other Missions reveal the presence now and in the past of numerous Indian centenarians. The ages of Fernando and Placido, who died at Los Angeles, were estimated at 102 and 137. The latter danced at a fandango a short time prior to his decease. Justiniano Roxas, who died at Santa Cruz in 1878, was baptized at that Mission in 1792, and his age then was put down by the officiating padre as about forty. Within the last few years there have died in Kern county four Indians, each of whom was undoubtedly over 100 years old. They were Canillo (Alcalde of Tejon), Alfonso, Rafael, and Francisco. They helped to build the Mission of San Fernando. An Indian named Gabriel died in Monterey some time ago who was reported to have been 140 years of age. Dr. Remondino, in a paper read before the State Society in 1890, gives some interesting experi-

PLATE XIV

a. AGUIDA

b. MARTINIA

AGED INDIANS AT SAN JUAN CAPISTRANO, FROM PHOTOGRAPHS BY MISS GRACE NICHOLSON

ences of prolonged savage life in San Diego county. At the Mission of San Tomás there lived an old Indian 140 years old. On the Sweetwater was an Indian man 115 years old, and one died at the county seat 109 years old. At Capitan Grande were several Indian women over 100 years old. Warner's ranch furnishes one 130 years of age. The present chief of the almost extinct local tribe at San Buenaventura, Juan de Jesus, is an active old centenarian, who can be seen on the streets every day. As an evidence of his virility it may be said that the last of his series of squaws presented him ten years ago with twin papooses. Dr. Ferguson of Bakersfield informs me that an old Indian named Sebastian lives there who at the age 90 rides forty to fifty miles a day."

Throughout the country the Indians have left quite a number of picture writings. One of the most noted groups of these is found east of the San Marcos pass, about sixteen miles northwest of Santa Barbara. Owing to color having been used, and the pictographs being located in a cave, the location is known as the Painted Cave. The pictographs are in red, white, yellow, and black, and show crosses, conventionalized forms of the sun, human figures, circular designs, snake-like figures, tree-forms, centipedes, etc.

Possibly these pictographs had something to do with their early worship, but as far as I know, no endeavor was ever made to find out from the Indians themselves. In matters pertaining to their inner thought they are always exceedingly reticent. This is one secret of the vast amount of error and misunderstanding that has passed current as fact concerning them.

Few men have known the Indian more sympathetically than John Comfort Fillmore, the great authority on aboriginal music, and in the following words he expresses my own thought so much better on this subject than I can that I quote him in full:

"Of course there are serious difficulties in the way of acquiring this knowledge. The Indian is always suspicious of the white man, until his confidence has been completely won. He is always expecting his white visitor to look on his religious ideas and feelings, not with respect and sympathy, but with more or less of contempt. 'You will not believe me,' said a Sioux priest to a friend of mine who was his guest at the great Sun-dance, 'but I pray to God, and I am answered.' ' 'Certainly,' was the reply, 'why not?' The priest looked surprised and said: "But your people think my people are dogs!' Whoever would study the Indian must absolutely divest himself of all feeling of superiority of any kind, and think of his red brethen simply as men like himself, differing, to be sure, in their bringing-up and in their inherited ideas, but as well-intentioned and living up to the light they have quite as well, on the average, as the men of his own race. If he can show himself brotherly and sympathetic he will, sooner or later, overcome the natural suspicion with which the Indian at first regards him, and then the way is open for an intelligent comprehension of the Indian character."

The religion of these tribes was very simple. It was a rude kind of Nature worship with personified divinities; some of whom were undoubted human heroes possessing mythical histories. In the " Journal of American Folk-Lore " for October, 1903, I have related the story of one of these demigods, Algoot by name, who slew a cannibal monster, Tauquitch, and who still terrorizes the superstitious Indians of the region about Mount San Jacinto.

Their ceremonies consisted of smoking the propitiatory pipe — the ascending smoke typifying the ascent of their prayers to Those Above — dancing, praying, and singing. Dancing always attracted the attention of the gods, and, having their interest thus aroused, they could not fail to pay heed to the petitions presented to them.

As a specimen of the beliefs of the old aborigines, here is part of a story once told to me by an aged Saboba Indian. After describing the coming of his people to Southern California, from some far-away land over the sea, and the varied adventures of these heroes, he continued:

" But when Siwash, the god of earth, looked around and saw everything revealed by the sun, he was displeased; for the earth was bare, level, and monotonous, and there was nothing to cheer the sight.   Who could love a world that was all one limitless plain, with no mountains, no trees, hills, rocks, rivers, waterfalls, creeks, animals, reptiles, no birds, nor flowers?   There were many of our people that were of no use.   So Siwash took these, and of some he made high mountains, of some, smaller mountains; of others he made rivers, creeks, lakes, and waterfalls; of still others coyotes, foxes, deer, antelope, bear, squirrels, porcupines, and all the other animals.   Then he made out of other people all the different kinds of snakes, insects, birds, and fishes.   Then he wanted trees, plants, and flowers, and so he turned some of the people into these.   Of every man or woman that he seized, he made something according to the person's value.

" When he finished his work, he had made a beautiful country of this, and there were many things that my people had never seen before.   But he had used up so many men and women that he was frightened.   So he made a new lot of people, some to live here, there, and anywhere.   And he gave to each family its own language and tongue, and its own place to live, and he told them all the sad distress that would come upon them if they mingled their tongues by intermarriage.   Each family was to live in its own place, and while all the different families were to be friends, one to the other, and live as brothers bound together by kinship and concord, there was to be no mixing of bloods.

" Thus were settled the original inhabitants on the coast of Southern California by Siwash, the god of the earth, under the leadership of Uuyot."

These Indians were polygamists, as a matter of course, but much of what the missionaries and others have called their obscenities and vile conversations were the simple and unconscious utterances of men and women whose instincts were not perverted.   It is the invariable testimony of all careful observers of every class that as a rule the aborigines were healthy, vigorous, virile, and chaste, until they became demoralized by the whites. With many of them certain ceremonies had a distinct flavor of sex worship: a rude phallicism which exists to the present day. To the priests, as to most modern observers, these rites were offensive and obscene, but to the Indians they were only the natural and simple prayers for the fruitfulness of their wives and of the other producing forces.

J. S. Hittell says of the Indians of California:

"They had no religion, no conception of a deity, or of a future life, no idols, no form of worship, no priests, no philosophical conceptions, no historical traditions, no proverbs, no mode of recording thought before the coming of the missionaries among them."

Seldom has there been so much absolute misstatement as in this quotation. Jeremiah Curtin, the translator of Sienkiewicz and a life-long student of the Indian, speaking of the same Indians, makes a remark which applies with force to these first three statements:

"The Indian, *at every step*, stood face to face with divinity as he knew or understood it. He could never escape from the presence of those powers who had made the first world. . . . The most important question of all in Indian life was communication with divinity, intercourse with the spirits of divine personages."

In his "Creation Myths of Primitive America," this studious author gives the names of a number of divinities, and the legends connected with them. He affirms positively that "the most striking thing in all savage belief is the low estimate put upon man, when unaided by divine, uncreated power. In Indian belief every object in the universe is divine except man!"

As to their having no priests, no forms of worship, no philosophical conceptions, no historical traditions, no proverbs, any one interested in the Indian of to-day knows that these things are untrue. Whence came all the myths and legends that recent writers have gathered, a score of which I myself hold still unpublished in my note-book? Were they all imagined after the arrival of the Mission Fathers? By no means! They have been handed down for countless centuries, and they come to us, perhaps a little corrupted, but still just as accurate as do the songs of Homer.

Every tribe had its medicine men, who were developed by a most rigorous series of tests; such as would dismay many a white man. As to their philosophical conceptions and traditions, Curtin well says that in them " we have a monument of thought which is absolutely unequalled, altogether unique in human experience. The special value of this thought lies, moreover, in the fact that it is primitive; that it is the thought of ages long anterior to those which we find recorded in the eastern hemisphere, either in sacred books, in histories, or in literature, whether preserved on baked brick, burnt cylinders, or papyrus."

And if we go to the Pueblo Indians, the Navahoes, the Pimas, and others, all of whom were brought more or less under the influence of the Franciscans, we find a mass of beliefs, deities, traditions, conceptions, and proverbs, which would overpower Mr. Hittell merely to collate.

Therefore, let it be distinctly understood that the Indian was not the thoughtless, unimaginative, irreligious, brutal savage which he is too often represented to be. He thought, and thought well, but still originally. He was religious, profoundly and powerfully so, but in his own way; he was a philosopher, but not according to Hittell; he was a worshipper, but not after the method of Serra, Palou, and their priestly coadjutors.

CHAPTER IV

THE INDIANS UNDER THE PADRES

THE first consideration of the padres in dealing with the Indians was the salvation of their souls. Of this no honest and honorable man can hold any question. Serra and his coadjutors believed, without equivocation or reserve, the doctrines of the Church. As one reads Serra's diary, his thought on this matter is transparent. In one place he thus naïvely writes: " It seemed to me that they (the Indians) would fall shortly into the apostolic and evangelic net."

This accomplished, the Indians must be kept Christians, educated and civilized. Here is the crucial point. In reading criticisms upon the Mission system of dealing with the Indians one constantly meets with such passages as the following: " The fatal defect of this whole Spanish system was that no effort was made to educate the Indians, or teach them to read, and think, and act for themselves."

To me this kind of criticism is both unjust and puerile. What is education? What is civilization?

All civilization is comparative; all happiness relative. The highest civilization, and, therefore, the most laudable object of ambition to one, is a burden and weariness of the flesh to another. And no thinker will deny that it is an exceedingly difficult matter for the objects of one kind of civilization to look with any but superior, haughty, and critical eyes upon the objects of every other civilization. It is only since the Congress of Religions in Chicago that the Western world has learned to look with rational eyes, and a little more tolerance, upon the civilization, thought, and religious life of the Orient. Hence, in dealing with this question of the condition of the Indians under the padres, we are met with widely differing opinions and standards. Without discussing the religious question — for all experience demonstrates that no reasoning or argument will remove sectarian prejudices — let us consider the matter of the education of the Indians. What is education? The teaching of the " three r's " and of various ologies? God forbid! There are more foolish things done to-day in the enlightened and civilized United States of America under the name of " education " than the Catholic missionaries in all the centuries have ever done. My definition of education is a common-sense one, according to my view of life. To educate is to *educere* — draw out — the recognition of what one should *do* and *be* in order to make the best of his life. Religious education, among other things, should give the inspiration of the will, the resolution to *do* what one sees is best.

According to these definitions and the light and experience they possessed, the padres went to work. They surveyed the ground to be covered, and made as good a study of the Indian as conditions permitted. Then they began at the bottom. They first taught the Indian how to live; how to wear clothes; how to deserve eating and clothing by working; and better still, how to raise and manufacture what they needed. Certainly this was good, viewed from any standpoint, and, anyhow, we have not improved upon it, for it is just what our government with all its boasted advancement is now doing for them. But along with this the padres taught (*what was really their prime business*), in accordance with their own belief, the most necessary lessons of all, namely (and here I quote one of them), " the knowledge of whence they came, whither they were finally going, and what was most essential to attain that end fixed by the Creator Himself." On this portion of their work the padres knew, as we know, the futility of expecting to find unanimity of opinion amongst people who have ten thousand different shades of theological and untheological belief. Now, to quote from a modern Franciscan missionary's recent letter to me: "The fathers soon discovered that so much was all the Indians could grasp, and all for which they could be led to take an interest, just like unreasoning children who live but for the present day. This was true education, which gave the word its proper meaning. It was the only education the Indians were capable of comprehending, and the only kind the same Indians are capable of grasping even now, as Uncle Sam has discovered at last. Book learning, except the rudimentary, is not for the Indians (the major portion of them) even at this date; and the United States government is going back to the methods of the old Catholic missionaries in their essential points. The fact is, this kind of education is the most suitable for the generality of the white people. It would make them contented and happy, whereas now they are being ' educated ' to an unfitness for performing the ordinary duties of a simple life.

" Nevertheless, the padres, despite the drawbacks of having no suitable teachers, no suitable books, no suitable material, such as are plentiful now, taught any of the Indian boys, that showed any inclination, how to read and write and figure, and many other useful things."

I believe this to be, from all the study I have given the subject, a true statement of the facts. Hence I regard the education given by the padres as eminently practical, even though I materially differ from them as to some of the things they regarded as *religious* essentials. Yet in honor it must be said that if I, or the church to which I belong, or you and the church to which you belong, reader, had been in California in those early days, your religious teaching or mine would have been entitled, justly, to as much criticism and censure as have ever been visited upon

PLATE XV

SQUARE BRICKED DOORWAY, SAN JUAN CAPISTRANO

that of the padres. They did the best they knew, and, as I shall soon show, they did wonderfully well, far better than the enlightened government to which we belong has ever done. Certain essentials stood out before them. These were, to see that the Indians were baptized, taught the ritual of the Church, lived as near as possible according to the rules laid down for them, attended the services regularly, did their proper quota of work, were faithful husbands and wives and dutiful children. Feeling that they were indeed fathers of a race of children, the priests required obedience and work, as the father of any well-regulated American household does. And as a rule these " children," though occasionally rebellious, were willingly obedient.

Under this régime it is unquestionably true that the lot of the Indians was immeasurably improved from that of their aboriginal condition. They were kept in a state of reasonable cleanliness, were well clothed, were taught and required to do useful work, learned many new and helpful arts, and were instructed in the elemental matters of the Catholic faith. All these things were a direct advance.

It should not be overlooked, however, that the Spanish government provided skilled laborers from Spain or Mexico, and paid their hire, for the purpose of aiding the settlers in the various pueblos that were established. Master mechanics, carpenters, blacksmiths, and stone masons are mentioned in Governor Neve's Rules and Regulations, and, as I show elsewhere, some of the Indians were taught by these skilled artisans. Under the guidance of the padres some of them were taught how to weave. Cotton was both grown and imported, and all the processes of converting it, and wool also, into cloth were undertaken with skill and knowledge.

At San Juan Capistrano the swing and thud of the loom were constantly heard, there having been at one time as many as forty weavers all engaged at once in this useful occupation.

San Gabriel and San Luis Rey also had many expert weavers.

Many women also became tailors and dressmakers. At San Gabriel, under the administration of Padres Zalvidea and Sanchez, there were four thousand Indians, all of whom were clothed by the work of Indian women. Eulalia Perez de Guillen, the first owner of the Rancho San Pasqual (the site of the modern Pasadena), taught the spinning, weaving, and tailoring. She herself cut out all the dresses and clothes, and then had general oversight of the work.

It is interesting to look back and note that perhaps the very first manual training attempted in California was given by convicts. Governor Fages proposed to the authorities that artisans imprisoned in Mexico and Guadalajara should have their sentences changed to exile to California on condition that they worked at the presidios, and on the expiration of their terms remained in the country as settlers. There is record of three such men being sent in 1791, and in that same year are references to a convict blacksmith teaching his trade to the Indians in San Francisco.

In the last decade of the century a decided and successful effort was made to promote manufactures. Skilled artisans were sent from Mexico under government pay to teach various trades to the neophytes. Between 1792 and 1795 about twenty of these " manual-training " teachers — themselves skilled artisans, came to California. Here, then, was the beginning of technical schools in California. The artisans were distributed among the presidios and Missions, and some of them travelled to and fro as occasion required. In 1793–4 several San Carlos Indians received expert instruction in stone-cutting, bricklaying, etc. After 1795 the padres no longer had the

PLATE XVI

STONE ARCHED DOORWAY, SANTA MARGARITA CHAPEL

services of the artisans free. They had to pay the military officers for all work done, and if they retained the services of the artisans for teaching the Indians they were required to pay their salaries. On the other hand, if they saw fit to send the Indians to the presidios they were educated there free of charge. But as this removed them from the moral control of the padres it was avoided as much as possible. By 1800 this plan of education had produced many good workmen, and the padres felt that they were now far better able to get along than they had been hitherto. Looms were set up at many of the Missions, and the wool sheared from the Mission sheep turned into blankets and fabrics for their own clothing. In fact, after 1797 no more blankets were brought from Mexico. A little cotton was brought up from San Blas, and this the Indians wove into cloth.

There is no definite record as to when grapes, oranges, and other fruits were brought into California, but it is possible they were all brought up by way of the peninsula in the earliest of the expeditions (between 1769 and 1773), as nearly all the varieties were in flourishing condition before Padre Serra's death in 1786. Wine was manufactured in several of the southern Missions before 1785.

In 1795 a special attempt was made at San José to introduce the cultivation of flax and hemp. After overcoming the first difficulties, samples were later sent to Mexico which gave satisfaction, and in 1800 it was deemed promising enough to send Joaquin Sanchez to superintend the industry in California.

At all the Missions the girls and women, as well as the men, had their share in the general education. They had always been seed gatherers, grinders, and preparers of the food, and now they were taught the civilized methods of doing these things. Many became tailors as well as weavers; others learned to dye the made fabrics, as in the past they had dyed their basketry splints; and still others

— indeed nearly all — became skilled in the delicate arts of lace-making and drawn-work. They were natural adepts at fine embroidery, as soon as the use of the needle and colored threads was shown them, and some exquisite work is still preserved that they accomplished in this field. As candy-makers they soon became experts and manifested judicious taste.

To return to the men. Many of them became cattle, horse, and sheep herders, teamsters, and butchers. At San Gabriel alone a hundred cattle were slaughtered every Saturday as food for the Indians. The hides of all slain animals were carefully preserved, and either tanned for home use or shipped East. Dana in "Two Years Before the Mast" gives interesting pictures of hide-shipping at San Juan Capistrano. A good tanner is a skilled laborer, and these Indians were not only expert makers of dressed leather, but they tanned skins and peltries with the hair or fur on. Indeed I know of many wonderful birds'-skins, dressed with the feathers on, that are still in perfect preservation. As workers in leather they have never been surpassed. Many saddles, bridles, etc., were needed for Mission use, and as the ranches grew in numbers they created a large market. It must be remembered that horseback-riding was the chief method of travel in California for over a hundred years. Their carved-leather work is still the wonder of the world. In the striking character of their designs, in the remarkable adaptation of the design, in its general shape and contour, to the peculiar form of the object to be decorated, — a stirrup, a saddle, a belt, etc., — and in the digital and manual dexterity demanded by its execution it left nothing to be desired. Equally skilful were they in taking the horn of an ox or mountain sheep, heating it, and then shaping it into a drinking-cup, a spoon, or a ladle, and carving upon it designs that equal those found upon the pottery of the ancient world.

PLATE XVII

a. STREET AT PALATINGWA (HOT SPRINGS), WARNER'S RANCH

b. BASKET-MAKERS AT WORK AT PALATINGWA

Shoemaking was extensively carried on, for sale on the ranches and to the trading-vessels. Tallow was tried out by the ton and run into underground brick vaults, some of which would hold in one mass several complete ship-loads. This was quarried out and then hauled to San Pedro, or the nearest port, for shipment. Sometimes it was run into great bags made of hides, that would hold from five hundred to a thousand pounds each, and then shipped.

A large amount of meat was cut into strips and jerked, or sun-dried, either with or without salt, — for home use, to sell, and to trade. The Indians taught this art to the padres, and it is common among the Mexicans to this day. A writer of November, 1818, says he remembers his mother travelling in a carreta " which had two hides for a floor and two more for a roof, where, after supping on half-roasted strips of dried meat without salt, she gathered around her the whole family."

Up to 1814 all the meal used in California was ground by the women by their old-fashioned methods of metate and meal-stone, but in that year Padre Zalvidea built the first water-power grist-mill in the State. The next was erected in 1839 in San Francisco. At San Gabriel the Indians became the millers, making a coarse, unbolted meal of wheat, corn, or barley. Then it was carried to the storerooms where the women put it through a simple process of sifting.

Soap was also made on a large scale, the ashes from the brick and tile works, the bake-ovens, and tallow-furnaces, being used to leach lye for the soap. At San Antonio, old, rusty, and discarded, is an old soap-kettle that was once capable of holding many gallons.

A large number of old-fashioned tallow-dip candles were made for home use, and for sale to the ranches and vessels.

An amount of lumbering was carried on that, for those days, was large. The Indians cut down the trees, trimmed them, and brought the logs to where they were required.

They then hewed or split them with axes, or sawed them by hand. Santa Anita Canyon, near Pasadena, is still, by the old people, called Saw-pit Canyon, for in the early days a saw-pit was established there; and Hugo Reid tells us that every old Indian who was accused of witchcraft was made a sawyer. These unfortunates were chained in couples and compelled to work, two on the saw above and two below. In 1810 or 1812, however, a water-power saw-mill was set in operation by Padre Zalvidea at San Gabriel, and soon the Indians did all the work there. Lumber was sawed for buildings, fences, carts, wine-vats, cooperage, candle and soap boxes, etc.

Many of them became expert carpenters, and a few even might be classed as fair cabinet-makers, as the chapter on woodwork will show. There were wheelwrights and cart-makers who made the " carretas " that are now the joy of the relic-hunter. These were clumsy ox-carts, with wheels made of blocks, sawed or chopped off from the end of a large round log, and then a big hole bored, chiselled, or burned through its centre, enabling it to turn on a rude wooden axle. Soap or tallow was sometimes used as a lubricant. This was the only wheeled conveyance in California as late as 1840. Other Indians did the woodwork in buildings, made fences, etc. Some were carvers, and there are not a few specimens of their work that will bear comparison with the work of far more pretentious artisans.

Many of them became blacksmiths and learned to work well in iron. In the Coronel Collection in the Los Angeles Chamber of Commerce are many specimens of the ironwork of the San Fernando neophytes. The work of this Mission was long and favorably known as that of superior artisans. The collection includes plough-points, anvils, bells, hoes, chains, locks and keys, spurs, hinges, scissors, cattle-brands, and other articles of use in the Mission communities. There are also fine specimens of hammered copper, showing their ability in this branch of the craftsman's art.

As there was no coal at this time in California, these metal-workers all became charcoal-burners.

Bricks of adobe and also burnt bricks and tiles were made at every Mission, I believe, and in later years tiles were made for sale for the houses of the more pretentious inhabitants of the pueblos.   As lime and cement were needed, the Indians were taught how to burn the lime of the country, and the cement work then done remains to this day as solid as when it was first put down.

Many of them became expert bricklayers and stone-masons and cutters, as such work as that found at San Luis Rey, San Juan Capistrano, San Carlos, Santa Inés, and other Missions most eloquently testifies.

It is claimed that much of the distemper painting upon the church walls was done by the Indians, though surely it would be far easier to believe that the Fathers did it than they.   For with their training in natural design, as shown in their exquisite baskets, and the work they accomplished in leather carving, I do not hesitate to say that the mural decorations would have been far more artistic in design, more harmonious in color, and more skilfully executed if the Indians had been left to their own native ability.

A few became silversmiths, though none ever accomplished much in this line.   They made better sandal-makers, shoemakers, and hatters.   As horse-trainers they were speedily most efficient, the cunning of their minds finding a natural outlet in gaining supremacy over the lower animal.   They braided their own riatas from rawhide, and soon surpassed their teachers in the use of them.   They were fearless hunters with them, often " roping " the mountain lion and even going so far as to capture the dangerous grizzly bears and bring them down from the mountains for their bear and bull fights with no other " weapon."   As vaqueros, or cow-boys, they were a distinct class.   As daring riders as the world has ever seen, they instinctively

6

knew the arts of herding cattle and sheep, and soon had
that whole field of work in their keeping. " H. H.," in
Ramona, has told what skilled sheep-shearers they were,
and there are Indian bands to-day in Southern California
whose services are eagerly sought at good wages because
of their thoroughness, skill, and rapidity.

Now, with this list of achievements, who shall say they
were not educated? Something more than lack of education must be looked for as the reason for the degradation
and disappearance of the Indian, and in the next chapter
I think I can supply that missing reason.

At the end of sixty years, more than thirty thousand
Indian converts lodged in the Mission buildings, under the
direct and immediate guidance of the Fathers, performing
their allotted daily labors with cheerfulness and thoroughness. There were some exceptions necessarily, but in the
main the domination of the missionaries was complete. In
the years 1803–1807 G. H. von Langsdorff, Aulic Coun-
cillor to the Emperor of Russia, journeyed around the
world with Captain Krusenstern, the first Russian circum-
navigator. He visited the San Francisco and Santa Clara
Missions in March, 1806, and says : " The monks conduct
themselves in general with so much prudence, kindness, and
paternal care toward their converts, that peace, happiness, and obedience universally prevail among them. . . .
There are seldom more than from three to five soldiers,
at a time, at any Mission, but this small number always
has been found sufficient to keep the Indians under proper
restraint."

Occasionally the priests went out in search of converts;
over their breasts and shoulders then they wore a short
leathern mantle made of deer-skin. This was to protect
them against the arrows of hostile Indians, for " by a
royal command, the ecclesiastics must not carry about them
any other weapons than the Bible and the Cross."

Of the girls and widows, the same traveller says:

"They live in separate houses, and are kept at work under lock and key; they are only sometimes permitted by their superiors to go out during the day, but never at night. As soon, however, as a girl is married, she is free, and lives with her husband in one of the villages of the Indians, called *rancherías*, which belong to the Mission. By such institutions, the ecclesiastics hope to bind their converts more closely to the establishment and to spread their religion more securely and extensively. . . . The number of converted Indians at this Mission is about twelve hundred."

It has often been asked, "What became of all the proceeds of the work of the Mission Indians? Did the padres claim it personally? Was it sent to the mother house in Mexico?" etc. These questions naturally enter the minds of those who have read the criticisms of such writers as Wilson, Guinn, and Scanland. In regard to the missionaries, they were under a vow of poverty. As to the mother house, it is asserted on honor that up to 1838 not even as much as a *curio* had been sent there. After that, as is well known, there was nothing to send. The fact is, the proceeds all went into the Indian Community fund for the benefit of the Indians, or the improvement of their Mission church, gardens, or workshops. The most careful investigations by experts have led but to one opinion, and that is that in the early days there was little or no foundation for the charge that the padres were accumulating money. During the revolution it is well known that the Missions practically supported the military for a number of years, even though the padres, their wards, and their churches all suffered in consequence.

CHAPTER V

THE SECULARIZATION OF THE MISSIONS

IT was not the policy or intention of the government of Spain to found Missions in the New World solely for the benefit of the natives. Philanthropic motives doubtless influenced the rulers to a certain degree; but to civilize barbarous peoples and convert them to the Catholic faith meant not only the rescue of savages from future perdition, but the enlargement of the borders of the Church, the preparation for future colonization, and, consequently, the extension of Spanish power and territory.

At the very inception of the Missions this was the complex end in view; but the padres who were commissioned to initiate these enterprises were almost, without exception, consecrated to one work only, — the salvation of souls.

In the course of time this inevitably led to differences of opinion between the missionaries and the secular authorities in regard to the wisest methods of procedure. In spite of the arguments of the padres, these conflicts resulted in the secularization of some of the Missions prior to the founding of those in California; but the condition of the Indians on the Pacific Coast led the padres to believe that secularization was a result possible only in a remote future. They fully understood that the Missions were not intended to become permanent institutions, yet faced the problem of converting a savage race into christianized self-supporting civilians loyal to the Spanish Crown, — a problem which presented perplexities and difficulties neither understood nor appreciated at the time by the government

authorities in Spain or Mexico, nor by the mass of critics
of the padres in our own day.

Whatever may have been the mental capacity, ability,
and moral status of the Indians from one point of view, it
is certain that the padres regarded them as ignorant, vile,
incapable, and totally lost without the restraining and educating influences of the Church. As year after year opened
up the complexities of the situation, the padres became
more and more convinced that it would require an indefinite
period of time to develop these untamed children into law-
abiding citizens, according to the standard of the white
aggressors upon their territory.

On the other hand, aside from envy, jealousy, and greed,
there were reasons why some of the men in authority honestly believed a change in the Mission system of administration would be advantageous to the natives, the Church,
and the State.

There is a good as well as an evil side to the great subject of " secularization." In England the word used is
" disestablishment." In the United States, to-day, for
our own government, the general sentiment of most of its
inhabitants is in favor of what is meant by " secularization," though of course in many particulars the cases are
quite different. In other words, it means the freedom of
the Church from the control or help of the State. In such
an important matter there is bound to be great diversity
of opinion. Naturally, the church that is " disestablished "
will be a most bitter opponent of the plan, as was the
church in Ireland, in Scotland, and in Wales. In England
the " dissenters " — as all the members of the nonconform-
ist churches are entitled — are practically unanimous for
the disestablishment of the State or Episcopal Church,
while the Episcopalians believe that such an act would
" provoke the wrath of God upon the country wicked
enough to perpetrate it." The same conflict — in a slightly
different field — is that being waged in the United States

to-day against giving aid to any church in its work of educating either white children or Indians in its own sectarian institutions. All the leading churches of the country have, I believe, at some time or other in their history, been willing to receive, and actually have received, government aid in the caring for and education of Indians. To-day it is a generally accepted policy that no such help shall be given.

But the question at issue is: Was the secularization of the Missions by Mexico a wise, just, and humane measure at the time of its adoption? Let the following history tell.

From the founding of the San Diego Mission in 1769, until about sixty years later, the padres were practically in undisturbed possession, administering affairs in accordance with the instructions issued by the viceroys and the mother house of Mexico. There were several endeavors by the secular authorities to interfere with them, and this book could be filled with the records of Serra's troubles with Fages and Neve, and those of his successors. These troubles largely sprang from jealousy; and this did not decrease when the military authorities saw the wonderful successes of the padres, not only in controlling the neophytes, but in accumulating property and making it valuable. On the other hand, the padres felt they were the stewards of this property for the Indians, and were determined to guard it to the utmost of their ability. What if they did enlarge their churches, workshops, fields, pastures, gardens, flocks, herds, crops, output from workshops? — were not all these things for the Indians? The better the church could be equipped, the better could the services for the Indians be conducted. The larger the fields, the more for the Indians when the time came to divide these up amongst them. In the meantime, as they had directed the accumulation of the wealth, they had fought the battles against ignorance, sloth, and barbarism; had taught the Indians how to work and live; what more natural than

PLATE XVIII

b. DISTRIBUTING ARCH OF ADOBE AT SAN ANTONIO

a. MAIN ENTRANCE ARCH AT SAN DIEGO MISSION

that they should feel that none could conduct the establishments — even their temporalities — as well as themselves? And I for one am not ready yet to believe that when any person has built up a large institution it is just to deprive him of its control on the ground that it is too large for him to handle. The creator of an enterprise that has taken many years to develop *prima facie* is the best person to control it. This was the secret of the trouble between Neve and Serra. The former wished to introduce into the government of the new Missions to be established during his incumbency the plan of pueblo-Missions (which I shall fully describe in the companion volume to this), which had resulted so disastrously on the Colorado River. Serra objected, urging that " well enough be left alone," especially seeing the results at Yuma.

In 1787 Inspector Sola claimed that the Indians were then ready for secularization; and if there be any honor connected with the plan eventually followed, it practically belongs to him. For, though none of his recommendations were accepted, he suggested the overthrow of the old methods for others which were somewhat of the same character as those carried out many years later.

In 1793 Viceroy Gigedo referred to the secularization of certain Missions which had taken place in Mexico, and expressed his dissatisfaction with the results. Three years later, Governor Borica, writing on the same subject, expressed his opinion with force and emphasis, as to the length of time it would take to prepare the California Indians for citizenship. He said: " Those of New California, at the rate they are advancing, will not reach the goal in ten centuries; the reason God knows, and men know something about it."

In 1813 came the first direct attack upon the Mission system from the Cortes in Spain. Prior to this time a bishop had been appointed to have charge over church affairs in California, but there were too few parish churches, and he had too few clergy to send to such a far-away field to think of disturbing the present system for the Indians.   But on September 13, 1813, the Cortes passed a decree that all the Missions in America that had been founded ten years should at once be given up to the bishop "without excuse or pretext whatever, in accordance with the laws." The Mission fathers in charge might be appointed as temporary curates, but, of course, under the control of the bishop instead of the Mission president as hitherto.   This decree, for some reason, was not officially published or known in California for seven or eight years; but when, on January 20, 1821, Viceroy Venadito did publish the royal confirmation of the decree, the guardian of the college in Mexico ordered the president of the California Missions to comply at once with its requirements. He was to surrender all property, but to exact a full inventoried receipt, and he was to notify the bishop that the missionaries were ready to surrender their charges to their successors.   In accordance with this order President Payeras notified Governor Sola of his readiness to give up the Missions, and rejoiced in the opportunity it afforded his coworkers to engage in new spiritual conquests among the heathen.   But this was a false alarm.   The bishop responded that the decree had not been enforced elsewhere, and as for him the California padres might remain at their posts.   Governor Sola said he had received no official news of so important a change, but that when he did he "would act with the circumspection and prudence which so delicate a subject demands."

With Iturbide's imperial regency came a new trouble to California, largely provoked by thoughts of the great wealth of the Missions.   The imperial decree creating the regency was not announced until the end of 1821, and, practically, all California acquiesced in it.   But in the meantime Agustin Fernandez de San Vicente had been sent as a special commissioner to "learn the feelings of the

Californians, to foment a spirit of independence, to obtain
an oath of allegiance, to raise the new national flag," and
in general to superintend the change of government.   He
arrived in Monterey September 26, but found nothing to
alarm him, as nobody seemed to care much which way
things went.   Then followed the " election " of a new governor, and the wire-pullers announced that Luis Argüello
was the " choice of the convention."

In 1825 the Mexican republic may be said to have
become fairly well established.   Iturbide was out of the
way, and the politicians were beginning to rule.   A new
" political chief " was now sent to California in the person
of José María Echeandía, who arrived in San Diego late
in October, 1825.   While he and his superiors in Mexico
were desirous of bringing about secularization the difficulties in the way seemed insurmountable.   The Missions were
practically the backbone of the country ; without them all
would crumble to pieces, and the most fanatical opponent
of the system could not fail to see that without the padres
it would immediately fall.   As Clinch well puts it : " The
converts raised seven eighths of the farm produce ; — the
Missions had gathered two hundred thousand bushels in a
single harvest.   All manufacturing in the province —
weaving, tanning, leather-work, flour-mills, soap-making
— was carried on exclusively by the pupils of the Franciscans.   It was more than doubtful whether they could be
got to work under any other management, and a sudden
cessation of labor might ruin the whole territory."

Something must be done, so, after consultation with
some of the more advanced of the padres, the governor
issued a proclamation July 25, 1826, announcing to the
Indians that those who desired to leave the Missions might
do so, provided they had been Christians from childhood, or
for fifteen years, were married, or at least not minors, and
had some means of gaining a livelihood.   The Indians must
apply to the commandante at the presidio, who, after ob-

taining from the padre a report, was to issue a written permit entitling the neophyte and his family to go where they chose, their names being erased from the Mission register. The result of this might readily be foreseen. Few could take advantage of it, and those that did soon came in contact with vultures of the " superior race " who proceeded to devour them and their substance.

Between July 29 and August 3, 1830, Echeandía had the California *diputacion* discuss his fuller plans, which they finally approved. These provided for the gradual transformation of the Missions into pueblos, beginning with those nearest the presidios and pueblos, of which one or two were to be secularized within a year, and the rest as rapidly as experience proved practicable. Each neophyte was to have a share in the Mission lands and other property. The padres might remain as curates, or establish a new line of Missions among the hitherto unreached Indians as they should choose. Though this plan was passed, it was not intended that it should be carried out until approved by the general government in Mexico.

All this seems singular to us now, reading three quarters of a century later, for, March 8, 1830, Manuel Victoria was appointed political chief in Echeandía's stead; but as he did not reach San Diego until November or December, and in the meantime a new element had been introduced into the secularization question in the person of José María Padrés, Echeandía resolved upon a bold stroke. He delayed meeting Victoria, lured him up to Santa Barbara, and kept him there under various pretexts until he had had time to prepare and issue a decree. This was dated January 6, 1831. It was a political trick, " wholly illegal, uncalled for, and unwise." He decreed immediate secularization of all the Missions, and the turning into towns of Carmel and San Gabriel. The ayuntamiento of Monterey, in accordance with the decree, chose a commissioner for each of the seven Missions of the district. These were Juan B. Al-

varado for San Luis Obispo, José Castro for San Miguel,
Antonio Castro for San Antonio, Tiburcio Castro for Soledad, Juan Higuera for San Juan Bautista, Sebastian
Rodriguez for Santa Cruz, and Manuel Crespo for San
Carlos. Castro and Alvarado were sent to San Miguel and
San Luis Obispo respectively, where they read the decree
and made speeches to the Indians; at San Miguel Alvarado
made a spread-eagle speech from a cart and used all his
eloquence to persuade the Indians to adopt the plan of
freemen. " Henceforth their trials were to be over. No
tyrannical priest could compel them to work. They were
to be citizens in a free and glorious republic, with none to
molest or make them afraid." Then he called for those
who wished to enjoy these blessings of freedom to come
to the right, while those who were content to remain under
the hideous bondage of the Missions could go to the left.
Imagine his surprise and the chill his oratory received when
all but a small handful quickly went to the left, and those
who at first went to the right speedily joined the majority.
At San Luis and San Antonio the Indians also preferred
" slavery."

By this time Victoria began to see that he was being
played with, so he hurried to Monterey and demanded the
immediate surrender of the office to which he was entitled.
One of his first acts was to nullify Echeandía's decree, and
to write to Mexico and explain fully that it was undoubtedly owing to the influence of Padrés, whom he well knew.
But before the end of the year Echeandía and his friends
rose in rebellion, deposed, and exiled Victoria. Owing to
the struggles then going on in Mexico, which culminated
in Santa Anna's dictatorship, the revolt of Echeandía was
overlooked and Figueroa appointed governor in his stead.

Prior to this, however, Padre Duran had written (August, 1831) to the fathers, asking them for their opinion of
a plan of virtual secularization, which gave freedom from
Mission supervision to the Indians, division of property so

that it would provide for the services of the Church, the support of the padres, and help found new Missions. Only three replies are extant. These are interesting. Bancroft thus summarizes these letters:

" Padre Juan Cabot writes from San Miguel August 24th, that while he would be glad to be freed from his cares, he can see no way of distributing the estates without producing ruin. The Indians of his mission would have to be scattered at long distances in order to get a living, and he could not be responsible for their spiritual care. Padre José Sanchez deemed the execution of the project probably inevitable, but sure to result, as it was intended to, in total destruction to the missions. Taking into consideration what had happened in Baja California, and Sonora, he could see no possibility of good results here. ' So far as it concerns me personally,' he writes, ' would that it might be to-morrow, that I might retire between the four walls of a cell to weep over the time I have wasted in behalf of these miserables.' Padre José Joachin Jimenez of Santa Cruz wrote in October that in view of the reasons urged by the government, and of the fact that the burden was becoming insupportable to the friars, it would be wisest to free the Indians and distribute the property on the basis proposed; but also that the Indians should be obliged to keep their share and to work."

One matter of importance must not be forgotten. In 1833 ten padres from the college of Zacatecas were sent to California. It must be remembered that all the padres of the old régime were Spaniards. Mexico had revolted from Spain, and there were not a few who constantly agitated their fears that the Spanish padres of California would not fail to intrigue for the restoration of Spanish control. Orders of banishment were issued against them, but the governors found it practically impossible to enforce them. The padres were growing old, and new blood was required; so, as the Zacatecans were all Mexicans, their college was required to send priests to supply the vacant places. They were given control of all the seven Missions north, includ-

PLATE XIX

b. DOORWAY AT PRESIDIO CHURCH, MONTEREY

a. DOORWAY TO SACRISTY, SAN CARLOS CARMELO

ing San Carlos. Their superior, who had the title of Commissary, was Francisco García Diego, and he went to reside at Santa Clara.

In the meantime the Californian delegate to the Mexican Congress, Carlos Carrillo, was making strenuous efforts to keep the Missions and the Pious Fund intact. His zeal delayed any immediate action on the Missions, but a decree was passed May 25, 1832, empowering the executive to rent out the properties owned by the Pious Fund for the period of seven years, the proceeds to be paid into the national treasury. There can be no doubt whatever but that this fund excited the cupidity of the Mexican politicians. These moneys and the prosperous condition of the California Missions were the chief causes of their downfall.

With Figueroa the battle grew fiercer. So much time and attention did he give to it that he finally published a " Manifesto " to the Mexican people, explaining *in extenso* his action. This, better than anything else, shows how the vultures at that time were flying towards the declining Missions. The successive blows had been subversive of discipline, of everything worth preserving, and the end was not far off.

At first the new governor was inclined to follow Echeandía's plans (who, by the way, was still in California, posing as a preserver of peace and respecter of authority), but he soon saw that too rapid secularization would demoralize everything. He reported to Mexico that the Indians were but as children with a natural predilection for the customs of their ancestors, and for a savage life without work. During their " reduction " they had learned, perforce, only to cultivate the soil imperfectly, to practice some rude industries, and to manage horses. If freed at once from their present state of mild servitude, they would soon from proprietors become beggars, after having bartered away their possessions for liquors and gewgaws. They would then return to the wilderness and join the wild Indians in stealing cattle and horses, in order to sell them to the New Mexicans and foreigners. Nevertheless he issued a series of provisional regulations on gradual emancipation, awaiting instructions from the general government.

It was at this time that Don José María de Hijar appeared in company with the exiled Padrés upon the scene. Figueroa's ill health had led him to resign. Doubtless knowing of this through his official " pulls " in Mexico, Padrés had intrigued with such success that the Cortes passed, August 17, 1833, the law of secularization by which the final crash was brought about. The act also provided for the colonization of both the Californias, the expenses of this latter move to be borne by the proceeds gained from the distribution of the Mission property. Hijar was to be made governor of Upper California for the purpose of carrying this law into effect.

But in the meantime Figueroa's health having been restored, he was continued in office, so that, when Hijar and Padrés appeared on the scene with a number of colonists, he met the former's instructions to take the political chieftainship, with later instructions from the supreme government requiring of him " that you must not deliver up the said command, and that you must continue in discharge of the government."

Here, indeed, was a pretty kettle of fish. It cannot be denied that it was awkward for all concerned. Hijar and Padrés had started out on an elaborate expedition, the initial cost financed by the government, and a law passed providing for the later expenses. They had come a long distance, and had brought the colonists into a foreign land, these latter necessarily relying upon the good faith of the supreme government and assured of the integrity of their leaders, and then, suddenly, they find their high hopes blasted by a complete reversal of the government's plans. Their position was critical and embarrassing. Regardless of who or what they were, we cannot fail to sympathize

with them in their situation.   Yet, equally so, can we realize
the position of Figueroa and honor him for his determined
stand, not to allow the Missions to be spoliated, and the
Indians robbed because of the bungling, or worse, of the
politicians in the colonization scheme.   The " Manifesto " is
Figueroa's statement of what transpired between himself
and Hijar in the hot and sore controversy that ensued.
Had he manfully stood by his first position he would have
been regarded as a sincere defender of the Missions; but
after a long period of quarrelling with Hijar and Padrés,
he exiled them on the ground of their complicity in a revolution which sought his overthrow, and then published the
" Manifesto " to the Californian and Mexican peoples to
explain his action.

There is strong reason, however, to doubt Figueroa's
sincerity.   Just as Echeandía had forestalled the government's action, so did he.   Even though he had deemed his
own plans of secularization superior to those of Mexico,
he was sworn to carry out the laws.   If he could not consci-
entiously do this he should have resigned.   To his own
high-handed breaking of the law much subsequent lawlessness must be attributed.

As to what was actually accomplished under his orders,
the records give uncertain knowledge.   It is known that
ten of the Missions were fully secularized.   Bancroft summarizes all the information he found about the year 1834
somewhat as follows: " There is nothing in relation to San
Diego.   At San Luis Rey, Captain Portilla was commissioner in November, and the accounts turned over by Padre
Fortuni showed assets of $46,613 and liabilities of $14,429.
In December the Indians refused to work, and ran away,
taking most of the horses and killing many cattle; but in
January they began to come back and behave better.
There is no record for San Juan Capistrano, except that
Juan José Rocha, probably the commissioner, acknowl-
edges on November 22 receipt of resolution to secularize

the Mission.   At San Gabriel an inventory was made in November, 1834, and Lieutenant-colonel Gutierrez was doubtless the commissioner, being in charge early next year. Lieutenant Antonio del Valle was the commissioner at San Fernando, and was engaged in October in making inventories.   At Santa Barbara Alf. Anastasio Carillo was commissioner from September, with José María García as majordomo from October.   Domingo Carillo was commissioner of Purísima in November.   There are no records for San Luis, San Miguel, San Antonio, San Carlos, San Juan, or Soledad.   Santa Cruz, which was now known as Pueblo de Figueroa, was delivered to Alf. Ignacio del Valle as commissioner on August 24; and Juan Gonzalez was majordomo from October.   There is no record of secularization this year at Santa Clara or San José.   At San Francisco de Asis Joaquin Estudillo took charge as commissioner in September.   At San Rafael an inventory was taken in September, the pueblo was marked out in October by Ignacio Martinez, who was probably the commissioner, and stock was distributed in December.   San Francisco Solano was perhaps not fully secularized until next year."

In 1835 it is noted that six additional Missions were secularized, — San Diego, San Luis Obispo, San Antonio, Soledad, San Juan Bautista, and San Francisco Solano. So far as the records show, nothing had yet been done to definitely change the status of San Buenaventura, Santa Inés, San Miguel, Santa Clara, and San José.   In 1836–37, however, these were secularized, the first two owing to a quarrel the padres had with the new governor, Chico, and the others by order of the assembly.

Figueroa was now dead, but the plan he had illegally set in motion was at work.   The old padres, who, as it will be remembered, were now south of San Carlos, generally accepted the situation in good faith.   They had fought a good and long fight, had lost, and, as gentlemen and christians, were accepting the result.   It is said the new padres from Zacatecas were not so complaisant; but there are so many wild rumors and exaggerated statements as the natural outcome of the strained political conditions of the time that it is almost impossible to get at the truth.

There have been hundreds of pages written about the wild slaughtering of cattle by the padres in order that they might turn into money everything under their control. That the officials of the province believed that something of this kind was going on is evident by the two decrees they passed upon the subject, and Bancroft thinks there was some foundation for the general belief, though much exaggerated. As to the further charge that the padres wantonly injured the Mission buildings, I cannot believe there is the slightest foundation of truth in it. They may have neglected the gardens and orchards, as who would not, not knowing at what moment they might be sent away, and the Indians feeling, as the slaves did in the South during the Civil War, all the unsettling influences of the time, and, therefore, making the task of controlling them especially hard.

It is possible that if things could have gone on for a decade as Figueroa had planned, all would have ended much more happily than it did. But fresh and worse disasters were ahead.

To attempt to recount them all is impossible. Mexico being in such a whirl of revolution, California was equally afflicted, and there came governor after governor, " each worse than the other," as a Hibernian might express it. Rival political factions outdid each other in their spoliation policies towards the Missions. Under any circumstances, — even of the very best, — the secularization plan would have required great wisdom to carry it out. As it was, it seems as if no combination of circumstances could have been worse. All writers are unanimous in saying that Governor Alvarado's rule from 1836 to 1842 was one of plunder and ruin in Mission history. Bancroft says " the methods of spoliation were substantially as follows: The governor and subordinate officials by his authority used the cattle and grain of the Missions as freely as they used the revenues from other sources. If the government contracted a debt to a trader, the governor gave in payment an order on any Mission for wheat, tallow, or hides, just as he would draw a check on the treasury. The majordomo, being an employé of the government, obeyed the order as a rule whenever the articles called for existed at his Mission."

Governor Alvarado also " loaned " Mission cattle to private individuals, on the condition that the same number of cattle be returned later. In nine cases out of ten the loans were never repaid.

Of the methods too generally followed by the administrators of the order of secularization, too strong words of censure cannot be spoken. They were selfishly cruel, wantonly wicked, and diabolically inhuman. There was no pretence to any care for the rights or interests of the Indians. The Mission establishments were merely objects of legalized pillage, or, at least, if the pillage were not legalized, it was overlooked and tacitly condoned. As business men they were incompetent and stupid, deliberately allowing valuable properties to drift to ruin without the slightest attempt to save them. " Others were vicious as well as incompetent, always ready to sell any article of Mission property, not only live-stock, but kitchen utensils, farm implements, tools from the shops, and tiles from the roofs, for money with which to gratify their propensity for gambling. Still others were dishonest and able, devoting their energies to laying the foundation of future wealth for themselves and friends, oppressing the Indians, quarrelling with such padres, officials, and assistants as they could not control or deceive, and disposing of the Mission wealth without scruple for their own interests. Finally, there were, I suppose, some honest, faithful, and tolerably efficient managers, who did as well as was possible under difficult circumstances."

When Pio Pico became governor, there were few funds with which to carry on the affairs of the country, and he prevailed upon the assembly to pass a decree authorizing the renting or the sale of the Mission property, reserving only the church, a curate's house, and a building for a court-house. From the proceeds the expenses of conducting the services of the church were to be provided, but there was no disposition made as to what should be done to secure the funds for that purpose. Under this decree the final acts of spoliation were consummated, as will be seen from a study of the chapter devoted to each Mission.

The padres took the matter in accordance with their individual temperaments. Some were hopefully cheerful, and did the best they could for their Indian charges; others were sulky and sullen, and retired to the chambers allotted to them, coming forth only when necessary duty called; still others were belligerent, and fought everything and everybody, and, it must be confessed, generally with just cause.

As for the Indians, elsewhere I have shown the effect of the change upon them. It was exactly as all thoughtful men had foreseen. Those who received property seldom made good use of it, and soon lost it. Cattle were neglected, tools unused, for there were none to compel to their care or use. Consequently it was easy to convert them into money, which was soon gambled or drank away. Rapidly they sank from worse to worse, until now only a few scattered settlements remain of the once vast number, 30,000 or more, that were reasonably happy and prosperous under the rule of the padres.

A laudable effort is now being made to save some of the things scattered at the time of secularization. One collection has been bought by the Southern California Archæological Society, and it is eventually to be placed on permanent exhibition in Los Angeles. It is thus described:

"There is in Los Angeles, an invaluable collection of oil paintings, mostly very old, which formerly hung in the Franciscan Missions of Southern California; and a collection of books which were once in the libraries of those Missions. At the time of the secularization these articles were pillaged, even as the tiles were stolen to roof sheds and pig-pens. About twenty years ago, a man with the right feeling — a poor man, it hardly needs be said — began gathering up these scattered articles, buying them at his own proper cost from the families into whose hands they had fallen."

When it was known that the United States had designs on California the last scramble came. Lands, churches, everything was sold at whatever price it would fetch; in some cases given away by the last honorable governor. Properties were sold for as many tens as they were worth thousands.

When, finally, the United States gained possession, and a land court adjudicated the questions of title, all the Mission buildings were returned to the custody of the Church, and some of the lands. But their glory was departed; their sun was set; and we look upon them now as we look on their ruined temples of Assyria, the Nile, and India, — memorials of a time and conditions that are past.

CHAPTER VI

SAN DIEGO DE ALCALÁ

THE story of the founding of San Diego by Serra has already been given. It was the beginning of the realization of his fondest hopes. The early troubles with the Indians delayed conversions, but in 1773 Serra reported that some headway had been made. He gives the original name of the place as *Cosoy*, in 32° 43', built on a hill two gunshots from the shore, and facing the entrance to the port at Point Guijarros. The missionaries left in charge were Padres Fernando Parron and Francisco Gomez.

About the middle of July ill health compelled Parron to retire to Lower California and Gomez to Mexico, and Padres Luis Jayme and Francisco Dumetz took their places.

San Diego was in danger of being abandoned for lack of provisions, for in 1772 Padre Crespí, who was at San Carlos, writes that on the 30th of March of that year "the mail reached us with the lamentable news that this Mission of San Diego was to be abandoned for lack of victuals." Serra then sent him with "twenty-two mules, and with them fifteen half-loads of flour" for their succor. Padres Dumetz and Cambon had gone out to hunt for food to the Lower California Missions. The same scarcity was noticed at San Gabriel, and the padres, "for a considerable time, already, had been using the supplies which were on hand to found the Mission of San Buenaventura; and though they have *drawn their belts tight* there remains to them provisions only for two months and a half." Later, Crespí asks:

"What are we to do if there is not wherewith we can maintain ourselves? If the escort for a long time is maintaining itself with the sole ration of half a pint of corn, and of only twenty ounces of Flour daily; and the Fathers the same, with a little milk — how are they to be able to endure? We are without pottage whatever, more than the little Corn and Flour aforesaid. And they say that thus they have passed most of the year — without lard, without tallow, and without one candle of this sort, nor even wine for masses — since only on Sundays and feast days is Mass said. God grant that Father Dumetz arrive promptly with the Succor for these Missions, and that the Barque bring it to us. For otherwise we are Lost."

Fortunately help came from both sources; so the work continued.

The region of San Diego was well peopled. At the time of the founding there were eleven rancherías within a radius of ten leagues. They must have been of a different type from most of the Indians of the coast, for, from the first, as the old Spanish chronicler reports, they were insolent, arrogant, and thievish. They lived on grass seeds, fish, and rabbits.

In 1774, the separation of the Mission from the presidio was decided upon, in order to remove the neophytes from the evil influences of the soldiers. The site chosen was six miles up the valley (named *Nipaguay* by the Indians), and so well did all work together that by the end of the year a dwelling, a storehouse, a smithy built of adobes, and a wooden church eighteen by fifty-seven feet, and roofed with tiles, were completed. Already the work of the padres had accomplished much. Seventy-six neophytes rejoiced their religious hearts, and the herds had increased to 40 cattle, 64 sheep, 55 goats, 19 hogs, 2 jacks, 2 burros, 17 mares, 3 foals, 9 horses, 22 mules, — 233 animals in all.

The presidio remained at Cosoy (where the old palms

PLATE XX

a. OUR LADY AS QUEEN OF HEAVEN,
SANTA BARBARA

b. THE HOLY VIRGIN MOTHER

c. SANTA LUCIA

d. SANTA INÉS

now are at Old San Diego), and four thousand adobes that had been made for the Mission buildings were turned over to the military. A rude stockade was erected, with two bronze cannon, one mounted towards the harbor, the other towards the Indian ranchería.

The experiments in grain raising at first were not successful. The seed was sown in the river bottom and the crop was destroyed by the unexpected rising of the river. The following year it was sown so far from water that it died from drought.

There were several changes, arrivals, and departures among the padres during the first few years, but the most important was the arrival on August 30, 1773, of Francisco Palou with seven others from Lower California.

In the meantime Serra, having had difficulties with Governor Fages, went to Mexico to plead the cause of the Missions, and, returning, arrived at San Diego March 13, 1774. On the 6th of April he left for Monterey. Slowly things began to improve. In the fall of 1775 all seemed to be bright with hope. New buildings had been erected, a well dug, and more land made ready for sowing. The Indians were showing greater willingness to submit themselves to the priests, when a conflict occurred that revealed to the padres what they might have to contend with in their future efforts towards the christianizing of the natives. The day before the feast of St. Francis (October 4), 1775, Padres Jayme and Fuster were made happy by being required to baptize sixty new converts. Yet a few days later they were saddened by the fact that two of these newly baptized fled from the Mission and escaped to the mountains, there to stir up enmity and revolt. For nearly a month they moved about, fanning the fires of hatred against the " long gowns," until on the night of November 4 (1775) nearly 800 naked savages, after dusk, stealthily advanced and surrounded the Mission where the inmates slept unguarded, so certain were they of their security.

Part of the force went on to the presidio, where, in the absence of the commander, the laxity of discipline was such that no sentinel was on guard.

An hour after midnight the whole of the Mission was surrounded. The quarters of the christianized Indians were invaded, and they were threatened with instantaneous death if they gave the alarm. The church was broken into and all the vestments and sacred vessels stolen. Then the buildings were fired. Not until then did the inmates know of their danger. Imagine their horror, to wake up and find the building on fire and themselves surrounded by what, in their dazed condition, seemed countless hordes of savages, all howling, yelling, brandishing war clubs, firing their arrows, — the scene made doubly fearful by the red glare of the flames.

In the guard-house were four soldiers, — the whole of the Mission garrison; in the house the two priests, Jayme and Fuster, two little boys, and three men (a blacksmith and two carpenters). Father Fuster, the two boys, and the blacksmith sought to reach the guard-house, but the latter was slain on the way. The Indians broke into the room where the carpenters were, and one of them was so cruelly wounded that he died the next day.

Father Jayme, with the shining light of martyrdom in his eyes, and the fierce joy of fearlessness in his heart, not only refused to seek shelter, but deliberately walked towards the howling band, lifting his hands in blessing with his usual salutation: " Love God, my children! " Scarcely were the words uttered when the wild band fell upon him, shrieking and crying, tearing off his habit, thrusting him rudely along, smiting him with stones, sticks, and battle-axe, until at the edge of the creek his now naked body was bruised until life was extinct, and then the corpse filled with arrows.

During this time the fierce attack on the guard-house continued. Soon it was in flames. Six men and two children defended it against not less than four hundred screeching, vindictive, avowedly murderous savages. One of the soldiers, who in the flurry had forgotten his leathern cuirass, was soon disabled; thus three only of the soldiers and the carpenter were the firing squad, with Father Fuster and the two boys loading the guns for them. When the heat grew unbearable this brave band rushed into a kitchen close by, which had one side open. Its roof consisted of boughs thrown loosely over to protect those inside from the sun's rays. Into the open space the Indians hurled firebrands, discharged their arrows, and sent whirling stones with crashing force. To afford a little more protection, the defenders raised a small barricade with chests, boxes, etc., from the adjoining storeroom.

Soon the Indians who had gone to storm the presidio returned. They had not reached their destination when the glare of the flames apprised them that the attack on the Mission had begun; and, fearing lest the garrison should thereby be warned and prepared for them, they decided to return. The loud shout that went up from the Indians at this great reinforcement would have sent terror into the stoutest heart; yet, though only two of the soldiers and the padre were left in fighting trim, the grim defence still went on. So successful were the shots of the defenders that they managed to keep the foe at bay until morning, when, giving up the fight, the attacking force gathered up their dead and wounded and retired to the mountains.

No sooner were they gone than the neophytes came rushing up to see if any were left alive. Their delight at finding Father Fuster was immediately changed into sadness as others brought in the awfully mutilated and desecrated body of Father Jayme. Not until then did Father Fuster know that his companion was dead, and deep was the mourning of his inmost soul as he performed the last offices for his dear companion.

Strange to say, so careless was the garrison that not

until a messenger reached it from Father Fuster did they know of the attack. They had placed no guards, posted no sentinels, and, indifferent in their foolish scorn of the prowess and courage of the Indians, had slept calmly, though they themselves might easily have been surprised, and the whole garrison murdered while asleep.

It was a melancholy procession that marched from the smoking ruins to the presidio, — the wounded and disabled, the murdered padre, the charred remains of the black-smith, and the few animals that remained of the Mission herds, accompanied by the saddened padre and his faithful few.

Investigation revealed that after the last baptismal ceremony two of the neophytes, Carlos and Francisco, had run away and started on a tour of all the rancherías, inciting the Indians to rise and kill the Spaniards. As to the participation of the other neophytes, there seems to be disagreement. Anza believed that these planned the uprising, deceiving the padres, and made the surprise possible.

When the news reached Serra it brought a song of praise from his heart, instead of a wail of regret: "God be thanked; now the soil is watered; now will the reduction of the Dieguinos be complete." In the meantime letters were sent for aid to Rivera at Monterey, and Anza, the latter known to be approaching from the Colorado River region; and in suspense until they arrived, the little garrison and the remaining priests passed the rest of the year. The two commanders met at San Gabriel, and together marched to San Diego, where they arrived January 11, 1776. It was not long before they quarrelled. Anza was for quick, decisive action; Rivera was for delay; and, when news arrived from San Gabriel that the food supply was running short, Anza left in order to carry out his original orders, which involved the founding of San Francisco. Not long after his departure Carlos, the neophyte who had been concerned in the insurrection, returned to San Diego, and, doubtless acting under the suggestion of the padres, took refuge in the temporary church at the presidio. The law of sanctuary for many centuries operated in nearly all — if not all — European countries. Any debtor or person suspected of crime was allowed to postpone his arrest by entering a church. It was the old Hebrew law that a criminal was safe if he took hold of the two horns upon the altar. In all Spanish-speaking countries the civil law forbade the magistrates or their officers from laying their hands upon any person inside a church without the permission of the clerical authorities. The proper and authorized method of procedure was to make a sworn declaration, and with this in hand given to the priest, the obstacle was removed.

In the case of the Indian Carlos, Padre Fuster notified Rivera and informed him what was to be done. The Governor, instead of sending the sworn document which would have ended the matter, sent an officer with a letter demanding the surrender of the Indian on two grounds, namely: that his offence was such as not to entitle him to sanctuary; and that the room where mass was said could not be called a church. The padre held a consultation with his brother priests, and as a result the Governor was told that, except on the sworn statement, they dare not give up the man, save by orders of their superior, Serra, and that, therefore, if he attempted to make the arrest by force they would be under the necessity of excommunicating him. Immediately on receipt of this answer, Rivera called for a lighted candle, his baton of office, and, his sword by his side, entered the church, seized the skulking Indian, took him outside and delivered him to the guard. Padre Fuster protested against this violation of both civil and church law, but all the answer he got was: " Protest away, your reverence, for there goes the protest before you." And he pointed to the prisoner that his officers were taking away.

On the next feast day Padre Lasuen (who afterwards

became Padre presidente of the California Missions), had to say mass, but before he did so declared that those who had violated the sanctuary must depart, and Rivera and his officers, who had participated in the affair, were obliged to retire before the service proceeded.

It was not until after the intervention of Padre Serra that the ban of excommunication was removed from Rivera, and this was doubtless one of the causes that led him to annoy the priests whenever occasion arose.

In his method of dealing with the rebel Indians, Serra saw a great hindrance to his spiritual work. It had been found by long years of missionary labor that prompt and decisive measures, and then the exercise of a kindly spirit, worked far better than long continued retaliatory measures. Rivera, on the other hand, went in for extensive campaigns, long examinations, and rigorous punishment of those he deemed guilty. All this interfered with resumption of work on the church; so Serra himself went to San Diego, and, finding the ship " San Antonio " in the harbor, made an arrangement with Captain Choquet to supply sailors to do the building under his own direction. Rivera was then written to for a guard, and he sent six soldiers. On August 22, 1777, the three padres, Choquet with his mate and boatswain and twenty sailors, a company of neophytes, and the six soldiers went to the old site and began work in earnest, digging the foundations, making adobes, and collecting stones. The plan was to build a wall for defence, and then erect the church and other buildings inside. For fifteen days all went well. Then an Indian went to Rivera with a story that hostile Indians were preparing arrows for a new attack, and this so scared the gallant officer that he withdrew his six men. Choquet had to leave with his men, as he dared not take the responsibility of being away with so many men without the consent of Rivera; and, to the padre's great sorrow, the work had to cease.

PLATE XXI

a. ST. JOHN THE EVANGELIST, SANTA CLARA

b. ST. STEPHEN, SANTA CLARA

c. PROCESSIONAL CROSS (FRONT), SANTA INÉS

d. PROCESSIONAL CROSS (REVERSE), SANTA INÉS

A few days later a native reported that soldiers were marching up the peninsula from Velicatá. These were found to be extra soldiers for guards, so it was not long before work was resumed, and the buildings were in condition for occupancy.

In March of 1778 Captain Carrillo was sent to chastise hostile Indians at Pamó who had sent insolent messages to Captain Ortega. Carrillo surprised the foe, killed two, burned others who took refuge in a hut, while the others surrendered and were publicly flogged. The four chiefs, Aachel, Aalcuirin, Aaaran, and Taguagui, were captured, taken to San Diego, and there shot, though the officer had no legal right to condemn even an Indian to death without the approval of the governor. Ortega's sentence reads: " Deeming it useful to the service of God, the King, and the public weal, I sentence them to a violent death by two musket-shots on the 11th at 9 A. M., the troops to be present at the execution under arms, also all the Christian rancherías subject to the San Diego Mission, that they may be warned to act righteously."

Ortega then instructed Padres Lasuen and Figuer to prepare the condemned. "You will co-operate for the good of their souls in the understanding that if they do not accept the salutary waters of baptism they die on Saturday morning; and if they do — they die all the same!" This was the first public execution in California.

In 1779 Indians were chosen as alcaldes and regidores. This was a wise procedure, and one which, perhaps better than any other, if persisted in, would have taught the responsibilities of citizenship to the Indians. To have members of their own society act as magistrates, and, under the direction of the padres until they were wise enough to work alone, administer their laws, would have taught them far more than paternalism could have done. It is a great pity that this system, thus wisely begun, was not persisted in and introduced at all the Missions.

In 1780 the new church, built of adobe, strengthened and roofed with pine timbers, ninety feet long and seventeen feet wide and high, was completed.

In 1782 fire destroyed the old presidio church.

All communication with Mexico was either by water or overland down the peninsula. When Governor Neve left California he recommended that a new and better route to the south be found, and this was evidently done, as in 1786 General Rengel gave his approval to a new route which was said to save ten or twelve leagues of distance and avoid some dangerous bands of coast Indians.

It was also attempted, in 1783, to find an inland route by way of the desert and the Colorado River to Sonora, but the officer sent out — Alférez Velasquez — soon wearied and returned. In 1785 Governor Fages himself made the trip, having one or two brushes with the Indians. He, by the way, was the first white man who crossed from the Colorado River to San Diego. He made this trip in 1782.

In 1783 Lasuen made an interesting report on the condition of San Diego. At the Mission there were church, granary, storehouse, hospital, men's house, shed for wood and oven, two houses for the padres, larder, guest-room, and kitchen. These, with the soldiers' barracks, filled three sides of a square of about 160 feet, and on the fourth side was an adobe wall, nearly ten feet high. There were 740 neophytes at that time under missionary care, though Lasuen spoke most disparagingly of the location as a Mission site.

In May, 1790, José Antonio Romeu was appointed governor of the Californias, and in August of 1791 he reached San Diego on his way to Monterey. His rule was short, for he died in April of the following year, and was succeeded by Arrillaga, who was the lieutenant-governor.

In 1800 the number of neophytes at San Diego was 1523. There had been 1320 baptisms and 628 deaths. It was now the most populous Mission in California. In the year 1797 there were 554 baptisms, the banner year in the whole history of the Missions except 1803, when, at Santa Barbara, 831 received the water of the holy sacrament.

The Mission herds multiplied in this decade from 1730 to 6960 head, and its flocks from 2100 to 6000. The harvest of agricultural products in 1800 was 2600 bushels, the largest crops having been 9450 bushels in 1793 and 1799. A large tile-roofed granary was built, 96 by 24 feet. In 1794 the Mission wall was constructed, and the vineyard surrounded by five hundred yards of adobe wall. In 1795 work was begun on a newly discovered source of water-supply for irrigation. This is believed by some to have been the extensive work now in ruins; though others claim it was not begun until after the ruinous drought of 1809.

The dam is in a rocky gorge at the west end of the Cajon Valley, about three and a half miles above the Mission. It is built of gray granite and cement, more than twelve feet thick, and is almost as perfect as when completed, though the sand has filled it up nearly to the level. A three-inch tile opened into the acequia, which is made of cement and stones, with a concave tile for the bottom. It is two feet across and two feet in depth.

There were places where the aqueduct had to be carried over cross-gulches, but the fall of the channel was so perfectly engineered that it delivered the water in full flow at the spot required. In 1817 Governor Sola visited San Diego, and he says the padres " had now begun to bring water through conduits," so it may be possible these works were not finished until about that time.

From the top of the dam a glorious view may be had of Cuyamaca Peak, about forty miles away, where the timbers were secured for the Waste Gate and the Mission; and about a mile above the dam, on a hill commanding a wonderful outlook, is an old fortified sentinel post that gives view over the whole Cajon Valley. It was a circular enclosure of stone between huge boulders, and the old Indians have told me it was constantly used for years on account of the hostile tendencies of the mountain Indians.

Considerable excitement was caused in 1803 by the appearance of the " Lelia Byrd," Captain Cleveland, which tried to do some illegal bargaining for otter-skins, trade in which was absolutely forbidden by the Spanish government. Cleveland had learned that some of the soldiers had skins to sell if they could dispose of them secretly; so in the night two boats were sent off. One came back in due time with a few skins; the other was captured and its men made prisoners. Next morning Cleveland went ashore with four men, rescued the captives, returned to his vessel, and then, setting sail, attempted to run out past the guns of the fort. It should not be forgotten that when the commandant came on board to investigate the reason for the visit of Cleveland he left a sergeant and five men on board as a guard. These men were made to occupy as conspicuous a position on the fleeing vessel as possible, but this did not prevent the officers at the fort from sending several well-directed shot at the vessel, one of which made an ugly hole just above the water line. But she made her escape, after landing the six Spaniards. One amusing sequence to the affair was the overhauling of one of the corporals and his men for their share in the trading. They were compelled to give up the goods they had received for their contraband otter-skins, and they were eventually sold at auction for $212, the proceeds of which were divided among the men who made the capture of the sailors of Cleveland's boat.

May 25, 1803, an earthquake slightly damaged the Mission church, and then, or later, a new church was begun. It was finished and dedicated on San Diego's day, November 12, 1813.

In 1824 San Diego registered its largest population, being then 1829.

When Spanish rule ended, and the Mexican empire and

republic sent its first governor, Echeandía, he decided to make San Diego his home; so for the period of his governorship, though he doubtless lived at or near the presidio, the Mission saw more or less of him. As is shown in the chapter on secularization, he was engaged in a thankless task when he sought to change the Mission system, and there was no love lost between the Governor's house and the Mission.

In 1833, from February to June, there was considerable excitement caused by a rumor that Indians in El Cajon were to gather together and make an onslaught upon the Mission. A small force was sent out to capture the chief, Tajochi, and other ringleaders. He was sentenced to two years of public work, and three of his associates received shorter sentences.

In 1833 Governor Figueroa visited San Diego Mission in person, in order to exhort the neophytes to seize the advantages of citizenship which the new secularization regulations were to give to them; but, though they heard him patiently, and there and at San Luis Rey one hundred and sixty families were found to be duly qualified for " freedom," only ten could be found to accept it. Nevertheless he appointed Captain Argüello as comisionado to carry out the new law, though the Mission itself was not formally secularized until 1834. In April of that year Joaquin Ortega became the majordomo. How many Indians were allotted lands we do not know, though the pueblo of San Pascual, with thirty-four families, was in existence in November. These were doubtless San Diego neophytes. But the decline of the Mission had begun. Though in November, 1835, the decree was issued that the temporal control should be restored to the padres, nothing seems to have been done.

In 1836 complaints were frequent and loud against the Indians, and the citizens made several expeditions against them, in one of which seven Indians were killed. In April

8

or May of 1837 the Indians made a raid on the frontier ranchos, and at Jamul several whites were killed, and the majordomo's two grown-up daughters were carried away into captivity, from which they were never released. The San Diegans were in great terror, but protection was afforded by the ship " Alert "; and later, Juan Bandini, whose rancho of *Tecate* was one of the plundered, returned from Los Angeles, marched against the foe, and in a campaign of ten days is said to have killed several Indians, — all he could find. Thus already the work of the demoralization and destruction of the Indians had begun, as the result of the secularization plans. Another excitement in 1837 was caused by the rumor of a plot to attack the town and kill all the Spanish inhabitants. Indian servants were to co-operate by opening doors, but one of them revealed the plot, and three out of the dozen servants were immediately arrested and shot.

December 11, 1841, saw the arrival of the newly appointed Bishop of California. García Diego was the prefect of the band of Zacatecanos who, it will be remembered, came to take charge of the seven northern Missions in 1833. When secularization made parishes of the Missions, even the politicians saw that it was no longer reasonable to suppose that the ecclesiastical affairs of California could be administered by the bishop in Sonora; so Diego was appointed, with a large salary (on paper) and control of the Pious Fund.

On the 29th of March, 1843, Governor Micheltorena issued a decree which restored San Diego Mission temporalities to the management of the padre. He explained in his prelude that the decree was owing to the fact that the Mission establishments had been reduced to the mere space occupied by the buildings and orchards, that the padres had no support but that of charity, etc. Mofras gives the number of Indians in 1842 as 500, but an official report of 1844 gives only 100. The Mission retained the ranchos of

Santa Isabel and El Cajon until 1844–45, and then, doubt-less, they were sold or rented in accordance with the plans of Pio Pico.

In 1852 Bartlett visited San Diego Mission. He says:

"It is a spot possessing great picturesque beauty, and sur-rounded by fertile and well watered lands. It was the last of the California Missions that was abandoned; and but five years ago its ancient library and its priest still remained. The build-ings, which are of adobe, are not extensive, but are in good pres-ervation. The Mission is at present occupied by United States troops, under the command of Col. J. B. Magruder, and in consequence is kept in good repair."

To-day nothing but the *fachada* of the church remains, and that has recently been braced or it would have fallen. The photograph shows its condition in 1904. There are a few portions of walls also, and a large part of the adobe wall around the garden remains. The present owner of the orchard, in digging up some of the old olive trees, has found a number of interesting relics: stirrups, a gun-barrel, hollow iron cannon-balls, metates, etc. These are all preserved and shown as " curios," together with beams from the church, and the old olive-mill. Carter says:

"In this orchard is an old abandoned well, and from it, tradi-tion affirms, is an underground passage leading to the Mission. This was used when the padres and their company were besieged, at various times, by the Indians. Whether there be such a pas-sage, no one knows for a certainty; but it seems more than likely, for there are remains of some sort of a passage to be seen in the well, a few feet below the surface of the ground, which has been explored for a short distance, where the way was found to be caved in and blocked."

Instead of being an underground passage, it may be that this is one of the vaults for storing tallow, of which, as I have elsewhere shown, the Missions made great quantities.

By the side of the ruined church a newer and modern

brick building now stands.   It destroys the picturesqueness of the old site, but it is engaged in a good work.   Father Ubach, the indefatigable parish priest of San Diego, is possessed with much of the spirit of the old padres, and he it is who has erected this building for the training of the Indian children of the region.   On one occasion I asked the children if they knew any of the " songs of the old," the songs their Indian grandparents used to sing; and to my delight, they sang two or three of the old chorals taught their ancestors in the early Mission days by the padres.

CHAPTER VII

SAN CARLOS BORROMEO

A BRIEF account of the founding of San Carlos at Monterey, June 3, 1770, was given in an earlier chapter. What joy the discovery of the harbor and founding of the Mission caused in Mexico and Spain can be understood when it is remembered that for two centuries this thing had been desired. In the Mexican city the bells of the Cathedral rang forth merry peals as on special festival days, and a solemn mass of thanksgiving was held, at which all the city officials and dignitaries were present. A full account of the event was printed and distributed there and in Spain, so that, for a time at least, California occupied a large share of public attention.

Padre Crespí reports an interesting event in connection with the second expedition, that found the Bay of Monterey. He says:

" After a journey of three leagues, we arrived at one of the salty lagunas of Punta Piños, where a cross had been erected. Before alighting from our horses, the Governor, a soldier, and myself approached the cross, seeking to discover some signs of the expedition which had set out for water, but we found none. The cross was surrounded by arrows, and little rods tipped with feathers, which had been set in the ground by Indians; suspended from a stick, at one side of the cross, was a string of half-spoiled sardines, a pile of mussels, and a piece of meat. This astonished us not a little; but we failed to comprehend the significance of it; however, as soon as the neophytes were capable of expressing themselves in Spanish, they assured us that the first time they saw the Spaniards, their attention was attracted by a beautiful shining cross which each one wore on his breast; that when they departed they left on the shore this large cross, which seemed at night to almost touch the sky, and was surrounded with rays of heavenly light; but in the daytime, seeing it in its usual proportions, and, to propitiate it, they had offered it flesh-meat and fish; observing that it partook not of their feast, they presented arrows and feathers, as a token that they were at peace with the holy cross, and with those who had planted it."

The result of the news of the founding of San Carlos was that all were enthused for further extension of the Missions. The indefatigable Galvez at once determined that five new Missions should be founded, and the Guardian of the Franciscan College was asked for, and agreed to send, ten more missionaries for the new establishments, as well as twenty for the old and new Missions on the peninsula.

Prior to the arrival of these missionaries Serra was not inactive. He soon decided, after a careful survey of the country, that the location of the Monterey Mission could be bettered. Look at him! The old priest, with a lame leg, on foot, garbed in his long gray gown, tramping over the hills around Monterey, seeking for a new site. It is a picture to arouse the lazy blood of some of us to-day who would never think of walking from Hotel del Monte to the Carmelo Valley. Religious zeal is indeed a great incitement to labor. When the permission was duly given, Serra set to work at his new site on the banks of the Rio Carmelo. There he left three sailors and forty Indians (Bancroft says four) from the peninsula, at work cutting timber, while five soldiers looked on and lent occasional assistance. Travelling overland, he established the Mission of San Antonio de Padua, and then returned; and after several months of labor in preparing the new buildings, the formal transfer took place in December of 1771. Palou says that during this time " his dwelling was a poor hut. He erected a large cross, which he visited and venerated at an early hour every morning; here too the soldiers would assemble and sing an alabado or hymn; then, after matins and prime, Padre Junipero would offer the holy sacrifice of the mass, at which the soldiers and servants attended with great devotion. Then all commenced to labor, Junipero everywhere directing. Often during the day he would cease his labors, venerate the cross, and recite his rosary, this being the only recreation he allowed himself. The Indians visited him daily, and he delighted them by offering them strings of beads and little trinkets; afterwards he made the sign of the cross on their foreheads, and accustomed them to kiss that holy emblem. He also tried to pick up a few words of their language; he taught them to salute one another by saying: ' Amar a Dios,' ' to love God; ' and this custom became so general that it was adopted even by the Indians, who would thus salute the Spaniards when they met."

Thus did the zealous Junipero in his desire to win the heathen to the Cross.

At the end of the year 1773 Serra made his report to Mexico, and then it was found that there were more converts at San Carlos than at any other Mission. Three Spanish soldiers had married native women. The buildings are thus described, according to Bancroft:

" A line of high strong posts, set in the ground close together, encloses the rectangular space which contains the simple wooden buildings serving as church and dwellings, the walls of which also in most instances take the stockade form. At San Carlos the rectangle is seventy yards long and forty-three wide, with ravelins at the corners. For want of nails the upright palisades are not secured at the top, and the ease with which they can be moved renders the strong gate locked at night an unnecessary precaution. Within, the chief building, also of palisade walls plastered inside and out with mud or clay, is seven by fifty yards and divided into six rooms. One room serves as a church, another as the minister's dwelling, and another as a storehouse, the best rooms being whitewashed with lime. This building is roofed with mud, supported by horizontal timbers. A slighter structure used as a kitchen is roofed with grass. The quarters of the soldiers are distinct from the mission and are enclosed by a separate palisade, while outside of both enclosures are the simple huts of the rancheria."

A little later, as the mud roofs were not successful in keeping out the winter rains, a new church was built, partly of rough and partly of worked lumber, and roofed with tules. The lumber used was the pine and cypress for which the region is still noted.

There was little agriculture, only five fanegas of wheat being harvested in 1772. Each Mission received eighteen head of horned cattle at its founding, and San Carlos reported a healthy increase.

In 1772 Serra left for Mexico, to lay matters from the missionary standpoint before the new viceroy, Bucareli. He arrived in the City of Mexico in February, 1773. With resistless energy and eloquence he pleaded for the preservation of the shipyard of San Blas, the removal of Fages, some of whose irritations I have elsewhere referred to, the correction of certain abuses that had arisen as the result of Fages's actions, and for further funds, soldiers, etc., to prosecute the work of founding more Missions. In all the main points his mission was successful. Captain Rivera y Moncada, with whose march from the peninsula we are already familiar, was appointed governor; and at the same time that he received his instructions, August 17, 1773, Captain Juan Bautista de Anza was authorized to attempt the overland journey from Sonora to Monterey. Full particulars of this and subsequent trips over the sandy deserts of Arizona will be given in the companion volume to this.

Here, then, were three parties starting from Mexico to California at about the same time: Serra, Rivera, and Anza. They all arrived in due course, — Anza at San

Gabriel, March 22, Serra at Monterey, May 9, and Rivera at Monterey, May 23, 1774.

Successful in his first trip, Anza returned to Mexico to report to the Viceroy, who immediately gave him orders to prepare for a second. He was to recruit soldiers and settlers for a new presidio to be established at San Francisco, and two new Missions on the Colorado River, the latter being deemed a necessary step towards making the route overland across Arizona practical. In the chapter on San Francisco full particulars of this expedition will be given.

The Colorado River Missions were duly established, attacked, and destroyed, with much loss of life, as elsewhere recorded. But prior to this, Anza had met Rivera at San Gabriel, had gone to San Diego to help suppress the rebellion there, and had met Serra at Monterey, where a special service of thanksgiving was held. San Francisco was duly founded, and Anza returned to Sonora, and Rivera to the Colorado River, where his murder by the Indians took place a little later.

It should not be overlooked that, prior to the arrival of Anza, the viceroy wrote both to Serra and Rivera of his intention to found a new presidio at San Francisco. He required Lieutenant Ayala to explore the bay to find out whether the mouth seen by Fages three years before was a navigable entrance, and also to learn whether the bay was suitable for a port. As Ayala had no boat he set to work to make a *cayuco*, or dugout, from the trunk of a redwood, on the shores of the Carmelo River, doubtless availing himself of the Indians there, who were experts in such work. This canoe, after serving its purpose, was finally wrecked on the beach below the cliff, where it was stranded after breaking loose from its moorings.

In 1776 Serra's heart was joyed with the thought that he was to wear a martyr's crown, for there was a rumor of an Indian uprising at San Carlos; but the presence of troops sent over from Monterey seemed to end the trouble.

In July, 1776, Felipe de Neve, who, since March, 1775, had been governing the Californias at Loreto, was ordered to transfer his capital to Monterey. Already the importance of the new California was beginning to shadow the old. Rivera was to become lieutenant-governor and rule Lower California. But another power than that of king and viceroy was directing his affairs, and he did not live to assume his office. Neve, however, arrived at Monterey on the 3d of February, 1777. It was not long before Neve and Serra were at loggerheads on matters pertaining to the Church. Serra received a patent in 1778, entitling him to perform the sacred rite of confirmation, — a rite generally reserved to no office lower than that of bishop. Serra was not a bishop; the nearest bishop to California was thousands of miles away. To overcome the difficulty the Holy Father in Rome authorized this special patent. In 1779 Neve, as the representative of the Crown of Spain, called upon him for his authority for the exercise of the office. The quarrel was long and severe, and, as might have been foreseen, ultimated in Neve receiving orders to refrain from interference with Serra.

In 1779 a maritime event of importance occurred. The padres at San Carlos and the soldiers at Monterey saw a galleon come into the bay, which proved to be the "San José," from Manila. It should have remained awhile, but contrary winds arose, and it sailed away for San Lucas. But the King later issued orders that all Manila galleons must call at Monterey, under a penalty of four thousand dollars, unless prevented by stress of weather.

This same year Serra chose two each, alcaldes and regidores, from the Indian neophytes to aid in the administration of justice at San Carlos. Great improvements had been made at the presidio at Monterey, and at the Mission things were slowly improving. For the next two or three years there was much working at cross purposes between Serra and Neve, the latter wanting new Missions to be established on the plan which had proven so disastrous on the Colorado River; but in 1782, while Neve and his lieutenant, Fages, were near Yunna on a campaign against the Indians, orders came appointing Neve to a higher office in Mexico, and making Fages governor of California. Fages and Serra had never agreed when Fages held the office before, but as he showed a better disposition than heretofore, it was hoped that all would prove for the best.

In 1784, however, Serra was called upon to lay down all earthly burdens and receive his heavenly reward. His personal work was ended. The year before his beloved co-worker and friend, Padre Crespí, had died. Crespí had aided Serra in the founding of San Carlos, and for some time had worked there. In 1781 the two had journeyed together to visit San Francisco and Santa Clara, and it was on their return that he was taken with his fatal illness. Serra himself administered the last rites to his friend when he died, January 1. He was buried in the church at San Carlos, on the gospel side of the sanctuary. Now Serra's own end had come. August 28 he passed away so quietly that all thought he was sleeping. He was buried, as was his expressed wish, by the side of Crespí, in the sanctuary at San Carlos, Palou performing the rites.

For a short time after Serra's death the duties of padre presidente fell upon Palou; but in February, 1785, the college of San Fernando elected Lasuen to the office, and thereafter he resided mainly at San Carlos.

September 14, 1786, the eminent French navigator, Jean François Galaup de la Pérouse, with two vessels, appeared at Monterey, and the Frenchman gives us a vivid picture of his reception at the Mission of San Carlos that is worth transcribing.

"The padres of San Carlos Mission, two leagues from Monterey, soon came to the presidio; as kind to us as the officers of fort and frigates they insisted on our going to dine with them, and promised to acquaint us in detail with the management of their mission, the Indian manner of living, their arts and customs, in fact all that might interest travellers. We accepted with eagerness . . . M. Fages wished to accompany us. . . . After having crossed a little plain covered with herds of cattle . . . we ascended the hills and heard the sound of bells announcing our coming. We were received like lords of a parish visiting their estates for the first time. The president of the missions, clad in cope, his holy-water sprinkler in hand, received us at the door of the church illuminated as on the grandest festivals; led us to the foot of the altar; and chanted a Te Deum of thanksgiving for the happy issue of our voyage. Before entering the church we had crossed a plaza where Indians of both sexes were ranged in line; their faces showed no surprise and left room for doubt if we should be the subject of their conversation for the rest of the day."

After leaving the church the visitors spent a short time in examining the Mission and in making a careful, though necessarily brief, study of the Franciscan régime and its effects upon the natives. They probably visited San Carlos more than once.

La Pérouse's companion, M. de Langle, presented San Carlos with a hand-mill for grinding wheat, which would enable four of the neophyte women to do the work of a hundred in the old way; but it is very doubtful whether they used it long.

In 1791 Fages retired from the governorship with honors, and José Antonio Romeu was named his successor. He arrived at Monterey in ill-health, October 13, and on April 9, 1792, he passed away, and was buried at San Carlos the next day. The Lieutenant-Governor Arrillaga was thereupon called up from Loreto to act as temporary governor until a new appointment was made. He reached Monterey early in July, 1793.

In the meantime the English navigator, Vancouver, had visited San Francisco, and Santa Clara, and San Carlos. Lasuen had entertained him as hospitably as he did La Pérouse six years before. The natives gave an exhibition

PLATE XXII

RUINED CORRIDORS AT SAN ANTONIO DE PADUA

of their skill in killing deer by stratagem, and there was a grand dinner at the presidio, and even fireworks. The governor, on his arrival, was much chagrined at the fact that Vancouver had been allowed to discover the weakness of the Spanish defences in California, and he administered a general rebuke to his officers. Consequently, when Vancouver returned at the end of 1793 he was not received so warmly, though it was only by contrast with his former reception that he could have justly made any complaint. But before he sailed away, the British captain gave to Padre Lasuen a handsome barrel-organ as a gift for San Carlos. There is such an organ at San Juan Bautista as is recorded in the chapter devoted to that Mission, and it may be that it is the very one thus contributed.

On his second visit he went to San Carlos (Sunday, December 2, 1792), and while he gives no detailed description, he presents a drawing which shows four buildings irregularly arranged and partially enclosing a square. From this picture Bancroft makes up the following description:

"The old church, partly thatched and partly tiled, stands on the left of the picture, and probably on the west side of the square. Three bells hang on a frame raised on a stone foundation; a lofty cross, bearing a close resemblance to a modern telegraph-pole, rears its head near the centre of the plaza, and just beyond, almost in contact with, and apparently northeastward from the old church, are the rising stone walls of a new one. Beyond, on an eminence, may be seen a corral for cattle, while at the right are the conical huts of the neophytes. The new church was being built of a soft, straw-colored stone, which was said to harden on exposure to the air. The lime used was made from sea-shells. This church, the ruins of which are still to be seen on the banks of the Carmelo, was completed and dedicated in September 1797."

While the description thus given shows the new church, it is possible it was not added in his drawing until his third visit, which occurred in 1794, for Padre Lasuen states that the first stone was laid July 7, 1793, a year after Vancouver's visit.

The troubles in Europe caused by Napoleon sent a tiny ripple which was felt at Monterey; but his act in placing his brother Joseph on the throne of Spain was never recognized. On March 5, 1809, Ferdinand the Seventh was duly hailed as " Our king and natural lord," and on the 10th of August Governor Arrillaga swore loyalty to him before President Tapis (who had taken the place of the deceased Lasuen) in the church at San Carlos.

In 1810 Spanish South America began to revolt against Spanish rule. In 1818 Monterey and California generally felt a wave from this sea of revolt in the coming of Captain Bouchard, who professed to be waging war against Spain and her possessions in the interests of the South American insurgents. October 6, 1818, the American brig " Clarion " arrived at Santa Barbara, and alarmed the commandante, Guerra, by telling him that two vessels were outfitting at the Hawaiian Islands for the devastation of the California settlements. Immediately Guerra sent warnings north and south, which, when received by Governor Sola, led that active official to issue most explicit instructions to all the various officials and the padres at the Missions, as to what they were to do if the enemy actually hove in sight. A month passed, and the people had begun to forget their fears, when, on the afternoon of November 20, the sentinel on Point Piños reported two vessels in sight approaching Monterey. On their arrival and anchoring there were parleyings and evasions, and finally next morning a conflict resulted, in which the insurgents lost several men. Bouchard then made a demand for the immediate surrender of the province, which Sola indignantly refused. Then followed the landing of four hundred men with four field pieces, and as Sola had only twenty-five men to oppose it, he ordered his guns spiked and beat a retreat, taking everything he could with him to the rancho del rey, where

Salinas City now stands. The insurgents set the presidio and fort on fire, and destroyed supplies to the value of $5000, and also took private property of the officers to the same value. The orchard and garden were entirely ruined. Possibly they did not go over to San Carlos Mission, for nothing there was injured. They sailed away November 26, or early in the morning of November 27, and we shall hear further from them at several of the other Missions.

In due time the officials and people returned, and by April, 1819, possibly earlier, Monterey had resumed its old-time aspect.

About this time the chapel adjoining the church, on the south side, in honor of the " pasion del señor," was erected, though the exact date of its dedication is not known.

San Carlos felt the troubles of the Mexican revolution somewhat, in that Prefect Sarría was regarded as under arrest for some time as a recalcitrant Spaniard. In 1830 the report shows that it was rapidly declining in Indian population. In 1833 the Zacatecan padre, José María del Refugia Sagrado Suarez del Real, took the place of the Franciscan Abella. In 1834–35 the Mission was secularized, Joaquin Gomez being appointed commissioner, and succeeded by José Antonio Romero as majordomo. The spoliation was rapid: there being little property left in 1834, and none at all but the ruined buildings in 1840. At the time of secularization Serra's army of converts had dwindled down to 150, and at the end of the decade there were only about 30 left, with perhaps 50 more out at service at the ranches and in the town.

When Pico issued his decrees in 1845 San Carlos was regarded as a pueblo, or abandoned Mission, Padre Real residing at Monterey and only holding services occasionally. The little property that remained was to be sold at auction for the payment of debts and the support of worship, but there is no record of property, debts, or sale. The glory of San Carlos was departed.

For many years no one cared for the building, and it was left entirely to the mercy of the vandal and relic hunter. In 1852 the tiled roof fell in, and all the tiles save about 1000 were either then broken, or afterwards stolen. The rains and storms beating in soon brought enough sand to form a lodgment for seeds, and ere long a dense growth of grass and weeds overgrew the dust of California's great apostle.

In " Glimpses of California," by " H. H.," Mr. Sandham, the artist, has a picture which well illustrates the original spring of the roof and curve of the walls. There were three buttresses, *from which* sprang the roof arches. The curve of the walls was made by increasing the thickness at the top, as can be seen from the window spaces on each side, which still remain in their original condition. The building is about 150 feet long by 30 feet wide.

In 1868 Rev. Angelo D. Cassanova became the pastor of the parish church at Monterey, and though Serra's home Mission was then a·complete mass of ruins, he determined upon at least its preservation from further demolition. The first step was to clear away the débris that had accumulated since its abandonment, and then to locate the graves of the missionaries. On July 3, 1882, after due notice in the San Francisco papers, over 400 people assembled at San Carlos. There, from the original records, he read aloud to the assembled people the following entries, both in the original Spanish, and then in English:

" Rev. F. Francisco Lasuen, second President of the missions ; born in Spain, died here, and is buried in the sanctuary, on the Gospel side, in a stone tomb near the main altar, June 28th, 1803."

Father Cassanova thus describes what follows:

" The heavy stone slab having been removed before the ceremony, the coffin of each stone tomb or grave was left visible. A man then went down and raised the lid of each coffin. The coffins were simple red wood, unplaned, and in a good state of preservation. The people all looked at the remains, first of Father Juan Crespí, the first that died, then on the remains of Father Junipero Serra. The skeletons were in a good state, the ribs standing out in proper arch, part of the vestment in good order, also the heavy silk stole which is put only on a priest, in good order and in one piece, two yards and a half long, with the silk fringes to it as good as new. We did not raise the coffins, but only viewed them and their contents to the satisfaction of all present. We did the same to the four corpses; anything more would have been improper, especially as the coffin of the last buried, the Rev. Father Lasuen, was going to pieces. Then the tombs were covered as before with stone slabs. The tomb of Father Junipero Serra, for better security, was filled with earth, so as to make it more difficult for any vandal to disturb his resting-place, and over that was placed the stone slab broken in four pieces."

The discovery of the bodies of Serra, Crespí, Lopez, and Lasuen aroused some sentiment and interest in Father Cassanova's plan of restoration; and as he had himself worked with a devotion that should have produced better results, sufficient aid came to enable him to properly restore and roof the building. On the 28th of August, 1884, the rededication took place, and the building was left as it is found to-day (1905).

It is the earnest desire of the writer of these pages that all his readers should have a share in completing the work Father Cassanova began. The roof should be retiled in the original style. The cost of this will be about two thousand dollars. If each reader of this book would send a dollar to the publishers, with the request that it be kept for this purpose, I am satisfied a tiled roof could be put on before the end of 1907. And I hereby make appeal to that end. I will undertake to send an autographed photograph of the restored and retiled Mission (when the work is done) to all who will contribute a dollar for the purpose named.

9

In the architectural chapter certain interesting things about San Carlos are noted.

The old pulpit still remains. It is reached by steps from the sacristy through a doorway in the main side wall. It is a small and unpretentious structure of wood, with wooden sounding board above. It rests upon a solid stone pedestal, cut into appropriate shaft and mouldings. The door is of solid oak, substantially built.

In the sacristy is a double lavatory of solid sandstone, hewn and arranged for flowing water. It consists of two basins, one above the other, the latter one well recessed. The lower basin is structurally curved in front, and the whole piece is of good and artistic workmanship.

In the neighborhood of San Carlos there are enough residents to make up a small congregation, and it is the desire of Father Mestris to establish a parish there, have a resident minister, and thus restore the old Mission to its original purpose.

THE PRESIDIO CHURCH AT MONTEREY

Before leaving San Carlos it will be well to explain the facts in regard to the church at Monterey, elsewhere pictured in these pages. Many errors have been perpetuated about this church. It is not properly a Mission, though dating back to Mission days.

In the establishment of the Missions, as has been shown, the presidios were founded to be a means of protection to the padres in their work of civilizing and christianizing the natives. These presidios were at San Diego, Monterey, San Francisco, and Santa Barbara. Each was supposed to have its own church or chapel, and the original intention was that each should likewise have its own resident priest. For purposes of economy, however, this was not done, and the mission padres were called upon for this service, though it was often a source of disagreement between the military and the missionaries. The Monterey church is the successor to the old presidio chapel. I have been unable to learn when it was built, but about fifty years ago Governor Pacheco donated the funds for its enlargement. The original building was extended back a number of feet, and an addition made, which makes the church of cruciform shape, the original building being the long arm of the cross. It is in the two walls of this addition — one on the left and one on the right — that the two ornate doorways elsewhere presented are placed. The walls are built of sandstone rudely quarried at the rear of the church.

The view from this church is now destroyed by the presence immediately before it of the school, conducted by the sisters of St. Joseph, but it formerly must have been commanding. It stands about half a mile from the bay, the deep blue waters and far-away hills of the Coast Range, the verdure-clad sandhills below and near by, combining with the long stretch of gray sand of the beach to make an unusually lovely setting in a country full of beauty. To the left are the pine-clad hills, and to the rear and beyond, the foothills of the Gabilan Range. The Mission faces almost north; the old town of Monterey nestles in the lower folds of the hills which rise to the west, on the point of which, nearest to the sea, the Sloat monument is slowly rising.

Here are a large number of interesting relics and memorials of Serra and the early Mission days. Some are described in the chapters on Saints, Woodwork, and Silverware.

Another interesting relic is a reliquary case, made by an Indian at San Carlos to hold certain valuable relics which Serra highly prized. Some of these are bones from the Catacombs, and an Agnus Dei of wax. Serra himself wrote the list of contents on a slip of paper, which is still intact on the back of the case. This reliquary used to be carried in procession by Serra on each 4th of November, and is now used by Father Mestris in like ceremonials.

In the altar space or sanctuary are five chairs, undoubtedly brought to California by one of the Philippine galleons from one of those islands, or from China. The bodies are of teak, ebony, or iron wood, with seats of marble, and with a disk of marble in the back.

In the sacristy is the safe in which Serra used to keep the sacred vessels, as well as the important papers connected with his office. It is an interesting object, sheeted with iron, wrapped around with iron bands and covered all over with bosses. It is about three feet wide and four feet high. In the drawers close by are several of the copes, stoles, maniples, and other vestments which were once used by Serra at the old Mission.

CHAPTER VIII

SAN ANTONIO DE PADUA

THE third Mission of the series was founded in honor of San Antonio de Padua, July 14, 1771, by Serra, accompanied by Padres Pieras and Sitjar. One solitary Indian heard the dedicatory mass, but Serra's enthusiasm knew no bounds. He was assured that this " first fruit of the wilderness " would go forth and bring many of his companions to the priests. Immediately after the mass he hastened to the Indian, lavished much attention on him, and gave him gifts. That same day many other Indians came and clearly indicated a desire to stay with such pleasant company. They brought pine-nuts and acorns, and the padres gave them in exchange strings of glass beads of various colors.

At once buildings were begun, in which work the Indians engaged with energy, and soon church and dwellings, surrounded by a palisade, were completed. From the first the Indians manifested confidence in the padres, and the fifteen days that Padre Serra remained were days of intense joy and gladness at seeing the readiness of the natives to associate with him and his brother priests. Without delay they began to learn the language of the Indians, and when they had made sufficient progress they devoted much time to catechising them. In two years 158 natives were baptized and enrolled, and instead of relying upon the missionaries for food, they brought in large quantities of acorns, pine-nuts, squirrels, and rabbits. The Mission being located in the heart of the mountains, where pine and oak trees grew luxuriantly, the pine-nut and acorn were abundant. Before the end of 1773 the church and dwellings were all built, of adobe, and three soldiers, who had married native women, were living in separate houses.

In August of 1774 occurred the first trouble. The gentile Indians, angered at the progress of the Mission and the gathering in of so many of their people, attacked the Mission and wounded an Indian about to be baptized. When the news reached Rivera at Monterey, he sent a squad of soldiers, who captured the culprits, gave them a flogging, and imprisoned them. Later they were flogged again, and, after a few days in the stocks, they were released.

In 1779 an alcalde and regidore were chosen from the natives to assist in the administration of justice. In 1800 the report shows that the neophyte population was 1118, with 767 baptisms and 656 deaths. The cattle and horses had decreased from 2232 of the last report to 2217, but small stock had slightly increased. In 1787 the church was regarded as the best in California, though it was much improved later, for in 1797 it is stated that it was of adobes with a tiled roof. In 1793 the large adobe block, eighty varas long and one vara wide, was constructed for friars' houses, church and storehouse, and it was doubtless this church that was tiled four years later.

In 1805 it gained its highest population, there being 1296 Indians under its control. The lands of the Mission were found to be barren, necessitating frequent changes in cultivated fields and stock ranges.

In 1808 the venerable Buenaventura Sitjar, one of the founders of the Mission, and who had toiled there continuously for thirty-seven years, passed to his reward, and was buried in sight of the hills he had loved so long. The following year, or in 1810, work was begun on a newer and larger church of adobes, and this is doubtless the building the ruins of which remain. Though we have no record of its dedication, there is no question but that it took place

PLATE XXIII

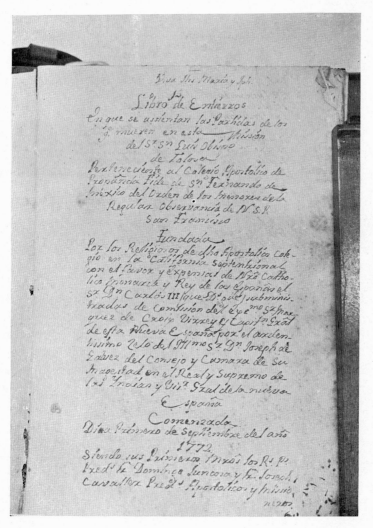

TITLE-PAGE OF REGISTER OF SAN LUIS OBISPO, IN THE HANDWRITING
OF PADRE PALOU

prior to 1820, and in 1830 references are made to its arched corridors, etc., built of brick. Robinson, who visited it in this year, says the whole Mission is built of brick, but in this he is in error. The *fachada* is of brick, as is shown in the chapter on architecture, but the main part of the building is of adobe. Robinson speaks thus of the Mission and its friar: "Padre Pedro Cabot, the present missionary director, I found to be a fine, noble-looking man, whose manner and whole deportment would have led one to suppose he had been bred in the courts of Europe, rather than in the cloister. Everything was in the most perfect order: the Indians cleanly and well dressed, the apartments tidy, the workshops, granaries, and storehouses comfortable and in good keeping."

In 1834 Cabot retired to give place to Padre Jesus María Vasquez del Mercado, one of the newly arrived Franciscans from Zacatecas. In this year the neophyte population had dwindled to 567, and five years later Visitador Hartwell found only 270 living at the Mission and its adjoining ranches. It is possible, however, that there were fully as many more living at a distance of whom he gained no knowledge, as the official report for 1840 gives 500 neophytes.

Manuel Crespo was the comisionado for secularization in 1835, and he and Padre Mercado had no happy times together. Mercado made it so unpleasant that six other administrators were appointed in order to please him, but it was a vain attempt. As a consequence, the Indians felt the disturbances and discord, and became discontented and unmanageable.

The inventories required by the secularization decrees show that September 10, 1835, the produce, implements, furniture, and goods were valued at $7883. Another inventory, dated April 27, 1836, says: Credits (whatever that means, supposedly accounts owing to the Mission), $18,642; buildings, $11,197; vineyards, implements, furniture, and goods in store, $22,671; 8 ranches, $32,834; live-stock, $1000; total, $93,122, besides church property, $7617; but there should be deducted $16,886 for property distributed among the Indians. On Hartwell's visit he reported the Mission accounts in sad confusion (no wonder, seven administrators in half that number of years), and the Indians full of complaints. At San Bernabé was a " gente de razon," who was responsible for much disease among the natives. Alas! not only ruin to the Mission, but demoralization and destruction to the Indians had already set in.

In 1843, according to Governor Micheltorena's order of March 29, the temporal control of the Mission was restored to the padre. But, though the order was a kindly one, and relieved the padre from the interference of officious, meddling, inefficient, and dishonest " administrators," it was too late to effect any real service.

As far as I can learn, Pico's plan did not affect San Antonio, and it was not one of those sold by him in 1845–6. In 1848 Padre Doroteo Ambris was in charge as curate. For thirty years he remained here, true to his calling, an entirely different kind of man from the quarrelsome, arrogant, drinking, and gambling Mercado. He finally died at San Antonio, and was buried in the Mission he guarded so well.

At his death there was no pastor who could be sent to take charge, and the few remaining Indians and whites had to be content with such services as the priests from San Miguel and casual visitors could render. These were not always of the best. One of the residents of Jolon informed me of one of them, who, after mass, drank more than was good for him, retreated in disgrace, and left one of the old manuals of the Mission in his room, which it was evident he intended to take away with him.

San Antonio appeals to me more than any other of the Missions. There is a pathetic dignity about the ruins,

an unexpressed claim for sympathy in the perfect solitude
of the place that is almost overpowering.   In the whirl of
railroading San Antonio has been completely sidetracked,
— far more so than San Juan Bautista, — and, unlike
San Juan, it stands out in the fields, alone, deserted, forgotten.   Across the way from San Juan is a hotel, across
from San Antonio there is nothing; indeed, there is no
across, for there is not traffic enough to make a way.   Here
is what I wrote in the shadow of the walls that still stand,
one exquisite Sunday in May of 1904: Oh, the infinitude
of care and patience and work and love shown in this
old building.   Everything was well and beautifully done;
it is so evidently a work of love and pride.   This builder
was architect and lover, maker of history and poet, for
power, strength, beauty, and tenderness are revealed on
every hand.   Every arch is perfect; every detail in harmony with every other; and in location and general sur-
roundings it is ideal.   San Antonio Creek is at the rear,
— exquisite views of fertile valley, rolling foothills, and
tree-covered mountains on every side.   It is enclosed in a
picturesque bower of beauty, — God's quiet nook in His
great out-of-doors.

And all, now, is silent and deserted.   Birds fly in and
out, and sing in the towers that once sent forth sweet
sounds of evening bell.   Horses wander up and down the
corridors where monks were wont to tell their beads, and
even the monastery, consecrated by prayers, songs, and
the holy toil of daily labor, and the rooms in which Indian
maidens and youths learned the handicrafts of the white
man, are now used as places of shade for the cattle that
roam through the valley.

Inside the ruined church all is still.   There is no droning
voice of drowsy padre intoning his early morning mass; no
resounding note of the same padre's voice when fired with
martial ardor, as soldier of the Cross, preaching to Indians whose souls have been imperilled by some recent re-

lapse. All, all is silent! In the surrounding ruins where once was heard the ring of iron and hammer on anvil, the saw and plane on wood, the tap of the hammer on leather, the scrape of the tool on hide, the cutting of the graver on wood, and the busy hum of active workers of every kind, — everything now is hushed and still. The olive-oil mill is dismantled; its standards gone; only two of the olive trees remain; the fields no longer see the Indians; the plough is idle; the rancherías are deserted. Like a gray-haired mother of sons and daughters, whose life-work is accomplished, and who sits in her capacious arm-chair awaiting the last summons, so seems San Antonio to sit, calm and serene among the hills, silently voicing the questions: "Have I, too, not accomplished? May I not also pass in peace?"

At Jolon is the old stage station and hotel, owned for many years by George C. Dutton, cousin of Clarence Dutton, whose prose poems on the Grand Canyon I have always regarded as among the classics of the English language. During the past years Mr. Dutton has seen San Antonio's slow degradation and demolition. The illustration elsewhere shown pictures it as he remembers it, with roof still on, pulpit in place, altar, statues, confessionals, benches, chairs, — all there. Now, alas! what is it but a "shapeless cairn." Roofless and dismantled, Nature and Humanity have both buffeted the sacred building. The owls and bats have long made it their nesting place, and Man has despoiled it of everything portable. To save somewhat from the general pillage, Mr. Dutton brought to a room of safety a few of the more important objects, which he now holds ready to turn over to the proper authorities on demand.

In 1904 the California Historic Landmarks League (Inc.) undertook the preservation of San Antonio, and on my visit there in 1904 lumber was on the ground for roofing it. A little work had already been accomplished, but much more is immediately necessary if the walls are to be kept from falling.

CHAPTER IX

SAN GABRIEL, ARCÁNGEL

WE have already seen that San Gabriel, the fourth Mission, was founded September 8, 1771. The natives gave cheerful assistance in bringing timber, erecting the wooden buildings, covering them with tules, and constructing the stockade enclosure which surrounded them. They also brought offerings of acorns and pine-nuts. In a few days so many of them crowded into camp that Padre Somero went to San Diego for an addition to the guard, and returned with two extra men. It was not long before the soldiers got into trouble, owing to their treatment of the Indian women, and an Indian attack, as before related, took place. A few days later, Fages appeared on the scene from San Diego with sixteen soldiers and two missionaries, who were destined as guard and priests for the new Mission of San Buenaventura. But the difficulty with the Indians led Fages to postpone the founding of the new Mission. The offending soldier was hurried off to Monterey to get him out of the way of further trouble. The padres did their best to correct the evil impression the soldiers had created, and, strange to say, the first child brought for baptism was the son of the chief who had been killed in the dispute with the soldiers.

But the San Gabriel soldiers were not to be controlled. They were insolent to the aged priests, who were in ill-health; they abused the Indians so far as to pursue them to their rancherías " for the fun of the thing "; and there have additional sport by lassoing the women and killing such men as interfered with their lusts. No wonder

Serra's heart was heavy when he heard the news, and that he attributed the small number of baptisms — only seventy-three in two years — to the wickedness of the men who should have aided instead of hindering the work.

In his first report to Mexico, Serra tells of the Indian population around San Gabriel. He says it was larger than at any other Mission, though, unfortunately, of several different tribes who were at war with one another; and the tribes nearest to the sea would not allow others to fish, so that they were often in great want of food. Of the prospects for agriculture he was most enthusiastic. The location was a well-watered plain, with plenty of water and natural facilities for irrigation; and though the first year's crop was drowned out, the second produced one hundred and thirty fanegas of maize and seven fanegas of beans. The buildings erected were of the same general character as those already described at San Carlos, though somewhat smaller.

When Captain Anza reached California from Sonora, by way of the Colorado, on his first trip in 1774, accompanied by Padre Garcés, he stayed for awhile to recuperate at San Gabriel; and when he came the second time, with the colonists for the new presidio of San Francisco, San Gabriel was their first real stopping place after that long, weary, and arduous journey across the sandy deserts of Arizona and California. Here Anza met Rivera, who had arrived the day before from Monterey. It will be remembered that just at that time the news came of the Indian uprising at San Diego; so, leaving his main force and the immigrants to recuperate, he and seventeen of his soldiers, with Padre Font, started with Rivera for the South. This was in January, 1776. He and Rivera did not agree as to the best methods to be followed in dealing with the troublesome Indians; so, when advices reached him from San Gabriel that provisions were giving out, he decided to allow Rivera to follow his own plans, and that, as for him, he would return to the North and do the work for which he came. When he arrived at San Gabriel, February 12, he found that three of his muleteers, a servant, and a soldier belonging to the Mission had deserted, taking with them twenty-five horses and a quantity of Mission property. His ensign, Moraga, was sent after the deserters; but, as he did not return as soon as was expected, Anza started with his band of colonists for the future San Francisco, where they duly arrived, as is recorded in the San Francisco chapter.

In 1777-8 the Indians were exceedingly troublesome, and on one occasion came in large force, armed, to avenge some outrage the soldiers had perpetrated. The padres met them with a shining image of Our Lady, when, immediately, they were subdued, and knelt, weeping, at the feet of the priests.

In 1779 Indians were chosen as alcaldes and regidores to aid in the administration of discipline. The same year the crops were large, as it is reported that they had 2000 bushels of surplus maize.

Being the natural meeting place for overland parties coming from the peninsula northwards, and from Sonora west and north, San Gabriel was made the rendezvous of all the colonizing expeditions. When Neve's recommendations for the founding of the so-called Channel Missions were being carried out, a party of colonists, consisting of thirty-five soldiers and thirty families, arrived at San Gabriel by way of the Colorado River from Sonora, on July 14, 1781; and on August 18 of the same year another party, which had come from Mexico by crossing the Gulf at Guaymas and up the peninsula, consisting of seventeen men, probably soldiers, and eleven settlers and their families also arrived. As some of the children of the latter band had recently had smallpox, they were quarantined at a distance of a league from the Mission as a preventive measure. On the 26th of August Governor Neve issued, at San

Gabriel, his instructions for founding the pueblo of La Reina de los Angeles. The impossibility of transporting needed supplies and making necessary preparations before the rainy season set in compelled delay in founding the channel settlements. The return of Ensign Limon, — the officer who, with his nine soldiers had escorted the settlers from the Colorado River to San Gabriel, and had then started back for Sonora, but had been attacked by hostile Yuma Indians and two of his men killed and himself wounded, — while causing great excitement, gave no reason for a delay in proceeding with the founding of Los Angeles, so that on September 4 it was formally accomplished. In 1782 the council determined to punish the murderous Yumas, and, accordingly, plans were laid with a great deal of official red tape, but practically nothing was done until August 21, when Governor Neve set out from San Gabriel with Fages and sixty men. Three days before reaching the river, despatches reached Fages which led him to return and assume the duties of governor, to which office he had just been appointed, while Neve proceeded to Sonora to assume his new and higher office. Captain Romeu, who had come from Sonora with one hundred and eight men, was left to chastise the Yumas; but, after a few days' skirmish, in which a few Indians were killed, the place was abandoned, as far as the Spaniards were concerned, practically forever.

During the whole of this time, the forces that were to be employed at the new Channel Missions had been quartered at San Gabriel, giving quite a martial appearance to the place. In the spring of 1782, however, they moved, and established Santa Barbara.

In 1784 the venerable Serra, on a tour to all the Missions, stopped at San Gabriel, and there was so ill that his end was daily expected. But he rallied and succeeded in returning to San Carlos, where he died. In 1790 the number of neophytes had increased from 638, in 1783, to 1040;

large stock from 860 to 4221, and small stock from 2070 to 6013. The harvest in the year 1790 was 6150 bushels. In 1800 it had 9400 bushels.

Gigedo, speaking of the condition of affairs at the close of the eighteenth century, says of the Colorado River and San Gabriel:

" This point and the Mission of San Gabriel form the circle within which swarm pagan Indians, who may be persuaded to accept our holy religion and the mild dominion of our sovereign, and so contribute to the important object of making the peninsula of the Californias one of the most respectable colonies on the frontier of New Spain."

But Fate decreed otherwise of the Colorado River, and the Indians at San Gabriel, having more or less contact with those of the Colorado and the Mohave regions, and, doubtless being incited to lawlessness by these unsubjugated peoples, gave considerable trouble to the Spaniards. Neophytes conspired with gentiles, and the Mission storehouse was robbed, cattle and horses driven off. In 1810 the padres report that a force of 800 hostile Indians of the Mohave and Yuma tribes marched to San Gabriel with the avowed intention of destroying it and San Fernando, but the timely arrival of forces prevented the attack.

In October, 1785, trouble was caused by a woman tempting (so they said) the neophytes and gentiles to attack the Mission and kill the padres. The plot was discovered, and the corporal in command captured some twenty of the leaders and quelled the uprising without bloodshed. Four of the ringleaders were imprisoned, the others whipped with fifteen or twenty lashes each, and released. The woman was sentenced to perpetual exile, and possibly shipped off to one of the peninsula Missions.

In 1810 the settlers at Los Angeles complained to the Governor that the San Gabriel padres had dammed up the river at Cahuenga, thus cutting off their water supply;

and they also stated that the padres refused to attend to the spiritual wants of their sick. The padres offered to remove the dam if the settlers were injured thereby, and also claimed that they were always glad to attend to the sick when their own pressing duties allowed.

On January 14, 1811, Padre Francisco Dumetz, one of Serra's original compadres, died at San Gabriel. At this time, and since 1806, Padre José María Zalvidea, that strict martinet of padres, was in charge, and he brought it up to its highest state of efficiency. He it was who began the erection of the stone church that now remains, and the whole precinct, during his rule, rang with the busy hammer, clatter, chatter, and movement of a large number of active workers.

It was doubtless owing to the earthquake of December 8, 1812, which occurred at sunrise, that a new church was built. The main altar was overthrown, several of the figures broken, the steeple toppled over and crashed to the ground, and the sacristy walls were badly cracked. The padres' house as well as all the other buildings suffered.

One of the adjuncts to San Gabriel was *El Molino Viejo*, — the old mill. Indeed there were *two* old mills, the first one, however, built in Padre Zalvidea's time in 1810 to 1812, being the one that now remains. It is about two miles from the Mission. It had to be abandoned on account of faulty location. Being built on the hillside, its west main wall was the wall of the deep funnel-shaped cisterns which furnished the water head. This made the interior damp. Then, too, the chamber in which the water-wheel revolved was so low that the powerful head of water striking the horizontal wheel would splash all over the walls and work up through the shaft holes to the mill stones and thus wet the flour. This necessitated the constant presence of Indian women to carry away the meal to dry storerooms at the Mission, where it was bolted by a hand process of their own devising. On this account the mill was abandoned, and for several years the whole of the meal for the Mission was ground on the old-style metates.

The main building is 24 by 55 feet, with walls of solid masonry nearly five feet thick at the base and sloping to a little over three feet at the top, and resting on a foundation of stone and cement. There were two great arches in the lower story (east front), where the water-wheel was placed. The south wheel-chamber was never used. An earthquake in 1812 cracked the north fore-bay, and thus rendered it useless as a water storage. The water was conveyed from Los Robles Canyon in a ditch to the fore-bay, which is a funnel-shaped cement cistern, 12 feet deep. From the bottom of this cistern a narrow spout-flume extended through the thick stone wall into the brick-arched wheel-chamber, and the water poured through the spout horizontally against the buckets of the water-wheel. The water from Mill Canyon was also brought in by ditch. After its use here the water flowed into the dam below, where it was used again for power to operate a saw-mill, also erected by the indefatigable Zalvidea. The grinding stones of the old mill were 2½ feet in diameter and 7 to 8 inches thick, and are now used as a horse-block at San Marino, the residence of the Hon. J. De Barth Shorb. From under the buttress at the northeast corner of the mill, in the wheel-chamber, flows a tiny stream of water, and many writers have made much mystery out of this. When all the circumstances are considered the mystery is easily solved. The San Gabriel Indians were all made to work by Padre Zalvidea, who, being austere with himself, was austere with all who were in his keeping. There were about thirty classes of workers, all under the direction of the famous *mayordomo*, Claudio Lopez. Claudio appointed his deputies, who took actual charge of the bands, armed with bull-whips made of strips of rawhide, which they did not hesitate to use if any of the men and women failed to do their allotted tasks. This harsh treatment led to frequent

10

escapes into the mountains, where the aggrieved Indians would organize into bands of hostiles. Uprisings, attacks, murders were not entire strangers to the padres, so Zalvidea made both his Mission and the mill strong enough for fortresses of defence in case of need. And lest they should be so needed, he wisely provided a supply of water by means of this cunningly devised water-way. Fortunately it was never needed.

In 1859 Col. E. J. C. Kewen, one of the members of the noted Walker filibustering expedition, and an ex-attorney-general of California, bought the old mill and converted it into a comfortable residence; but at his death in 1879 it was abandoned and its later owner used it as a bunk-house for tools, etc.

The region adjacent to the mill was once largely inhabited by Indians, for the foreman of the mill ranch declares that he has hauled from the adjacent bluff as many stone pestles and mortars, metates and grinders as would load a four-horse wagon.

It should not be forgotten that originally the mill was roofed with red tiles made by the Indians at the Mission; but these have entirely disappeared.

It was the habit of Padre Zalvidea to regularly send certain of his most trusted neophytes over to the Islands of San Clemente and Catalina with a bolt or two of woven serge, made at the Mission San Gabriel, to exchange with the Island Indians for their soapstone cooking vessels, — mortars, etc. These traders invariably embarked from a point where Redondo now is, and started always at midnight.

In 1819 the Indians of the Guachama rancho, called San Bernardino, petitioned for the introduction of agriculture and stock raising, and this was practically the beginning of that *asistencia*, as will be recorded in the chapter on the various chapels. A chapel was also much needed at Puente, where Zalvidea had six hundred Indians at work in 1816.

In 1822 San Gabriel was fearfully alarmed at the rumor that one hundred and fifty Indians were bearing down upon that Mission from the Colorado River region. It transpired that it was a band of Ópatas with despatches, and that they had no hostile intent. But Captain Portilla met them and sent them back, not a little disconcerted by their inhospitable reception.

In the wild, political chaos that occurred in California after Mexico became independent of Spain, San Gabriel felt occasional waves. When the people of San Diego and the southern part of the State rebelled against Governor Victoria, and the latter confident chief came to arrange matters, a battle took place near Los Angeles, in which he was severely wounded. His friends bore him to San Gabriel, and, though he had entirely defeated his foes, so cleverly did some one work upon his fears that he made a formal surrender, December 6, 1831. On the 9th the leader of the rebels, the former governor Echeandía, had a conference with him at San Gabriel, where he pledged himself to return to Mexico without giving further trouble; and on the 20th he left, stopping for awhile at San Luis Rey with Padre Peyri. It was at this time the venerable and worthy Peyri decided to leave California, and he therefore accompanied the deposed governor to San Diego, from which port they sailed January 17, 1832.

After secularization San Gabriel was one of the Missions that slaughtered a large number of her cattle for the hides and tallow. Pio Pico states that he had the contract at San Gabriel, employing 10 vaqueros and 30 Indians, and that he thus killed over 5000 head. Robinson says that the rascally contractors secretly appropriated two hides for every one they turned over to the Mission.

In 1834 occurred the destruction of the chapel at San Bernardino, and the survivors fleeing to San Gabriel brought a considerable feeling of unrest; but the uprising was quelled, as is related in the chapter on chapels.

In this year Colonel Gutierrez was the comisionado to carry into effect the order of secularization; but up to 1838 he had three successors, and when, in 1840, the last administrator, Juan Bandini, handed over the live-stock there were but 72 cattle and 700 sheep, though in 1839 there were 1700 horses, 1100 cattle, and 1000 sheep.

The old registers practically close in 1831, and they state that from 1771 there had been 7709 baptisms, 5494 burials, and 1877 marriages.

In 1843, March 29, Micheltorena's order, restoring San Gabriel to the padres, was carried out, and in 1844 the official church report states that nothing is left but its vineyards in a sad condition, and 300 neophytes. The final inventory made by the comisionados under Pio Pico is missing, so that we do not know at what the Mission was valued; but June 8, 1846, he sold the whole property to Reid and Workman in payment for past services to the government. When attacked for his participation in what evidently seemed the fraudulent transfer of the Mission, Pico replied that the sale " did not go through." The United States officers, in August of the same year, dispossessed them, and the courts finally decreed the sale invalid.

In 1847 Padre Estenega died, and Blas de Ordaz was appointed. He died in 1850, and since then the church has been a regular parish church, under the direction of the bishop of the diocese.

There are a few portions of the old cactus hedge still remaining, planted by Padre Zalvidea. Several hundreds of acres of vineyard and garden were thus enclosed for purposes of protection from Indians and roaming bands of horses and cattle. The fruit of the prickly pear was a prized article of diet by the Indians, so that the hedge was of benefit in two ways, — protection and food.

The Mission church is nearly 140 feet long, 26 feet wide, and 30 feet high, inside measurement. The foundations and walls are of rubble stones and cement as far as the windows; above that brick is used. At the floor the walls are five feet thick. Originally the building had an arched roof, but this was partially destroyed in one of the earthquakes and a tile roof substituted in its stead.

On the altar are several of the old statues, and there are some quaint pictures upon the walls.

In the baptistery is a font of hammered copper, probably made either at San Gabriel or San Fernando. There are several other interesting vessels. At the rear of the church are the remains of five brick structures, where the soap making and tallow rendering of the Mission was conducted. Five others were removed a few years ago to make way for the public road. Undoubtedly there were other buildings for the women and male neophytes as well as the workshops.

The San Gabriel belfry is well known in picture, song, and story. Yet the fanciful legends about the casting of the bells give way to stern fact when they are examined. Upon the first bell is the inscription: "Ave María Santisima. S. Francisco. De Paula Rvelas, me fecit." The second: "Cast by G. H. Holbrook, Medway, Mass., 1828." The third: "Ave Maria, Sn Jvan Nepomvseno, Ruelas me fecit, A. D., '95." The fourth: "Fecit Benitvs a Regibvs, Ano D. 1830, Sn. Frano."

In the year 1886 a number of needed repairs were made; the windows were enlarged, and a new ceiling put in, the latter a most incongruous piece of work.

CHAPTER X

SAN LUIS, OBISPO DE TOLOSA

FOUNDED, as we have seen, by Serra himself, September 1, 1772, by the end of 1773 it could report only twelve converts. Serra left the day after the founding, leaving Padre Cavaller in charge, with two Indians from Lower California, four soldiers and their corporal. Their only provisions were a few hundred pounds of flour and wheat, and a barrel of brown sugar. But the Indians were kind, in remembrance of Fages's goodness in shooting the bears, and brought them venison and seeds frequently, so they " managed to subsist " until provisions came.

Padre Cavaller built a neat chapel of logs and apartments for the missionaries, and the soldiers soon erected their own barracks. While the Indians were friendly they did not seem to be particularly attracted to the Mission, as they had more and better food than the padre, and the only thing he had that they particularly desired was cloth. There was no ranchería in the vicinity, but they were much interested in the growth of the corn and beans sown by the padre, and which, being on good and well-watered land, yielded abundantly.

In 1776 certain gentiles, who were hostile to some Indians who were sheltered by the padres, attacked the Mission by discharging burning arrows upon the tule roof of the buildings, and everything was destroyed, save the church and the granary. Rivera came at once, captured two of the ringleaders, and sent them for punishment to the Monterey presidio. The success of the gentiles on this

PLATE XXIV

SIX ARCHES AT SAN JUAN CAPISTRANO

occasion led them to repeat it by setting fire to the Mission twice during the next ten years, and it was these calamities that led one of the San Luis padres to attempt the making of roof tiles. Being successful, it was not long before all the Missions were so roofed.

In 1794 certain of the neophytes of San Luis and La Purísima conspired with some gentiles to incite the Indians at San Luis to revolt, but the arrest and deportation of fifteen or twenty of the ringleaders to Monterey, to hard labor at the presidio, put a stop to the revolt.

Padres Lasuen and Tapis both served here as missionaries, and in 1798 Luis Antonio Martinez, one of the best known of the padres, began his long term of service at San Luis. In 1794 the Mission reached its highest population of 946 souls. It had 6500 head of cattle and horses, 6150 sheep. In 1798 it raised 4100 bushels of wheat, and in this same year a water-power mill was erected and set in motion. San Luis was also favored by the presence of a smith, a miller, and a carpenter of the artisan instructors, sent by the King in 1794. Looms were erected, and cotton brought up from San Blas was woven. A new church of adobes, with a tile roof, was completed in 1793, and that same year a portico was added to its front.

In 1818, when Bouchard, the South American revolutionist, came North to harass the California coast, he stopped at Refugio, a sea-coast rancho about opposite to San Luis. A force was at once raised to go and drive off the " pirates," and Padre Martinez rose from a sick bed to lead thirty-five of his neophytes to the scene of action. After the destruction of the ranch house Bouchard sailed for Santa Barbara, leaving three of his men, however, prisoners in the hands of the Spaniards.

A little prior to this time, Martinez visited the Indians of the great valley of the Tulares, and found them willing to have a Mission established; and had not controversy arisen on the question of the presence of soldiers, it is possible the San Joaquin Valley would have had several Missions established in the course of a few years.

To the sailors and traders along the coast early in the century, few figures were better known and better liked than that of the picturesque Padre Luis Martinez. "Portly of figure and gruff of speech" he was jolly, hail-fellow-well-met, hospitable, and, if reports and suspicions count for anything, always ready to trade for his own advantage. Anyhow, in the spring of 1830, on the charge of smuggling, he was banished, and, with many tears and much regret, he was compelled to say farewell to the Mission he so much loved, and the Indians he had sought to benefit, to return in disgrace to old Madrid, where he spent the remainder of his days.

" H. H.," in Ramona, in describing the wedding tour and festivities of General and Señora Moreno, tells a good story which perfectly illustrates the jolly character of Padre Martinez. She says:

" On the morning of their departure, the good padre, having exhausted all his resources for entertaining his distinguished guests, caused to be driven past the corridors for their inspection, all the poultry belonging to the Mission. The procession took an hour to pass. For music there was squeaking, cackling, hissing, gobbling, crowing, and quacking of the fowls, combined with the screaming, scolding, and whip-cracking of the excited Indian marshals of the lines. First came the turkeys, then the roosters, then the white hens, then the black, and then the yellow; next the ducks, and at the tail of the spectacle long files of geese, some struggling, some half flying and hissing in resentment and terror at the unwonted coercion to which they were subjected. The Indians had been hard at work all night capturing, sorting, assorting, and guarding the rank and file of their novel pageant. It would be safe to say that a droller sight never was seen, and never will be, on the Pacific coast or any other. Before it was done with, the General and his bride had nearly died with laughter; and the General could never allude to it without laughing almost as heartily again."

At the time of Martinez's banishment the buildings at San Luis were already falling into decay, as the padre, with far-seeing eye, was assured that the politicians had nothing but evil in store for them. Consequently, he did not keep up things as he otherwise would have done. He was an outspoken, frank, fearless man, and this undoubtedly led to his being chosen as the example necessary to restrain the other padres from too great freedom of speech and manner.

In 1834 San Luis had 264 neophytes, though after secularization the number was gradually reduced until, in 1840, there were but 170 left. The order of secularization was put into effect in 1835 by Manuel Jimeno Casarin. The inventory of the property in 1836 showed $70,000. In 1839 it was $60,000. In 1840 all the horses were stolen by " New Mexican traders," one report alone telling of the driving away of 1200 head. The officers at Los Angeles went in pursuit of the thieves and one party reported that it came in full sight of the foe retiring deliberately with the stolen animals, but, as there were as many Americans as Indians in the band they deemed it imprudent to risk a conflict.

In 1842 a distribution of land to the most worthy neophytes took place; one, named Odon, receiving 75 varas of land, the house occupied by him, a copper pot and two troughs. The fruit of the trees on his land, however, was to remain community property.

Two years later the report of the padre presidente Duran states that at San Luis there are neither lands, nor cattle, and its neophytes are scattered for want of a minister. It had been completely secularized by Micheltorena's decree in 1843, converted into a pueblo, the neophytes freed, the Mission house turned into a parsonage, and the other buildings dedicated to public uses.

June 5, 1845, saw Pio Pico's decree issued offering San Luis for sale, and December 4 it was sold to Scott,

Wilson, and McKinley for $510, and this ended its history as a Mission.

In December of 1846, when Frémont was marching south to co-operate with Stockton against the Southern Californians, San Luis was thought to harbor an armed force of hostiles. Accordingly Frémont surrounded it one dark, rainy night, and took it by sudden assault. The fears were unfounded, for only women, children, and non-combatants were found.

In the baptismal register at San Luis Obispo, the first date of which is in 1772, the original names are given of many of the rancherías of that Mission, some of which are still retained in local names to this day. We find Tchena, Tgmaps, De Qmchechs, De Imipu, Chiminer, Lteguie, Chofuate, Sespala, Sesjala, Chapule, etc. Baptism 2087 is of an adult about 30 years of age, a native of Santa Margarita. His name was Csfoczo, and he was given the Christian name of Juan.

Six miles from San Luis is the Rancho Camado, where are some hot springs. Opposite these are to be found remnants of walls. These are ruins of the church of a vista or asistencia of San Luis, and a padre went regularly from the Mission to say mass for the Indians there.

The Book of Confirmations at San Luis has its introductory pages written by Serra. There is also a " Nota " opposite page 3, and a full page note in the back in his clear, vigorous and distinctive hand.

There are three bells at San Luis Obispo. The thickest is to the right, the smallest in the centre. On the largest bell is the following inscription: " Me fecit ano di 1818 Manvel Vargas, Lima. Mision de Sn Luis Obispo De La Nueba California," this latter in a circumferential panel about midway between the top and bottom of the bell. On the middle bell we read the same inscription, while there is none on the third. This latter was cast in San Francisco, from two old bells which were broken.

From a painting the old San Luis Obispo church is shown to have been raised up on a stone and cement foundation. The corridor was without the arches that are elsewhere one of the distinctive features, but plain round columns, with a square base and topped with a plain square moulding gave support to the roof beams on which the usual red-tiled roof was placed.

The *fachada* of the church retreats some 15 or 20 feet from the front line of the corridors. The monastery has been " restored," even as has the church, out of all resemblance to its own honest original self. The adobe walls are covered with painted wood, and the tiles have given way to shingles, just like any other modern and commonplace house. The building faces the southeast. The altar end is at the northwest. To the southwest are the remains of a building of boulders, brick, and cement, exactly of the same style as the asistencia building of Santa Margarita. It seems as if it might have been built by the same hands.

CHAPTER XI

SAN FRANCISCO DE ASIS

THE story of Bucareli's determination to found a presidio at San Francisco, and Anza's march with the colonists for it from Sonora, has already been recounted. When Serra and Galvez were making their original plans for the establishment of the three first Missions of Alta California, Serra expressed his disappointment that St. Francis was neglected by asking: " And for our founder St. Francis there is no Mission? " to which Galvez replied: " If St. Francis desires a Mission, let him show us his harbor and he shall have one." It therefore seemed providential that when Portolá, Fages, and Crespí, in 1769, saw the Bay of Monterey they did not recognize it, and were thus led on further north, where the great Bay of San Francisco was soon afterwards discovered and reasonably well surveyed.

As illustrating the way the Spaniards financially cared for the officers and soldiers of their frontier posts in Alta California, it is interesting here to note Governor Neve's provision for the post at San Francisco:

" The annual allowance for the Post of San Francisco shall be $8027.50, divided in this form :

Annual pay of the Lieutenant	$550.00
Ensign	400.00
Sergeant	262.50
4 Corporals at $225	900.00
26 Privates at $217.50	5655.00
Gratuity from Common Fund, $10 each . .	260.00
Total	$8027.50

To each settler in each of the two first years,
    for pay and rations $116.37½
For rations in each of the three following
    years, that they may be granted him . . . 60.00

Palou eventually established the Mission October 9, 1776. None of the Indians were present to witness the ceremony as they had fled, the preceding month, from the attacks of certain of their enemies. When they returned in December they brought trouble with them. They stole all in their reach; one party discharged arrows at the corporal of the guard; another insulted a soldier's wife; and some other attempted to kill the San Carlos neophyte who had been brought here. The officer shut up one of these hostiles, whereat a party of his comrades rushed to the rescue, fired their arrows at the Mission, and were only driven back when the soldiers arrived and fired their muskets in the air. Next day the sergeant went out to make arrests and another struggle ensued, in which one was killed and one wounded. All now sued for peace, which, with sundry floggings, was granted. For three months they now kept away from the Mission.

In 1777 they began to return, and on October 4 the Padre Serra, on his first visit, was able to say mass in the presence of seventeen adult native converts. Then, passing over to the presidio on October 10, as he stood gazing on the waters flowing out to the setting sun through the purple walls of the Golden Gate, he exclaimed with a heart too full of thanksgiving to be longer restrained: " Thanks be to God that now our father St. Francis with the Holy Cross of the Procession of Missions, has reached the last limit of the Californian continent. To go farther he must have boats."

General Vallejo states that the temporary building erected by Palou for a church was about a thousand varas to the northwest of the present site. The small lake of

Dolores, from which the Mission gained its popular name, was near by, but as the city has grown it has been drained, filled up, and is now built over.

On the 14th of September, 1779, two vessels, originally from San Blas, on an exploring expedition north, stopped at San Francisco on their return for six weeks, to recuperate the health of the scurvy-stricken sailors. One of the captains, Bodega y Cuadra, presented a bronze image of Nuestra Señora de los Remedios to the San Francisco Mission, and it was placed on the altar with most impressive ceremonies on the 3d of October. The next day three natives brought from the northern coast were baptized. Soon a courier arrived from Sonora, announcing the death of Viceroy Bucareli, and that war was declared between Spain and England. This made the vessels leave in haste.

In 1782, April 25, the corner-stone of a new church was laid at San Francisco. Three padres were present, together with the Mission guard and a body of troops from the presidio. In the Mission records it says: " There was enclosed in the cavity of said corner-stone the image of our Holy Father St. Francis, some relics in the form of bones of St. Pius and other holy martyrs, five medals of various saints, and a goodly portion of silver coin."

In 1785 Governor Fages complained to the Viceroy, among other things, that the presidio of San Francisco had been deprived of mass for three years, notwithstanding the obligation of the friars to serve as chaplains. Palou replied that the padres were under no obligation to serve gratuitously, and that they were always ready to attend the soldiers when their other duties allow.

In November, 1787, Captain Soler, who for a brief time acted as temporary governor and inspector, suggested that the presidio of San Francisco be abandoned and its company transferred to Santa Barbara. Later, as I have shown elsewhere, a proposition was again made for the abandonment of San Francisco; so it is apparent that Fate herself was protecting it for its future great and wonderful history.

In 1790 San Francisco reported 551 baptisms and 205 deaths, with a present neophyte population of 438. Large stock had increased to 2000 head and small to 1700.

Three years later, on November 14, the celebrated English navigator, George Vancouver, in his vessel " Discovery," sailed into San Francisco Bay. His arrival caused quite a flutter of excitement both at the presidio and Mission, where he was kindly entertained. The Governor was afraid of this elaborate hospitality to the hated and feared English, and issued orders to the commandante providing for a more frigid reception in the future, so, on Vancouver's second visit, he did not find matters so agreeable, and grumbled accordingly.

Vancouver gives a description of the Mission buildings, etc., which is quite interesting. He says that they form two sides of a square, without any apparent intention of completing the quadrangle, the architecture and material being as at the presidio, but the apartments larger, better constructed, and cleaner. At this time all the roofs were of thatch, and the dwellings of the Indians were huts of willow poles, basket-work of twigs, and thatch of grass and tules, about twelve feet high, six or seven feet in diameter, and abominably infested with every kind of filth and nastiness. One large room was occupied by Indians working looms, making blankets from native wool. " The looms," he says, " though rudely wrought, were tolerably well contrived, and had been made by the Indians. The produce is wholly applied to the clothing of the converted Indians. I saw some of the cloth, which was by no means despicable; and, had it received the advantages of fulling, would have been a very decent kind of clothing." Borica, however, though he ordered that Mission blankets should henceforth solely be used at the presidio, refused to allow the padres to erect a fulling-mill. A pottery was also established in 1796.

In March, 1795, certain neophytes having escaped across the bay from San Francisco, a band of their fellows was sent to bring them back. After two days of marching this band was attacked by gentile Indians and eight or ten of them slain. The Governor condemned the padres for their action in this matter and refused to avenge the death of the slain, as the gentiles, though warlike, had hitherto been friendly. In June, 1797, in spite of the attitude of the Governor, another party was sent out after runaways, and the result of this was that the Sacalanes threatened to attack the Mission San José. Sergeant Amador was sent from San Francisco to investigate, and he reported to the Governor that these Indians were threatening to kill the Christians if they continued to work, and the soldiers if they dared to interfere. The Governor then decided to teach these haughty savages what it meant to defy the Spanish power, and a force of twenty-two men was placed under the orders of Amador to capture the head men of the tribe, and also bring back the fugitives. In the fight which ensued two soldiers were wounded and seven natives killed; but Amador returned victorious with eighty-three of the escapes and nine gentiles. Borica was severe with some of the renegades, condemning them to receive from twenty-five to seventy-five lashes, and to work in shackles at the presidio from two months to a year. In the examination as to the cause of the neophytes running away, they gave as their reasons excessive flogging, hunger, and the death of relatives. Padre Dantí, one of the padres in charge at San Francisco, was undoubtedly very harsh and severe in his treatment of the Indians, but his associate Fernandez was the very reverse. All were glad when Dantí's term of service expired and he returned to Mexico.

Tiles were made and put on the church roofs in 1795; more houses were built for the neophytes, and all roofed with tiles. Half a league of ditch was also dug around the potrero (pasture ground) and fields.

In 1806 San Francisco was enlivened by the presence of the Russian chamberlain, Rezánof, who had been on a special voyage around the world, and was driven by scurvy and want of provisions to the California settlements. He was accompanied by Dr. G. H. von Langsdorff, from whom I have already quoted. Langsdorff's account of the visit and reception at several points in California is interesting. He gives a full description of the Indians and their method of life at the Mission; commends the zeal and self-sacrifice of the padres; speaks of the ingenuity shown by the women in making baskets; the system of allowing the cattle and horses to run wild, etc. Visiting the Mission of San José by boat, he and his companions had quite an adventurous time getting back, owing to the contrary winds.

In 1810 Moraga, the ensign at the presidio, was sent with seventeen men to punish the gentiles of the region of the Carquines Strait, who for several years had been harrassing the neophytes at San Francisco, and sixteen of whom they had killed. Moraga had a hard fight against a hundred and twenty of them, and captured eighteen, whom he soon released, " as they were all sure to die of their wounds." The survivors retreated to their huts and made a desperate resistance, and were so determined not to be captured that, when one hut was set on fire, its inmates preferred to perish in the flames rather than to surrender. A full report of this affair was sent to the King of Spain, and as a result he promoted Moraga and other officers, and increased the pay of some of the soldiers. He also tendered the thanks of the nation to all the participants.

Runaway neophytes gave considerable trouble for several years, and in 1819 a force was sent from San Francisco to punish these recalcitrants and their allies. A sharp fight took place near the site of the present Stockton, in which 27 Indians were killed, 20 wounded, and 16 captured, with 49 horses.

11

The Mission report for 1821–30 shows a decrease in neophyte population from 1252 to 219, though this was largely caused by the sending of neophytes to the newly founded Missions of San Rafael and San Francisco Solano.

San Francisco was secularized in 1834–35, with Joaquin Estudillo as comisionado. The valuation in 1835 was real estate and fixtures, $25,800; church property, $17,800; available assets in excess of debts (chiefly live-stock), $16,400, or a total of $60,000. If any property was ever divided among the Indians there is no record to show it.

On June 5, 1845, Pio Pico's proclamation was made, requiring the Indians of Dolores Mission to reunite and occupy it or it would be declared abandoned and disposed of for the general good of the department. A fraudulent title to the Mission was given, and antedated February 10, 1845; but it was afterwards declared void, and the building was duly returned to the custody of the archbishop, under whose direction it still remains.

After Commodore Sloat had taken possession of Monterey for the United States, in 1846, it was merely the work of a day or so to get despatches to Captain Montgomery, of the ship " Portsmouth," who immediately raised the stars and stripes, and thus the city of the Golden Gate entered into American possession. While the city was materially concerned in the events immediately following the occupation, the Mission was already too nearly dead to participate. In 1846 the bishop succeeded in finding a curate for a short period, but nothing in the records can be found as to the final disposition of the property belonging to the ex-Mission. In the political caldron it had totally disappeared.

The graveyard of Dolores is an interesting old place, and it is a great pity that it and the old Mission church are not made more accessible to visitors. Saturdays and Sundays only are they admitted. It is scarcely in keeping with the progressive spirit of the leaders of the great church that controls these sacred memorials of the past that such slight facilities are offered to the people who are the heirs of their history. At the least, certain hours — extended enough not to be prohibitive — should be set aside in each day of the week, when all who come in the proper spirit may have full — if not free — entrance to them.

In the early days the Mission Indians were buried in the graveyard, then the soldiers and settlers, Spanish and Mexican, and the priests, and, later, the *Americanos*. But all is neglected and uncared for, except by Nature, and, after all, perhaps it is better so. The kindly spirited Earth Mother has given forth vines and myrtle and ivy and other plants in profusion, that have hidden the old gravelled walks and the broken flags. Rose-bushes grow untrimmed, untrained, and frankly beautiful; while pepper and cypress wave gracefully and poetically suggestive over graves of high and low, historic and unknown. For here are names carved on stone denoting that beneath lie buried those who helped make California history. Just at the side entrance of the church is a stone with this inscription to the first governor of California: " Aqui yacen los restos del Capitan Don Luis Antonio Argüello, Primer Gobernador del Alta California, Bajo el Gobierno Mejicano. Naciòen San Francisco el 21 de Junio, 1774, y muri6en el mismo lugar el 27 de Marzo, 1830."

Farther along is a brown stone monument, erected by the members of the famous fire company, to Casey, who was hung by the Vigilantes — Casey, who shot James King of William. The monument, adorned with firemen's helmets and bugles in stone, stands under the shadow of drooping pepper sprays, and is inscribed: " Sacred to the memory of James P. Casey, who Departed this life May 23–1856 Aged 27 years. May God forgive my Persecutors. Requiescat en pace."

Poor, sad Dolores! How utterly lost it now looks, surrounded by parvenu buildings of pretentious greatness, and led up to by asphalt pavements and cement sidewalks. It is forlorn and neglected. The tiles on its roof and ridge are irregular and uneven. The wooden cross on the front is old and staggering. Even the *fachada* has been degraded with a new coat of whitewash, so that all its time-honored wrinkles are gone.

CHAPTER XII

SAN JUAN CAPISTRANO

ON the tragic events at San Diego that led to the delay in the founding of San Juan Capistrano I have already fully dwelt. The Mission was founded by Serra, November 1, 1776, and the adobe church recently restored by the Landmarks Club is said to be the original church built at that time.

Troubles began here early, as at San Gabriel, owing to the immorality of the guards with the Indian women, and in one disturbance three Indians were killed and several wounded. In 1781 the padre feared another uprising, owing to incitements of the Colorado River Indians, who came here across the desert and sought to arouse the local Indians to revolt.

In 1787 Governor Fages reported that San Juan was in a thoroughly prosperous condition; lands were fertile, ministers faithful and zealous, and natives well disposed. In 1800 the number of neophytes was 1046, horses and cattle 8500, while it had the vast number of 17000 sheep. Crops were 6300 bushels, and in 1797 the presidios of Santa Barbara and San Diego owed San Juan Mission over $6000 for supplies furnished. In 1794 two large adobe granaries with tile roofs, and forty houses for neophytes were built. In February, 1797, work was begun on the church, the remains of which are now to be seen. It is in the form of a Roman cross, ninety feet wide and a hundred and eighty feet long, and was planned by Fray Gorgonio. It was probably the finest of all the California Mission structures. Built of quarried stone, with arched roof of the same material and a lofty tower adorning its *fachada*, it justifies the remark that "it could not be duplicated to-day under $100,000."

The stone-work facings at San Juan Capistrano are more elaborate than at any other Mission. The few specimens illustrated show that the mason was a master craftsman, and he was given every opportunity to display his skill. In the ruins of the altar are many pieces of exquisite work, especially in the two arched doorways leading into the sacristy. The stone-work is well carved. Both doorways are now walled up. The window-frames are of stone, resting upon a three-membered sill. Above the frame is a similar three-membered detached cornice of stone. The master mason who did all this work was brought specially for the purpose from Culiacan, and under his direction the work slowly but steadily progressed for nine years.

The baptismal font and holy water receptacle were doubtless made here, and by the same artist that cut the stone for the building. It is scarcely to be assumed that such heavy objects as these stone baptismal fonts would be imported, when they could be manufactured on the ground much more easily.

A weaver, Mariano Mendoza, was sent down from Monterey to teach the Indians his art. This was in 1796. He was under contract to the government at thirty dollars a month, and the San Juan padre was instructed that if he neglected his work he was to be chained up at night. Soon the rattle and clatter of his rude loom was heard, and it was not long before many of the natives were making rude but serviceable cloth and blankets. In 1797, as a call was made for pay for his services, Mendoza was dismissed. The fact was his pupils had learned all he could teach.

The country was much agitated by fear of an English invasion in 1797, and, remembering that Vancouver had been there four years previously and had made careful observations, a sentinel was placed on the lookout at the

PLATE XXV

a. ARCHED CLOISTERS AT SAN JUAN CAPISTRANO

b. PRESIDIO CHURCH, MONTEREY

beach to watch for suspicious vessels. Nothing alarming, however, appears to have been reported.

It must be remembered that little or no communication was permitted between the Californians and any foreign vessel which might appear on the coast. Spain was very jealous of her Pacific possessions. Trade was either forbidden or very much restricted. Yet, being between the sea-coast presidios of San Diego and Santa Barbara, it seemed impossible to prevent vessels from stopping at San Juan Capistrano. And if a padre needed something that the captain had, and the captain needed something that the padre had, what more natural than that the exchange should take place? — purely as a friendly act, not as a matter of trade between people of different nationalities.

The carelessness of servants had an illustration here in March, 1801, when the storeroom was set on fire, and 2400 bushels of grain and six tons of tallow were lost, as well as considerable damage suffered by the other buildings.

The consecration of the beautiful new church took place, September 7, 1806. President Tapis was aided by padres from many Missions, and the scene was made gorgeous and brilliant by the presence of Governor Arrillaga and his staff, with many soldiers from San Diego and Santa Barbara. Large numbers of neophytes from other Missions were also permitted to be present at the rites, and it was one of the most elaborate and pretentious events in early Californian history. What congratulations and feastings indoors and out there must have been; the visiting padres and the Governor and other officials being regaled with the best the Mission afforded, and the hordes of Indians crowding the rancherías outside, and, likewise, feasting on the abundance provided for them on so auspicious an occasion.

The following day another mass was said and sermon preached, and on the 9th the bones of Padre Vicente Fuster were transferred to their final resting-place within the altar of the new church. A solemn requiem mass was chanted, thus adding to the solemnity of the occasion.

This altar had nine niches for statuary, all well executed. The ceiling was groined, and the apse being six-sided, it allowed the erection of five beautiful connecting arches above. Three steps led up from the church to the altar.

The church itself originally had seven domes. Only two now remain. In the earthquake of 1812, when the tower fell, one of the domes was crushed, but the others remained fairly solid and intact until the sixties of the last century, when, with a zeal that outran all discretion, and that the fool-killer should have been permitted to restrain, they were blown up with gunpowder by mistaken friends who expected to rebuild the church with the same material, but never did so.

This earthquake of 1812 was felt almost the whole length of the Mission chain, and it did much damage. It was on Sunday morning, December 8. At San Juan a number of neophytes were at morning mass; the day had opened with intense sultriness and heaviness; the air was hot and seemed charged with electricity. Suddenly a shock was felt. All were alarmed, but, devoted to his high office, the padre began again the solemn words, when, suddenly, the second shock came and sent the great tower crashing down upon one of the domes or vaults, and in a moment the whole mass of masonry came down upon the congregation. Thirty-nine were buried in the next two days, and four were taken out of the ruins later. The officiating priest escaped, as by a miracle, through the sacristy.

After he had made his pledges to leave California, Bouchard, the South American revolutionist, stopped two days at San Juan, but as all the valuables and the families had been removed to Trabuco rancho he found little. Nor could he have taken it without a fight, as Ensign Argüello, with thirty soldiers from San Diego, was there for the purpose of preventing any such effort.

It was in 1814 that Padre Boscana, who had been serving at San Luis Rey, came to reside at San Juan Capistrano, where he wrote the interesting account of the Indians that is so often quoted. In 1812 its population gained its greatest figure, 1361.

In November, 1833, Figueroa secularized the Mission by organizing a " provisional pueblo " of the Indians, and claiming that the padres voluntarily gave up the temporalities. There is no record of any inventory, and what became of the church property is not known. Lands were apportioned to the Indians by Captain Portilla. The following year, most probably, all this provisional work of Figueroa's was undone, and the Mission was secularized in the ordinary way, but in 1838 the Indians begged for the pueblo organization again, and freedom from overseers, whether lay or clerical. In 1840 Padre Zalvidea was instructed to emancipate them from Mission rule as speedily as possible. Janssens was appointed majordomo, and he reported that he zealously worked for the benefit of the Mission, repairing broken fences and ditches, bringing back runaway neophytes, clothing them and caring for the stock. But orders soon began to come in for the delivery of cattle and horses, applications rapidly came in for grants of the Mission ranches, and about the middle of June, 1841, the lands were divided among the ex-neophytes, about 100 in number, and some forty whites. At the end of July regulations were published for the foundation of the pueblo, and Don Juan Bandini soon thereafter went to supervise the work. He remained until March, 1842, in charge of the community property, and then left about half a dozen white families and twenty or more ex-neophytes duly organized as a pueblo.

In 1843 San Juan was one of the Missions the temporalities of which were to be restored to the padres, provided they paid one-eighth of all produce into the public treasury. In 1844 it was reported that San Juan had no minister, and all its neophytes were scattered. In 1845 Pico's decree was published, stating that it was to be considered a pueblo; the church, curate's house, and courthouse should be reserved, and the rest of the property sold at auction for the payment of debts and the support of public worship. In December of that year the ex-Mission buildings and gardens were sold to Forster and McKinley for $710, the former of whom retained possession for many years. In 1846 the pueblo was reported as possessing a population of 113 souls.

Of the present appearance of San Juan I have written in the chapter on architecture, and especially of its preservation in the chapter on the work of the Landmarks Club.

Twenty years ago there used to be one of the best of the Mission libraries at San Juan. The books were all in old-style leather, sheepskin and parchment bindings, some of them tied with leathern thongs, and a few having heavy home-made metal clasps. They were all in Latin or Spanish, and were well known books of divinity. The first page of the record of marriages was written and signed by Junipero Serra.

There are still several interesting relics; among others, two instruments, doubtless Indian-made, used during the Easter services. One is a board studded with handle-like irons, which, when moved rapidly from side to side, makes a hideous noise. Another is a three-cornered box, on which are similar irons, and in this a loose stone is rattled. In the service called " las tinieblas," — the utter darkness, — expressive of the darkness after the crucifixion, when the church is absolutely without light, the appalling effect of these noises, heightened by the clanking of chains, is indescribable.

In proof of the tireless industry of the priests and Indians of their charge, there are to be found at San Juan many ruins of the aqueducts, or flumes, some of brick, others of wood, supported across ravines, which conveyed the water needed to irrigate the eighty acres of orchard, vineyard, and garden that used to be surrounded by an adobe wall. Reservoirs, cisterns, and zanjas of brick, stone, and cement are seen here and there, and several remnants of the masonry aqueducts are still found in the village.

CHAPTER XIII

SANTA CLARA DE ASIS

RIVERA delayed the founding of San Francisco and Santa Clara for reasons of his own; and when, in September, 1776, he received a letter from Viceroy Bucareli, in which were references clearly showing that it was supposed by the writer that they were already established, he set to work without further delay, and went with Padre Peña, as already related. The Mission was duly founded January 12, 1777. A square of seventy yards was set off and buildings at once begun. Cattle and other Mission property were sent down from San Francisco and San Carlos, and the guard returned. But it was not long before the Indians developed an unholy love for contraband beef, and Moraga and his soldiers were sent for to capture and punish the thieves. Three of them were killed, but even then depredations occasionally continued. At the end of the year there had been sixty-seven baptisms, including eight adults, and twenty-five deaths.

The present is the third site occupied by Santa Clara. The Mission was originally established some three miles away, near Alviso, at the headwaters of the San Francisco Bay, near the river Guadalupe, on a site called by the Indians So-co-is-u-ka (laurel wood). It was probably located there on account of its being the chief rendezvous of the Indians, fishing being good, the river having an abundance of salmon trout. The Mission remained there only a short time, as the waters rose twice in 1779, and washed it out. Then the padres removed, in 1780–82, and built about 150

PLATE XXVI

a. ENTRANCE TO SAN JUAN CAPISTRANO CHAPEL

b. ELLIPTICAL ARCHES OF DIFFERING AXES, SAN JUAN CAPISTRANO

yards southwest of the present broad-gauge (Southern Pacific) depot, where quite recently traces were found of the old adobe walls. They remained at this spot, deeming the location good, until an earthquake in 1812 gave them considerable trouble. A second earthquake in 1818 so injured their buildings that they felt compelled to move to the present site, which has been occupied ever since. The Mission church and other buildings were begun in 1818, and finally dedicated in 1822. The site was called by the Indians *Gerguensun* — the Valley of the Oaks.

The corner-stone of the second church was laid November 19, 1781, and the building was completed in 1784. It was dedicated May 15, by Serra, Palou, and Peña, in the presence of Fages and Moraga. The occasion was a sad one for Serra, as only four days previously Palou had buried Murguia, its architect, within its walls. It was the most beautiful and elaborate church, up to that time, erected in California.

In agricultural advantages Santa Clara was deemed second only to San Gabriel, and crops of grain and fruit were both good, thus early foreshadowing the heavy harvests, especially of the latter, for which the whole valley is now noted throughout the world. In 1790 Santa Clara stood third in the number of its converts.

On the 29th of November, 1777, the pueblo of San José was founded. The padres protested at the time that it was too near the Mission of Santa Clara, and for the next decade there was constant irritation, owing to the encroachments of the white settlers upon the lands of the Indians. Complaints were made and formally acted upon, and in July, 1801, the boundaries were surveyed, as asked for by the padres, and landmarks clearly marked and agreed upon so as to prevent future disputes.

In 1793 Vancouver visited Santa Clara from San Francisco, and describes the Mission buildings as forming an incomplete square of about 100 by 170 feet. Even though this was the second site chosen, they were in a low, marshy spot, and quite recently the padres had been confined to their house with a flood. A roof of tiles was put on the church in 1795, and it was also lengthened twenty-four feet. The natives were busily engaged in weaving, tanning, and shoemaking.

In 1794 the eastern shore of the Bay of San Francisco was almost unknown, and in November the padres of Santa Clara petitioned to be allowed to go on a gentile hunting expedition, alleging that it would be an easy task, as the drought had made the supply of food very short; but the commandante at San Francisco refused, because the country was " almost unknown," the natives perverse, and the adventure too hazardous.

In 1800 Santa Clara was the banner Mission for population, having 1247. Live-stock had increased to about 5000 head of each (cattle and horses), and crops were good.

For several years after 1800 there was considerable trouble with the Indians, — hunting for a chief, sending after runaways, fights, and killings. In May, 1805, quite an alarm was caused by the discovery on the roof of the missionaries' house of a neophyte and a gentile who, it was alleged, were reconnoitring for a projected attack in which the whole Mission was to be burned and the padres killed. Troops were sent from San Francisco and Monterey, arrests made; but careful investigation showed the whole thing to be a *canard*, spread abroad by some lazy neophytes to frighten the padres so that they would escape certain promised floggings.

In 1802, August 12, a grand high altar, which had been obtained in Mexico, was consecrated with elaborate ceremonies.

Padre Viader was a very muscular and athletic man; and one night, in 1814, a young gentile giant, named Marcelo, and two companions attacked him. In the rough and tumble fight which ensued the padre came out ahead; and after giving the culprits a severe homily on the sin of attacking a priest, they were pardoned, Marcelo becoming one of his best and most faithful friends thereafter. Robinson says Viader was " a good old man, whose heart and soul were in proportion to his immense figure."

In 1820 the neophyte population was 1357, stock 5024, horses 722, sheep 12,060. The maximum of population was reached in 1827, of 1464 souls. After that it began rapidly to decline. The crops, too, were smaller after 1820, without any apparent reason.

In 1837 secularization was effected by Ramon Estrada. In 1839–40 reports show that two-thirds of the cattle and sheep had disappeared. The downfall of the Mission was very rapid. The neophyte population in 1832 was 1125, in 1834 about 800, and at the end of the decade about 290, with 150 more scattered in the district.

The totals of baptisms from 1777 to 1834 is 8640, of deaths 6950.

The old register of marriages records 3222 weddings from January 12, 1778, to August 15, 1863.

In 1833 Padre Viader closed his missionary service of nearly forty years in California by leaving the country, and Padre Francisco García Diego, the prefect of the Zacatecan friars, became his successor. Diego afterwards became the first bishop of California.

In July, 1839, a party called Yozcolos, doubtless after their leader, attacked the neophytes guarding the Santa Clara wheat-fields, killing one of them. The attackers were pursued, and their leader slain, and the placing of his head on a pole seemed to act as a deterrent of further acts for awhile.

In December of the same year Prado Mesa made an expedition against gentile thieves in the region of the Stanislaus River. He was surprised by the foe, three of his men killed, and he and six others wounded, besides losing a num-

ber of his weapons.   This Indian success caused great
alarm, and a regular patrol was organized to operate between San José and San Juan Missions for the protection
of the ranchos.   This uprising of the Indians was almost
inevitable.   Deprived of their maintenance at the Missions,
they were practically thrown on their own resources, and
in many cases this left them a prey to the evil leadership
of desperate men of their own class.

Santa Clara was one of the Missions immediately affected by the decree of Micheltorena, of March 29, 1843,
requiring that the padres reassume the management of the
temporalities.   They set to work to gather up what fragments they could find, but the flocks and herds were " lent "
where they could not be recovered, and one flock of 4000
sheep — the padre says 6000 — were taken by M. J. Vallejo, " legally, in aid of the government."

Pio Pico's decree of June 5, 1845, affected Santa Clara.
Andrés Pico made a valuation of the property at $16,173.
There were then 130 ex-neophytes, the live-stock had
dwindled down to 430 cattle, 215 horses, and 809 sheep.
The padre found it necessary to write a sharp letter to the
alcalde of San José on the grog-shops of that pueblo,
which encouraged drinking among his Indians to such
extent that they were completely demoralized.

Santa Clara saw exciting times both at the revolution
against Micheltorena and against the Americans after
Frémont had gone South.   In the latter there were about
200 native Californians to 100 of the Americans from San
Francisco; but the " fight " amounted to nothing, and
when the forces from San Francisco entered Santa Clara
Mission, a truce was arranged, the complaints of the Californians only listened to, recorded on paper, promised redress, and the conflict was over.

Santa Clara Mission was now a regular parish church,
Padre Real becoming the parish priest.   In 1846 he was
authorized to sell the Mission lands to pay debts and sup-

port himself and the church; and certain men afterwards claimed they bought the orchard and buildings belonging to it for $1200. But the courts afterwards decided that their pretended deed was fraudulent. Immigrants gave the padre considerable trouble by taking possession of the Mission buildings, but the Governor threatened to evict them by force, so they came to the padre's terms.

March 19, 1851, the parish priest, who was a cultivated and learned Jesuit, and who had prepared the way, succeeded in having the Santa Clara College established in the old Mission buildings. On the 28th of April, 1855, it was chartered with all the rights and privileges of a university. In due time the college grew to large proportions, and it was found imperative either to remove the old Mission structure completely, or renovate it out of all recognition. This latter was done, so that but little of the old church remains.

In restoring it in 1861–62 the nave was allowed to remain, but in 1885 it was found necessary to remove it. Its walls were five feet thick. The adobe bricks were thrown out upon the plaza behind the cross.

The present occupation of Santa Clara as a college as well as a church necessitated the adaptation of the old cloisters to meet the modern conditions. Therefore the casual visitor would scarcely notice that the reception-room into which he is ushered is a part of the old cloisters. The walls are about three feet thick, and are of adobe. In the garden the beams of the cloister roofs are to be seen.

The old Mission vineyard, where the grapes used to thrive, is now converted into a garden. A number of the old olive trees still remain. Two of the three original bells of the Mission still remain. One was broken and had to be recast in San Francisco.

On the altar, there are angels with flambeaux in their hands, of wooden carving. These are deemed the work of the Indians. There are also several old statues of the

12

saints, including San Joaquin, Santa Ana, San Juan Capistrano, and Santa Colette.   In the sodality chapel, also,
there are statues of San Francisco and San Antonio.   The
altar rail of the restored Santa Clara church was made
from the beams of the old Mission.   These were of redwood,
secured from the Santa Cruz mountains, and, I believe,
are the earliest specimens of redwood used for lumber in
California.   The rich natural coloring and the beauty
of the grain and texture have improved with the years.   The
old octagonal pulpit, though not now used, is restored and
honored, standing upon a modern pedestal.

Santa Clara was noted for the longevity of some of its
Indians.   One of them, Gabriel, who died in 1891 or 1892
at the hospital in Salinas, claimed he was a grandfather
when Serra came in 1767.   He must have been over 150
years old when he died.   Another, Inigo, was known to be
101 years of age at his death.

In a room in the college building is gathered together
an interesting collection of articles belonging to the old
Mission.   Here are the chairs of the sanctuary, processional candlesticks, pictures, and the best bound book in the
State — an old choral.   It rests on a stand at the end of
the room.   The lids are of wood, covered with thick leather
and bound in very heavy bronze, with bosses half an inch
high.   Each corner also has bronze protuberances, half an
inch long, that stand out on the bottom, or edge of the
cover, so that they raise the whole book.   The volume is
of heaviest vellum and is entirely hand-written in red and
black;   and though a century or more has passed since it
was written it is clear and perfect.   It has 139 pages.   The
brothers of the college have placed this inscription over it:
" Ancient choral, whose wooden cover, leather bound and
covered in bronze, came, probably, originally from Spain,
and has age of some 500 years."

In a case which extends across the room are ancient
vestments, the key of the old Mission, statuary brackets

PLATE XXVII

PAINTING OF THE MIRACLE OF THE LOAVES AND FISHES, SANTA CLARA

from the ancient altar, the altar bell, crown of thorns from the Mission crucifix, altar card-frames, and the rosary and crucifix that once belonged to Padre Magin Catala.

On the walls are some of the ancient paintings, one especially noteworthy. It is of Christ multiplying the loaves and fishes (John vi. 11). While it is not a great work of art, the benignity and sweetness of the Christ face redeems it from crudeness. With upraised right hand he is blessing the loaves which rest in his left hand, while the boy with the fishes kneels reverently at his feet.

CHAPTER XIV

SAN BUENAVENTURA

FOR thirteen years the heart of the venerable Serra was made sick by the postponements in the founding of this Mission. The Viceroy de Croix had ordered Governor Rivera " to recruit seventy-five soldiers for the establishment of a presidio and three Missions in the channel of Santa Barbara: one towards the north of the channel, which was to be dedicated to the Immaculate Conception ; one towards the south, dedicated to San Buenaventura, and a third in the centre, dedicated to Santa Barbara."

It was Serra's intense desire that the whole of the Indians along the two hundred leagues of Pacific Coast should be converted, and he argued that if Missions were established at convenient intervals of distance, they would be caught in one or another of them. Portolá, after he made his trip from San Diego to Monterey in 1769, reported fully to Serra the condition of the Indians he found on the shore of the Channel Coast, — how that they, by means of pictures made in the sand, showed that vessels had been there, and white men, with beards, also visited them ; thus, undoubtedly, recalling the traditions of the Vizcaino visit made nearly two hundred years before. Portolá described their huts and the arrangement of their villages. The one he named " Assumpta " was the site of the future San Buenaventura. There he found the Indians more industrious and athletic, and the women better clad, than elsewhere. They were builders of well-shaped pine canoes, and were expert fishermen. They were also stone-masons, using only tools made of flint. Exchanges were made by Portolá with them of curious trinkets for highly polished wooden plates, which showed that they were accomplished wood-workers. Each family lived in its own hut, which was conical in shape, made of willow poles and covered with sage and other brush. A hole was left in the top for the smoke to escape which rose from the fire, always built in the centre of the hut.

Reports such as these had kept Serra in a constant ferment to establish the long-promised Mission there, so we can imagine it was with intense delight that he received a call from Governor Neve, who, in February, 1782, informed him that he was prepared to proceed at once to the founding of the Missions of San Buenaventura and Santa Barbara. Although busy training his neophytes, he determined to go in person and perform the necessary ceremonies. Looking about for a padre to accompany him, and all his own coadjutors being engaged, he bethought him of Father Pedro Benito Cambon, a returned invalid missionary from the Philippine Islands, who was recuperating at San Diego. He accordingly wrote Padre Cambon, requesting him, if possible, to meet him at San Gabriel. On his way to San Gabriel, Serra passed through the Indian villages of the Channel region, and could not refrain from joyfully communicating the news to the Indians that, very speedily, he would return to them, and establish Missions in their midst. I have often wondered, and still wonder, what the thoughts of the Indians were, as this man — benignant, energetic, devout — talked with them and revealed his purposes towards them. Who can tell?

In the evening of March 18 Serra reached Los Angeles, and next evening, after walking to San Gabriel, weighed down with his many cares, and weary with his long walk, he still preached an excellent sermon, it being the feast of the patriarch St. Joseph. Father Cambon had arrived, and after due consultation with him and the Governor, the date for the setting out of the expedition was fixed for Tuesday, March 26. The week was spent in confirmation services and other religious work, and, on the date named, after solemn mass, the party set forth. It was the most imposing procession ever witnessed in California up to that time, and called forth many gratified remarks from Serra. There were seventy soldiers, with their captain, commander for the new presidio, ensign, sergeant, and corporals. In full gubernatorial dignity followed Governor Neve, with ten soldiers of the Monterey company, their wives and families, servants and neophytes.

At midnight they halted, and a special messenger overtook them with news which led the Governor to return at once to San Gabriel with his ten soldiers. He ordered the procession to proceed, however, found the San Buenaventura Mission, and there await his return. Serra accordingly went forward, and on the 29th inst. arrived at "Assumpta." Here, the next day, on the feast of Easter, they pitched their tents, " erected a large cross, and prepared an altar under a shade of evergreens," where the venerable Serra, now soon to close his life work, blessed the Cross and the place, solemnized mass, preached a sermon to the soldiers on the Resurrection of Christ, and formally dedicated the Mission to God, and placed it under the patronage of St. Joseph.

In the earlier part of this century the Mission began to grow rapidly. Padres Francisco Dumetz and Vicente de Santa María, who had been placed in charge of the Mission from the first, were gladdened by many accessions, and the Mission flocks and herds also increased rapidly. Indeed we are told that " in 1802 San Buenaventura possessed finer herds of cattle and richer fields of grain than any of her contemporaries, and her gardens and orchards were visions of wealth and beauty."

On his second visit to the California coast, Vancouver, when anchored off Santa Barbara, traded with Padre

PLATE XXVIII

a. INTERIOR OF SAN BUENAVENTURA MISSION

b. INTERIOR OF SAN ANTONIO DE PADUA MISSION

Santa María of San Buenaventura for a flock of sheep and as many vegetables as twenty mules could carry. The padre returned to his Mission in Vancouver's vessel, and the English captain visited with him for a day in his hospitable quarters. Said he:

"I found the Mission to be in a very superior style to any of the new establishments yet seen. The garden of Buenaventura far exceeding anything I had before met with in these regions, both in respect of the quantity, quality, and variety of its excellent productions, not only indigenous to the country, but appertaining to the temperate as well as torrid zone ; not one species having yet been sown or planted that had not flourished. These have principally consisted of apples, pears, plums, figs, oranges, grapes, peaches, and pomegranates, together with the plantain, banana, cocoanut, sugar-cane, indigo, and a great variety of the necessary and useful kitchen herbs, plants, and roots. All these were flourishing in the greatest health and perfection, though separated from the sea-side only by two or three fields of corn that were cultivated within a few yards of the surf."

It is to Vancouver, on this voyage, that we owe the names of a number of points on the California coast, as, for instance, Points Sal, Argüello, Felipe, Vicente, Dumetz, Fermin, and Lasuen.

Vancouver says that owing to a fire the buildings were being re-erected. The new church was of stone. It was about half finished in 1794, and three years later was reported nearly completed. Yet the work dragged on until September 9, 1809, when it was duly dedicated by Señan, assisted by five other friars and one priest. It was roofed with tiles.

In 1795 there was a fight between the neophyte and gentile Indians, the former killing two chiefs and taking captive several of the latter. The leaders on both sides were punished, the neophyte Domingo even being sentenced to work in chains.

In 1806 the venerable Santa María, one of the Mission

founders, died. His remains were ultimately placed in the new church.

In 1800 the largest population in its history was reached, with 1297 souls. Cattle and horses prospered, and the crops were reported as among the best in California.

The earthquake of 1812–13 did considerable damage at San Buenaventura. Afraid lest the sea would swallow them up, the people fled to San Joaquin y Santa Ana for three months, where a temporary *jacal* church was erected. The tower and a part of the *fachada* had to be torn down and rebuilt, and this was done by 1818, with a new chapel dedicated to San Miguel in addition.

Of course San Buenaventura felt all the alarm experienced by the other coast settlements at the time of Bouchard's attacks, and Padre Señan, with neophytes and guards, fled from the Mission to the canyada of New Purísima, where a temporary church was erected, and where they remained twenty-four days.

May 29, 1819, twenty-two Mohave Indians came from their home on the Colorado River to trade with the neophytes. This practice the authorities had given strict orders not to allow. Consequently the visitors were refused permission either to see the padre or the neophytes, and they were locked up in the guard-house until ready to depart the following day. The next day, while all were at mass in the church, one of the Indians insisted upon leaving the guard-house. The guard struck him and called for the corporal. The latter left the church with another soldier to quell the disorder, and both were attacked and killed with clubs. The padre then called upon the rest of the soldiers, and gave arms to the neophytes, bidding them defend themselves; and in the general mêlée that ensued ten Mohaves were killed and one neophyte. The rest of the Indians escaped, but were afterwards captured by a force from Santa Barbara. They were set to work at the presidio and again escaped. For a long time thereafter this caused an uneasy feeling throughout the whole region, as it was feared the Mohaves would come in force on a mission of vengeance. This feeling in time died away.

That San Buenaventura was prosperous is shown by the fact that in June, 1820, the government owed it $27,385 for supplies; $6200 in stipends, and $1585 for a cargo of hemp, — a total of $35,170, which, says Bancroft, " there was not the slightest chance of ever receiving."

In 1823 the president and vice-prefect Señan, who had served as padre at this Mission for twenty-five years, died August 24, and was buried by the side of Santa María. After his death San Buenaventura began rapidly to decline.

In 1822 a neophyte killed his wife for adultery. It is interesting to note that in presenting his case the fiscal said that as the culprit had been a Christian only seven years, and was yet ignorant in matters of domestic discipline, he asked for the penalty of five years in the chain gang and then banishment.

In the struggle between the rival claimants for gubernatorial honors in 1838 San Buenaventura was the scene of one of the " deadly conflicts." General Castro, who supported Governor Alvarado, marched with a force of a hundred men and a few cannon to meet the opposing forces of Castañeda (the supporter of Carrillo), who were intrenched in the Mission. After three separate demands for surrender and evacuation, all of which were refused, the cannonading began, lasting two days, in which one man was killed on the besieging side. At the close of the second day the defenders fled under cover of night. Sending a force in pursuit, seventy fugitives were caught, with fifty muskets and other arms. It was afterwards learned that so careless were the Carrillo forces that they had no sentinels or pickets out; they were completely surrounded before they were aware of it, their horses captured, and water supply cut off. Their valor for the next two days was kept up on Mission wine, and it is possible that they fled only when the supply gave out. In the cannonading two guns were placed on the shore-side, in the direction of the chapel, and one perhaps on the elevation back of the Mission. As late as 1874 the walls still bore the marks of the cannon-balls.

At the time of this struggle Carrillo was the comisionado to carry out the secularization decree at San Buenaventura. In 1834 the neophyte population had decreased to 626, but the live-stock and agricultural operations showed no decline. The decree was not made effective until the spring of 1837.

The baptisms for the whole period of the Mission's history, viz., for 1782–1834, is 3876. There is still preserved at the Mission the first register, which was closed in 1809. At that time 2648 baptisms had been administered. The padre presidente, Serra, wrote the heading for the Index, and the contents themselves were written in a beautiful hand by Padre Señan. There are four signatures which occur throughout in the following order: Pedro Benito Cambon, Francisco Dumetz, Vicente de Sta María, and José Señan.

The largest population was 1330 in 1816. The largest number of cattle was 23,400 in the same year. In 1814, 4652 horses; in 1816, 13,144 sheep.

Micheltorena's decree in 1843 restored the temporalities of the Mission to the padres. This was one of the two Missions, Santa Inés being the other, that was able to provide a moderate subsistence out of the wreck left by secularization. On the 5th of December, 1845, Pico rented San Buenaventura to José Arnaz and Narcisco Botello for $1630 a year. There are no statistics of the value of the property after 1842, though in April of 1843 Padre Jimeno reports 2382 cattle, 529 horses, 2299 sheep, 220 mules and 18 asses, 1032 fruit trees and 11,970 vines. In November of that same year the bishop appointed Presbyter Rosales, since which time the Mission has been the regular parish church of the city.

In 1893 the Mission church was renovated out of all its historic association and value by Father Rubio, who had a good-natured but fearfully destructive zeal for the " restoration " of the old Missions. Almost everything has been modernized. The fine old pulpit, one of the richest treasures of the Mission, was there several years ago; but when, in 1904, I inquired of the then pastor where it was, I was curtly informed that he neither knew nor cared. All the outbuildings have been demolished and removed in order to make way for the modern spirit of commercialism which in the last decade has struck the town. It is now an ordinary church, with little but its history to redeem it from the look of smug modernity which is the curse of the present age.

Before leaving San Buenaventura it may be interesting to note that a few years ago I was asked about two " wooden bells " which were said to have been hung in the tower at this Mission. I deemed the question absurd; but on one of my visits found one of these bells in a storeroom under the altar, and another still hanging in the belfry. By whom, or why, these dummy bells were made, I have not been able to discover.

CHAPTER XV

SANTA BARBARA

AFTER the founding of San Buenaventura Governor Neve arrived from San Gabriel, inspected the new site, and expressed himself as pleased with all that had been done. A few days later he, with Padre Serra, and a number of soldiers and officers started up the coast, and, selecting a site known to the Indians, after the name of their chief, *Yanonalit*, established the presidio of Santa Barbara. Yanonalit was very friendly, and as he had authority over thirteen rancherías he was able to help matters along easily. This was April 21, 1782.

Neve, in his report to the Viceroy, had long expressed himself in favor of Missions all along the channel. Here is part of his official declaration in regard to the determination to occupy the pass of Santa Barbara.

" This pass is 74 leagues (308 miles) from the Post of San Diego, and 70 from that of Monterey. It stretches between the coast and the Cieneguilla [meadow] Range about 26 leagues, its greatest width being half to three-fourths of a league. It is full of high hills, bluffs, and profound clefts. In this indispensable pass are 8000 to 10,000 Gentiles (Indians) who inhabit 21 Rancherías, situated at short distances on the heights and points contiguous to the Beach. Near the beach, some times on it and some times on the high ground, runs the Camino Real [King's Highway]. This evidences the risk to which small Parties are exposed on it ; and that if some incident makes those Gentiles treacherous or hostile, communication with the old and new settlements would be cut off. These urgent reasons have caused the determination to occupy this pass in the following form.

"The Post which shall be established midway the Pass shall be manned by Lieutenant, Ensign, and 29 Recruits, including a Sergeant and two Corporals.   It shall establish in its shelter a Reduction (Mission) which afterwards shall be removed to the neighboring spot which offers more land and sufficient water to irrigate the fields ; — and then it shall be given from the Garrison an Escort of a Corporal and five soldiers.   At the ends of said Pass, for its complete occupation, two other 'Reductions' shall be placed, each garrisoned with a Sergeant and 14 Soldiers.   Said Recruits will be considered supernumeraries to the Company at the Post, while they secure these settlements peace and good admission among the Gentiles.

"Attaining this with rapid progress that should be expected in the spiritual conquest, they shall be reduced proportionately to the regular Escort of a Corporal and five Soldiers each ; the Sergeants shall be incorporated with the Companies of San Diego and Monterey, and the 16 remaining Recruits shall be destined to garrison other 'Reductions' which it may be decided to found, in which case they shall be added to the companies nearest the spot."

With a fatuity as singular as it was determined, Neve advised and insisted that the new Missions be founded on the plan followed so disastrously on the Colorado River, which removed from the padres all control of the temporal affairs.   The superiors of the Franciscan college in Mexico refused to send their missionaries under any such plan ; the result was the long delay in the founding of Santa Barbara.   When Serra came to the establishment of the presidio he expected also to found the Mission, and great was his disappointment.   This undoubtedly hastened his death, which occurred August 28, 1784.

It was not until two years later that Neve's successor, Fages, authorized Serra's successor, Lasuen, to proceed. Even then it was feared that he would demand adherence to the new conditions ; but, as the guardian of the college had positively refused to send missionaries for the new establishments, unless they were founded on the old lines, Fages tacitly agreed.   On December 4, therefore, the

Cross was raised on the site called *Taynayan* by the Indians and *Pedragoso* by the Spaniards, and formal possession taken, though the first mass was not said until Fages's arrival on the 16th.   Lasuen was assisted by Padres Antonio Paterna and Cristobal Oramas.   Father Zephyrin has written a very interesting history of the Mission, some of which is as follows:

"The work of erecting the necessary buildings began early in 1787.   With a number of Indians, who had first to be initiated into the mysteries of house construction, Fathers Paterna and Oramas built a dwelling for themselves together with a chapel. These were followed by a house for the servants, who were male Indians, a granary, carpenter shop, and quarters for girls and unmarried young women.   This class of Indians were separated from their relatives and placed under the care of some elderly Indian woman, in order to withdraw them from the immoral influences of the camps.   The carpenter shop was utilized by boys and young men for the same reason, until suitable quarters had been provided.   All these structures were of adobe and the walls about one yard thick.   The roofing consisted of heavy rafters across which long poles or canes were tied with rawhide strips, over which a layer of soft clay or mud was spread, and then thatched with straw.   Tiles, however, were manufactured in the following year, and thereafter all the buildings covered with these.

" In succeeding years other structures arose on the rocky height as the converts increased and industries were introduced.   At the end of 1807 the Indian village, which had sprung up just southwest of the main building, consisted of 252 separate adobe dwellings harboring as many Indian families.   The present Mission building, with its fine corridor, was completed about the close of the eighteenth century.   The fountain in front arose in 1808.   It furnished the water for the great basin just below, which served for the general laundry purposes of the Indian village.   The water was led through earthen pipes from the reservoir north of the church, which to this day furnishes Santa Barbara with water.   It was built in 1806.   To obtain the precious liquid from the mountains, a very strong dam was built across ' Pedragoso ' creek about two miles back of the mission.

PLATE XXIX

INTERIOR OF SANTA BARBARA MISSION

It is still in good condition. Then there were various structures scattered far and near for the different trades, since everything that was used in the way of clothing and food had to be raised or manufactured at the Mission.

"The chapel grew too small within a year from the time it was dedicated, Sunday, May 21, 1787. It was therefore enlarged in 1788, but by the year 1792 this, also, proved too small. Converts were coming in rapidly. The old structure was then taken down, and a magnificent edifice took its place in 1793. Its size was 25 by 125 feet. There were three small chapels on each side, like the two that are attached to the present church. An earthquake, which occurred on Monday, December 21, 1812, damaged this adobe building to such an extent that it had to be taken down. On its site rose the splendid structure, which is still the admiration of the traveller. Padre Antonio Ripoll superintended the work, which continued through five years, from 1815 to 1820. It was dedicated on the 10th of September, 1820. The walls, which are six feet thick, consist of irregular sandstone blocks, and are further strengthened by solid stone buttresses measuring nine by nine feet. The towers to a height of thirty feet are a solid mass of stone and cement twenty feet square. A narrow passage leads through one of these to the top, where the old bells still call the faithful to service as of yore. Doubtless the Santa Barbara mission church is the most solid structure of its kind in California. It is 165 feet long, forty feet wide and thirty feet high on the outside. Like the monastery, the church is roofed with tiles which were manufactured at the mission by the Indians.

" Besides the buildings in the immediate neighborhood of the church, the missionaries had farm houses or cattle ranchos at considerable distances for the convenience of the herders and field hands. All the ranchos East of Santa Inés river, including San Marcos, down to the ' Rincon ' near Carpenteria, belonged to this mission. Thus we have the ranches of Tecolote, San Miguel, Canyada de las Armas-and San Marcos, at which places the stock was herded. The principal ranches for wheat, barley, and corn were : Dos Pueblos, or San Pedro y San Pablo (' Meke-guwe '), San Estévan ('Tokeene '), San Miguel ('Sagspileel' or 'Mescaltitlan'), San José or Abajo, San Juan Bautista or Sauzal. Sauzal is now part of the Hope Ranch. San Estévan was all that land north of the road beginning west of the arroyo ('Pedragoso Creek') at the new bridge and continuing to the Arroyo del Burro. The foundation of a large stone wall may yet be seen a little beyond the bridge west of 'Pedragoso Creek.' This was a large corral especially for tame horses."

The report for 1800 is full of interest. It recounts the activity in building, tells of the death of Padre Paterna, who died in 1793, and was followed by Estévan Tapis (afterwards padre presidente), and says that 1237 natives have been baptized, and that the Mission now owns 2492 horses and cattle, and 5615 sheep. Sixty neophytes are engaged in weaving and allied tasks; the carpenter of the presidio is engaged at a dollar a day to teach the neophytes his trade; and a corporal is teaching them tanning at $150 a year.

In 1801 a large number of the Indians died of an epidemic pulmonary disease. When the matter became serious, a neophyte reported to his fellows that he had had a dream in which Chupu, the channel deity, had appeared to him and warned him that all gentiles who were baptized would die of the epidemic unless they renounced Christianity and washed their faces in a certain water. The excitement was intense. The scared beings went secretly, but as speedily as possible, to the prophet's house with beads and grain to renounce anything and everything necessary. The movement reached to San Buenaventura and throughout the rancherías of the length of the channel. Fortunately for their peace of mind, the missionaries knew nothing of it until it was all over. Then they realized their danger; for had Chupu ordered their killing, there is no doubt but that it would have been attempted.

In 1803 the population was the highest the Mission ever reached, with 1792. In May, 1808, a determined effort of nine days was made to rid the region of ground squirrels, and about a thousand were killed.

The earthquakes of 1812 alarmed the people and dam-

aged the buildings at Santa Barbara as elsewhere. The
sea was much disturbed, and new springs of asphaltum
were formed, great cracks opened in the mountains, and the
population fled all buildings and lived in the open air.

On the 6th of December, in the same year, the arrival of
Bouchard " the pirate " gave them a new shock of terror.
The padres had already been warned to send all their valuables to Santa Inés, and the women and children were to
proceed thither on the first warning of an expected attack.
But Bouchard made no attack. He merely wanted to exchange " prisoners." He played a pretty trick on the
Santa Barbara commandante in negotiating for such exchange, and then, when the hour of delivery came, it was
found he had but one prisoner, — a poor drunken wretch
whom the authorities would have been glad to get rid of at
any price.

In 1824 the Indian revolt, which is fully treated in the
chapters on Santa Inés and Purísima, reached Santa Barbara. While Padre Ripoll was absent at the presidio the
neophytes armed themselves and worked themselves into a
frenzy. They claimed that they were in danger from the
Santa Inés rebels unless they joined the revolt, though they
promised to do no harm if only the soldiers were sent and
kept away. Accordingly Ripoll gave an order for the
guard to withdraw, but the Indians insisted that the soldiers leave their weapons. Two refused, whereupon they
were savagely attacked and wounded. This so incensed
Guerra that he marched up from the presidio in full force,
and a fight of several hours ensued, the Indians shooting
with guns and arrows from behind the pillars of the corridors. Two Indians were killed and three wounded, and
four of the soldiers were wounded. When Guerra retired
to the presidio the Indians stole all the clothing and other
portable property (carefully respecting everything, however, belonging to the church) they would carry, and fled to
the hills. That same afternoon the troops returned and,

13

spite the padre's protest, sacked the Indians' houses and killed all the stragglers they found, regardless of their guilt or innocence. The Indians refused to return, and retreated further over the mountains to the recesses of the Tulares. Here they were joined by escaped neophytes from San Fernando and other Missions. The alarm spread to San Buenaventura and San Gabriel, but few, if any, Indians ran away. In the meantime the revolt was quelled at Santa Inés and Purísima, as elsewhere recorded.

On the strength of reports to this effect, and not realizing the fact that Santa Barbara was still in a state of turmoil, Governor Argüello recalled the Monterey troops which had been aiding the padres at Santa Inés and Purísima; but this appeared to be a mistake, for, immediately, Guerra of Santa Barbara sent eighty men over to San Emigdio, where, on the 9th and 11th of April, severe conflicts took place, with four Indians killed, and wounded on both sides. A wind and dust storm arising, the troops returned to Santa Barbara.

In May the Governor again took action, sending Captain Portilla with a force of 130 men. The prefect Sarría and Padre Ripoll went along to make as peaceable terms as possible, and a message which Sarría sent on ahead doubtless led the insurgents to sue for peace. They said they were heartily sorry for their actions and were anxious to return to Mission life, but hesitated about laying down their arms in fear of summary punishment. The gentiles still fomented trouble by working on the fears of the neophytes, but owing to Argüello's granting a general pardon, they were finally, in June, induced to return, and the revolt was at an end.

After these troubles, however, the Mission declined rapidly in prosperity. Though the buildings under Padre Ripoll were in excellent condition, and the manufacturing industries were well kept up, everything else suffered.

In 1817 a girls' school for whites was started at the presidio of Santa Barbara, but nothing further is known of it. Several years later a school was opened, and Diego Fernandez received $15 a month as its teacher. But Governor Echeandía ordered that, as not a single scholar attended, this expense be discontinued; yet he required the commandante to compel parents to send their children to school.

The French voyager Duhaut-Cilly describes the Mission as follows: " As we advanced, the buildings of the Mission appeared under a finer aspect. From the roadstead we could have taken it for a château of mediæval times, with its lofty apertures and belfry. Coming nearer, the building grows, and, without losing anything of its beauty, takes on, little by little, a religious appearance; the turret becomes a spire; the brass, instead of announcing a knight's arrival, sounds the Office or the Angelus; the first illusion is destroyed, and the castle is a convent.

" In front of the building, in the middle of a huge square, is a playing fountain, the workmanship of which, imperfect as it was, surprised us more, since we had not expected to find in this country, otherwise so far removed from the fine things of Europe, this sort of luxury, reserved among us for the dwellings of the most wealthy."

" H. H." thus describes the christening of one of the towers of Santa Barbara at the wedding of the brother of the superior, the bride having told her the story:

" On the day after her wedding came the christening or blessing of the right tower of the church. She and her husband, having been chosen godfather and godmother of the tower, walked in solemn procession around it, carrying lighted candles in their hands, preceded by the friar, who sprinkled it with holy water and burned incense. In the four long streets of Indians' houses, then running eastward from the mission, booths of green boughs, decorated with flowers, were set up in front of all the doors. Companies of Indians from other missions came as guests, dancing and singing as they approached. Their Indian hosts went out to meet them, also singing, and pouring out seeds on the ground for them to walk on."

In 1835 all the Indians on San Nicholas Island were removed to the mainland, except one woman who escaped, and about whom many a page of wild fiction has since been written.

In 1833 Presidente Duran, discussing with Governor Figueroa the question of secularization, deprecated too sudden action, and suggested a partial and experimental change at some of the oldest Missions, Santa Barbara among the number.

When the decree from Mexico, however, came, this was one of the first ten Missions to be affected thereby. Anastasio Carrillo was appointed comisionado, and acted from September, 1833. His inventory in March, 1834, showed credits, $14,953; buildings, $22,936; furniture, tools, goods in storehouse, vineyards, orchards, corrals, and animals, $19,590; church, $16,000; sacristy, $1500; church ornaments, etc., $4576; library, $152; ranchos, $30,961; total, $113,960, with a debt to be deducted of $1000.

The statistics from 1786 to 1834, the whole period of the Mission's history, show that there were 5679 baptisms, 1524 marriages, 4046 deaths. The largest population was 1792 in 1803. The largest number of cattle was 5200 in 1809, 11,066 sheep in 1804.

Here, as elsewhere, the comisionados found serious fault with the pueblo grogshops. In 1837 Carrillo reports that he has broken up a place where Manuel Gonzalez sold liquor to the Indians, and he calls upon the commandante to suppress other places. In March, 1838, he complains that the troops are killing the Mission cattle, but is told that General Castro had authorized the officers to kill all the cattle needed without asking permission. When the Visitador Hartwell was here in 1839 he found Carrillo's successor Cota an unfit man, and so reported him. He finally suspended him, and the Indians became more contented and industrious under Padre Duran's supervision, though the latter refused to undertake the temporal management of affairs.

In 1841 García Diego was appointed bishop. He arrived in Santa Barbara from San Diego January 11, 1842, with the intention of making it his episcopal residence. Robinson, who witnessed his arrival, thus describes the event:

"The vessel was in sight in the morning, but lay becalmed and rolling to the ocean's swell. A boat put off from her side and approached the landing place. One of the attendants of his Excellency, who came in it, repaired to the Mission, to communicate with the Father President. All was bustle; men, women, and children hastening to the beach, banners flying, drums beating, and soldiers marching. The whole population of the place turned out to pay homage to this first Bishop of California. At eleven o'clock the vessel anchored. He came on shore, and was welcomed by the kneeling multitude. All received his benediction — all kissed the pontifical ring. The troops and civic authorities then escorted him to the house of Don José Antonio, where he dined. A carriage had been prepared for his Excellency, which was accompanied by several others, occupied by the President and his friends. The females had formed, with ornamental canes, beautiful arches, through which the procession passed; and as it marched along the heavy artillery of the 'Presidio' continued to thunder forth its noisy welcome. . . .

"At four o'clock the Bishop was escorted to the Mission, and when a short distance from the town the enthusiastic inhabitants took the horses from his carriage and dragged it themselves. Halting at a small bower on the road, he alighted, went into it, and put on his pontifical robes; then resuming his place in the carriage he continued on amidst the sound of music and the firing of guns till he arrived at the church, where he addressed the multitude that followed him."

Mexico made many financial and other pledges to the new bishop, including a salary of $6000 a year and the management of the pious fund. But she was too much in need of money herself to care for promises made to an outsider, and, consequently, his hopes and ambitions were speedily nipped in the bud. He found that tithe-gathering was not easy; and though he received the concession of the Mission buildings for episcopal purposes, and a site for a proposed cathedral, the latter never grew higher than a few piles of stone.

Micheltorena's decree of 1843 affected Santa Barbara, in that it was ordered returned to the control of the padres; but in the following year Padre Duran reported that it had the greatest difficulty in supporting its 287 souls. Pico's decree in 1845 retained the principal building for the bishop and padres; but all the rest and the orchards and lands were to be rented, which was accordingly done, the property being valued at $20,288, December 5, to Nicholas A. Den and Daniel Hill for $1200 per year. Padre Duran was growing old, and the Indians were becoming more careless and improvident; so, when Pico wrote him to give up the Mission lands and property to the renters he did so willingly, though he stated that the estate owed him $1000 for money he had advanced for the use of the Indians. The Indians were to receive one third of the rental, but there is no record of a cent of it ever getting into their hands. June 10, 1846, Pico sold the Mission to Richard S. Den for $7500, though the lessees seem to have kept possession until about the end of 1848. The land commission confirmed Den's title, though the evidences are that it was annulled in later litigation. Padre Duran died here early in 1846, a month after Bishop Diego. Padre Gonzalez Rubio still remained for almost thirty years longer to become the last of the old missionaries.

In 1853 a petition was presented to Rome, and Santa Barbara was erected into a Hospice, as the beginning of an Apostolic College for the education of Franciscan novitiates who are to go forth, wherever sent, as missionaries. St. Anthony's College, the modern building near by, was founded by the energy of Father Peter Wallischeck. It is for the education of aspirants to the Franciscan order. There are now thirty-five students.

Five of the early missionaries and three of later date are buried in the crypt, under the floor of the sanctuary, in front of the high altar; and Bishop Diego rests under the floor at the right hand side of the altar.

The small cemetery, which is walled in and entered from the church, is said to contain the bodies of 4000 Indians, as well as a number of whites. In the northeast corner is the vault in which are buried the members of the Franciscan community.

In the bell tower are two old bells made in 1818, as is evidenced by their inscriptions, which read alike, as follows: " Manvel Vargas me fecit ano d. 1818 Mision de Santa Barbara De la nveba California " — " Manuel Vargas made me Anno Domini 1818. Mission of Santa Barbara of New California." The first bell is fastened to its beam with rawhide thongs; the second, with a framework of iron. Higher up is a modern bell which is rung, the old ones being tolled only.

The Mission buildings surround the garden, into which no woman, save a reigning queen or the wife of the president of the United States, is allowed to enter. An exception was made in the case of the Princess Louise when her husband was the Governor-general of Canada. The wife of President Harrison also has entered. The garden, with its fine Italian cypress, planted by Bishop Diego about 1842, and its hundred varieties of semi-tropical flowers, in the centre of which is a fountain where goldfish play, affords a delightful place of study, quiet, and meditation for the Franciscans.

It is well that the visitor should know that this old Mission, never so abandoned and abused as the others, has been kept up in late years entirely by the funds given to the Franciscan missionaries, who are now its custodians. With no other revenues to rely upon, they have expended thousands of dollars in cash, and of their own skilled labor even more freely, to keep all these historic memorials in good condition. It is also to be remembered that each visitor, or group, requires a good deal of the time of the brother who is appointed as escort, hence it is an imposition to expect to be admitted and escorted around without the return of some honorarium. Every cent thus given is wisely expended, and it would be a good thing if a fund could thus be raised at each Mission to aid in its preservation and care.

The Mission library contains a large number of valuable old books gathered from the other Missions at the time of secularization. There are also kept here a large number of the old records from which Bancroft gained much of his Mission intelligence, and which, recently, have been carefully restudied by Father Zephyrin, the California historian of the Franciscan order with the purpose of writing a new history from the standpoint of the order. Father Zephyrin is a devoted student, and many results of his zeal and kindness are placed before my readers in this volume, owing to his generosity.

In the curio rooms are many objects of interest and value, some of which are pictured and described elsewhere in this volume.

The Santa Barbara fountain is the most ornate and beautiful piece of stone work, I believe, in the whole Mission chain. It consists of an upright octagonal standard, upon four sides of which are scrolled buttresses, divided into three fillets, giving added grace and lightness. Only one of these scrolls remains to show the beauty of the ornament, the others having been knocked off. This standard supports a bowl, some three feet around, sculptured into eight oval panels, each panel connected by a well-executed conventionalized leaf and wavy design above and below. From the centre of this bowl rises another octagonal stem supporting another and smaller bowl, carved in flutings. From this still another standard arises, circular in form, from which the water-pipe extends.

Just below the fountain, and now fenced into a corner of the garden, is a large reservoir, with sides that slightly slope to the edges. On these cement sides, which are nine or ten feet wide, the Indian women of the Mission were wont to bring their laundry. Let us try to imagine the .busy and interesting scene, — one that I fain would have come back again. A carved figure of a crouching bear spouts the water out of his mouth into this reservoir, which is seventy feet long by six feet wide. The cement sides are full of Indian women, each with her pile of clothes, splashing, soaping, scrubbing, sousing, rubbing them; at the same time laughing, chatting, scolding, gossiping, or, perhaps, even, sometimes serious and sad.

At the lower end of the cistern is another carved figure. The cistern itself is built of solid stone, well cemented, and made to endure.

CHAPTER XVI

LA PURÍSIMA CONCEPCIÓN

ALTHOUGH the date of the founding of this Mission is given as December 8, 1787, — for that was the day on which Presidente Lasuen raised the Cross, blessed the site, celebrated mass, and preached a dedicatory sermon, — there was no work done for several months, owing to the coming on of the rainy season. In the middle of March, 1788, Sergeant Cota of Santa Barbara, with a band of laborers and an escort, went up to prepare the necessary buildings; and early in April Lasuen, accompanied by Padres Vicente Fuster and José Arroita, followed. As early as August the roll showed an acquisition of seventy-nine neophytes. During the first decade nearly a thousand baptisms were recorded, and the Mission flourished in all departments. Large crops of wheat and grain were raised, and live-stock increased rapidly. In 1804 the population numbered 1522, the highest on record during its history, and in 1810 the number of live-stock reported was over 20,000; but the unusual prosperity that attended this Mission during its earlier years was interrupted by a series of exceptional misfortunes.

The first church erected was crude and unstable, and fell rapidly into decay. Scarcely a dozen years had passed, when it became necessary to build a new one. This was constructed of adobe and roofed with tile. It was completed in 1802, but although well built, it was totally destroyed by an earthquake, as we shall see later on.

The Indians of this section were remarkably intelligent as well as diligent, and during the first years of the Mission there were over fifty rancherías in the district. According

Plate XXX

a. BELLS OF SAN JUAN CAPISTRANO MISSION

b. RUINS OF LA PURÍSIMA MISSION

to the report of Padre Payeras in 1810 they were docile
and industrious. This indefatigable worker, with the assistance of interpreters, prepared a catechism and manual
of confession in the native language which he found very
useful in imparting religious instruction and in uprooting
the prevailing idolatry. In a little over twenty years the
entire population for many leagues had been baptized, and
were numbered among the converts.

This period of peace and prosperity was followed by
sudden disaster. The earthquake of 1812, already noted
as the most severe ever known on the Pacific Coast, brought
devastation to Purísima. The morning of December 21
found padres and Indians rejoicing in the possession of the
fruits of their labor of years, — a fine church, many Mission buildings, and a hundred houses built of adobe and
occupied by the natives. A few hours afterward little was
left that was fit for even temporary use. The first vibra-
tion, lasting four minutes, damaged the walls of the
church. The second shock, a half-hour later, caused the
total collapse of nearly all the buildings. Padre Payeras
reported that " the earth opened in several places, emitting
water and black sand." This calamity was quickly followed by torrents of rain, and the ensuing floods added to
the distress of the homeless inhabitants. The remains of
this old Mission of 1802 are still to be seen near Lompoc,
and on the hillside above is a deep scar made by the earthquake, this doubtless being the crack described by Padre
Payeras. But nothing could daunt the courage or quench
the zeal of the missionaries. Rude huts were erected for
immediate needs, and, having selected a new and more advantageous site — five or six miles away — across the river,
they obtained the necessary permission from the presidente,
and at once commenced the construction of a new church,
and all the buildings needed for carrying on the Mission.
Water for irrigation and domestic purposes was brought
in cement pipes, made and laid under the direction of the

padres from Salsperde Creek, three miles away. But other misfortunes were in store for these unlucky people. During a drought in the winter of 1816–1817 hundreds of sheep perished for lack of feed, and in 1818 nearly all the neophytes' houses were destroyed by fire.

In 1823 the Mission lost one of its best friends in the death of Padre Payeras. For nearly twenty years this wise, zealous, and much loved missionary had made his home at Purísima, and his firm hand had been felt in both calm and storm, guiding and controlling in the midst of every vicissitude. Had he lived another year it is quite possible his skill in adjusting difficulties might have warded off the outbreak that occurred among the Indians, — the famous revolt of 1824.

This revolt, which also affected Santa Inés and Santa Barbara (see their respective chapters), had serious consequences at Purísima. After the attack at Santa Inés the rebels fled to Purísima. In the meantime the neophytes at this latter Mission, hearing of the uprising, had seized the buildings. The guard consisted of Corporal Tapia with four or five men. He bravely defended the padres and the soldiers' families through the night, but surrendered when his powder gave out. One woman was wounded. The rebels then sent Padre Ordaz and Tapia to Santa Inés to warn Sergeant Carrillo not to come or the families would be killed. Before an answer was received, the soldiers and their families were permitted to retire to Santa Inés, while Padre Rodriguez remained, the Indians being kindly disposed towards him. Four white men were killed in the fight, and seven Indians.

Left now to themselves, and knowing that they were sure to be attacked ere long, the Indians began to prepare for defence. They erected palisades, cut loop-holes in the walls of the church and other buildings, and mounted one or two rusty old cannon. For nearly a month they were not molested. This was the end of February.

In the meantime the Governor was getting a force ready at Monterey to send to unite with one under Guerra from Santa Barbara. On the 16th of March they were to have met, but owing to some mischance, the northern force had to make the attack alone. Cavalry skirmishers were sent right and left to cut off retreat, and the rest of the force began to fire on the adobe walls from muskets and a four-pounder. The four hundred neophytes within responded with yells of defiance and cannon, swivel-guns, and muskets, as well as a cloud of arrows. In their inexperienced hands, however, little damage was done with the cannon. By and by the Indians attempted to fly, but were prevented by the cavalry. Now realizing their defeat, they begged Padre Rodriguez to intercede for them, which he did. In two hours and a half the conflict was over, three Spaniards being wounded, one fatally, while there were sixteen Indians killed and a large number wounded. As the Governor had delegated authority to the officers to summarily dispense justice, they condemned seven of them to death for the murder of the white men in the first conflict. They were shot before the end of the month. Four of the revolt ringleaders were sentenced to ten years of labor at the presidio and then perpetual exile, while eight others were condemned to the presidio for eight years.

There was dissatisfaction expressed with the penalties, — on the side of the padres by Ripoll of Santa Barbara, who claimed that a general pardon had been promised; and on the part of the Governor, who thought his officers had been too lenient.

An increased guard was left at Purísima after this affair, and it took some little time before the Indians completely settled down again, as it was known that the Santa Barbara Indians were still in revolt.

During all the years when contending with the destructive forces of earthquake, fire, flood, and battle, to say nothing of those foes of agriculture, — drought, frost,

grasshoppers, and squirrels, — the material results of
native labor were notable. In 1819 they produced about
100,000 pounds of tallow. In 1821 the crops of wheat,
barley, and corn amounted to nearly 8000 bushels. Between 1822 and 1827 they furnished the presidio with supplies valued at $12,921. The population, however, gradu-
ally decreased until about 400 were left at the time of
secularization in 1835. The Purísima estate at this time
was estimated by the appraisers to be worth about $60,000.
The inventory included a library valued at $655 and five
bells worth $1000. With the exception of the church prop-
erty this estate, or what remained of it, was sold in 1845
for $1110. Under the management of administrators ap-
pointed by the government the Mission property rapidly
disappeared, lands were sold, live-stock killed and scattered,
and only the fragments of wreckage remained to be turned
over to the jurisdiction of the padres according to the decree
of Micheltorena in 1843. The following year an epidemic
of smallpox caused the death of the greater proportion of
Indians still living at Purísima, and the final act in the
history of the once flourishing Mission was reached in 1845,
when, by order of Governor Pico, the ruined estate was
sold to John Temple for the paltry amount stated above.

Nearly forty years afterward Helen Hunt Jackson
visited the ruins, and thus vividly described the desolate
scene:

"Nothing is left there but one long, low adobe building, with
a few arches of the corridor; the doors stand open, the roof is
falling in; it has been so often used as a stable and sheepfold,
that even the grasses are killed around it. The painted pulpit
hangs half falling on the wall, its stairs are gone, and its sounding-board is slanting awry. Inside the broken altar-rail is a pile
of stones, earth and rubbish thrown up by seekers after buried
treasures; in the farther corner another pile and hole, the home
of a badger; mud-swallows' nests are thick on the cornice, and
cobwebbed rags of the old canvas ceiling hang fluttering over-

head. The only trace of the ancient cultivation is a pear-orchard a few rods off, which must have been a splendid sight in its day; it is at least two hundred yards square, with a double row of trees all around, so placed as to leave between them a walk fifty or sixty feet wide. Bits of broken aqueduct here and there, and a large, round stone tank overgrown by grass, showed where the life of the orchard used to flow in. It has been many years slowly dying of thirst. Many of the trees are gone, and those that remain stretch out gaunt and shrivelled boughs, which, though still bearing fruit, look like arms tossing in vain reproach and entreaty; a few pinched little blossoms seemed to heighten rather than lessen their melancholy look."

The Mission of La Purísima Concepción was built in a canyada not far from the river. It stands northeast to southwest, the southwest end buttressed with solid and well built masonry. The main walls are of adobe, plastered over. Parts of the buildings are in two stories, but everything now (1905) is in sad ruins. Though it is as solitary and deserted as San Antonio, it does not make the pathetic appeal that that venerable and dignified structure does. And it is hard to say why. The photograph shows that it is not so striking a building, still there seems to be no reason why one should not feel as sadly at its desolation as one does at San Antonio. It is pathetic enough. The tiles have been taken off the roof except where they have fallen in and been broken to pieces; some of the walls have tumbled down; others are rapidly crumbling away; some of the pillars of the corridors have fallen; weeds have grown everywhere, and, instead of giving the feeling of kindly covering the desolation, they serve only to accentuate it.

The corridors at La Purísima extended only in front of the building. The pillars are square with chamfered corners, and were evidently built of the material that happened to be readiest to hand at the moment, for some are of stone, others of burnt brick, and still others of adobe.

At the time of my last visit in May, 1904, eighteen pillars were still standing, and two had fallen. These pillars are about three feet square. The corridors are ten feet wide and extend the whole length of the building, which is about three hundred feet. The width, without the corridor, is about fifty feet.

The church is at the southwest end on the southeast side. It is about eighty feet long. The windows are low and arched, but there is little left to show what were the attractions of this church, so different from any of the others. At one corner, doubtless where interested neophytes have stood looking with luminous eyes upon the movements of the officiating padre, now stands a growing tree.

The peculiarity of La Purísima is in the architectural arrangement of the building. The church is a part, — one large room merely, — in a structure that contains many rooms. There is nothing that remains now of the wings that used to connect, and the ploughing up of the field near by has doubtless destroyed the foundations of walls, did any ever exist.

An extensive view of the valley, down to the ocean, can be had from the end of the corridor, or from the near-by hills. It was an attractive outlook, and gave the padres here more of a feeling of touch with the great outside when the glint of the sunshine upon the ocean greeted their watching eyes.

In regard to its present ownership and condition, a gentleman interested writes:

" The abandoned mission is on ground which now belongs to the Union Oil Company of California. The building itself has been desecrated and damaged by the public ever since its abandonment. Its visitors apparently did not scruple to deface it in every possible way, and what could not be stolen was ruthlessly destroyed. It apparently was a pleasure to them to pry the massive roof-beams loose, in order to enjoy the crash occasioned by the breaking of the valuable tile.

" On top of this the late series of earthquakes in that section threw down many of the brick pillars, and twisted the remainder so badly that the front of the building is a veritable wreck. During these earthquakes, which lasted several weeks, tile which could not be replaced for a thousand dollars were displaced and broken. To save the balance of the tile, as well as to avoid possible accidents to visitors, the secretary of the oil company had the remaining tile removed from the roof and piled up near the building for safety."

14

CHAPTER XVII

SANTA CRUZ

LASUEN found matters far easier for him in the founding of Missions than did Serra in his later years. The Viceroy agreed to pay $1000 each for the expenses of the Missions of Santa Cruz and La Soledad, and $200 each for the travelling expenses of the four missionaries needed. April 1, 1790, the guardian sent provisions and tools for Santa Cruz to the value of $1021. Lasuen delayed the founding for awhile, however, as the needful church ornaments were not at hand; but as the Viceroy promised them and ordered him to go ahead by borrowing the needed articles from the other Missions, Lasuen proceeded to the founding, as I have already related.

At the end of the year 1791 the neophytes numbered 84. In 1796 the highest mark was reached with 523. In 1800 there were but 492. Up to the end of that year there had been 949 baptisms, 271 couples married, and 477 buried. There were 2354 head of large stock, and 2083 small. In 1792 the agricultural products were about 650 bushels, as against 4300 in 1800.

The corner-stone of the church was laid February 27, 1793, and was completed and formally dedicated May 10, 1794 by Padre Peña from Santa Clara, aided by five other priests. Ensign Sal was present as godfather, and duly received the keys. The neophytes, servants, and troops looked on at the ceremonies with unusual interest, and the next day filled the church at the saying of the first mass. The church was about thirty by one hundred and twelve

PLATE XXXI

a. SANTA CRUZ MISSION

b. SANTA BARBARA MISSION AND FOUNTAIN

feet and twenty-five feet high. The foundation walls to
the height of three feet were of stone, the front was of
masonry, and the rest of adobes. The other buildings were
slowly erected, and in the autumn of 1796 a flouring-mill
was built and running. It was sadly damaged, however,
by the December rains. Artisans were sent to build the
mill and instruct the natives, and later a smith and a miller·
were sent to start it.

In 1798 the padre wrote very discouragingly. The
establishment of the villa or town of Brancifort, across the
river, was not pleasing. A hundred and thirty-eight neophytes also had deserted, ninety of whom were afterwards
brought in by Corporal Mesa. It had long been the intention of the government to found more pueblos or towns, as
well as Missions in California, the former for the purpose
of properly colonizing the country. Governor Borica
made some personal explorations, and of three suggested
sites finally chose that just across the river Lorenzo from
Santa Cruz. May 12, 1797, certain settlers who had been
recruited in Guadalajara arrived in a pitiable condition at
Monterey; and soon thereafter they arrived at the new
site under the direction of Comisionado Moraga, who was
authorized to erect temporary shelters for them. August
12 the superintendent of the formal foundation, Córdoba,
had all the surveying accomplished, part of an irrigating
canal dug, and temporary houses partially erected. In
August, after the Viceroy had seen the estimated cost of
the establishment, further progress was arrested by want
of funds. Before the end of the century everybody concerned had come to the conclusion that the villa of Brancifort was a great blunder, — the " settlers are a scandal to
the country by their immorality. They detest their exile,
and render no service."

In the meantime the Mission authorities protested vigor-
ously against the new settlement. It was located on the
pasture grounds of the Indians; the laws allowed the Mis-

sions a league in every direction, and trouble would surely result. But the Governor retorted, defending his choice of a site, and claiming that the neophytes were dying off, there were no more pagans to convert, and the neophytes already had more land and raised more grain than they could attend to.

In 1805 Captain Goycoechea recommended that as there were no more gentiles, the neophytes be divided between the Missions of Santa Clara and San Juan, and the missionaries sent to new fields. Of course nothing came of this.

On the 12th of October, 1812, Padre Quintana was found dead in his bed. On investigation it was decided that the friar, who for some time had been in poor health, unable to dress himself unaided, had died a natural death. Two years later, however, rumors led to a new investigation, and it was then learned that he had been called out of his bed to attend a dying man, set on, and brutally murdered and mutilated in an unnamable fashion, and then carefully placed in his bed and the door locked. The culprit neophytes were discovered, and five out of the nine arrested were sentenced to receive two hundred lashes each, and then to work in chains from two to ten years. Two others died in prison, and another died in 1817 in Santa Barbara. Only one survived the punishment. The plea of the murderers was that Quintana was excessively cruel, that he had beaten two neophytes almost to death, and was inventing a new instrument of torture, to prevent the use of which his death was determined upon. This charge was carefully investigated by the military authorities and denied with emphasis.

Bouchard's advent caused a flurry at Santa Cruz in 1818. Padre Olbés was ordered to pack up and send everything for safety to Soledad. In October he sarcastically wrote that all were astir both at the Mission and the villa of Brancifort, expecting the insurgents, " not to fight, but to join them, for such is the disposition of the inhabitants."

In November and December the irate padre reported that on the approach of the two vessels the people of Brancifort had deliberately sacked the Mission with the intention of charging it upon Bouchard. But, as the wind prevented a landing, they were left in the lurch. Olbés was excited and forceful in his charges. The scoundrels had stolen every movable article, had destroyed everything that could not be moved, and they had desecrated the church and the holy images. He declared he would abandon the establishment rather than longer submit to the outrages of such wretches.

Naturally such charges could not be neglected, and investigations were instituted, the Mission in the meantime being abandoned, and Olbés growing more violent as the " pretended investigation " proceeded. The upshot of it all was that the trouble grew out of Governor Sola's giving an order that Santa Cruz be abandoned, and then sending another order to Comisionado Buelna of Brancifort to the effect that he was to go to the Mission, and if it was abandoned he was to remove all the property. On the morning of the 23d of November Olbés with his neophytes set out for Santa Clara. On the 24th Buelna went as ordered, and found the buildings vacant, so he proceeded to carry out his orders, forcing some of the doors to do so. In the meantime the majordomo of the Mission and a few Indians, having doubtless heard that Bouchard had not landed, returned to the Mission to save some of the Mission goods. Imagine their amazement at finding Buelna already there, dismantling everything. When the Governor's order was understood, however, the two parties joined in the work; and as one or two casks of wine and aguardiente could not be carried away they were spilled. Possibly some of the liquor got into the throats of the workers. The result of this on the workers was not to promote care, and there is no doubt many reckless acts were performed. Some of the Mission goods were buried or otherwise concealed; others were taken by the majordomo in a cart to Santa Clara, and others listed by Buelna and removed to the villa. Among the latter things was a trunk of the padre's, which, unfortunately, was broken into; and certain stockings given to a young lady led to the detection of the criminals, two of whom were duly punished. This investigation calmed the wrath of the clerical authorities, who soon saw that Olbés had been unduly excited, and the irate padre in a short time dutifully returned to his work.

In February, 1819, however, he was again in trouble. All but three of his neophytes fled because some one had told them that the villa soldiers were coming to take them prisoners. But later on they returned and all was calm again. The crops were good, and the cattle and sheep herds increasing.

In the decade 1820–30 population declined rapidly, though in live-stock the Mission about held its own, and in agriculture actually increased. In 1823, however, there was another attempt to suppress it, and this doubtless came from the conflicts between the villa of Brancifort and the Mission. The effort, like the former one, was unsuccessful.

In 1834–35 Ignacio del Valle acted as comisionádo, and put in effect the order of secularization. His valuation of the property was $47,000, exclusive of land and church property, besides $10,000 distributed to the Indians. There were no subsequent distributions, yet the property disappeared, for, in 1839, when Visitador Hartwell went to Santa Cruz he found only about one sixth of the live-stock of the inventory of four years ago. The neophytes were organized into a pueblo, named Figueroa after the Governor; but it was a mere organization in name, and, the condition of the ex-Mission was no different from that of any of the others.

The statistics for the whole period of the Mission's existence, 1791–1834 are: baptisms, 2466; marriages, 847; deaths, 2035. The largest population was 644 in 1798.

The largest number of cattle was 3700 in 1828; horses, 900, in the same year; mules, 92, in 1805; sheep, 8300, in 1826.

In January, 1840, an earthquake and tidal wave brought disaster. The tower fell, and a number of tiles were carried off, a kind of premonition of the final disaster of 1851, when the walls fell, and treasure seekers completed the work of demolition.

The community of the Mission was completely broken up in 1841–42, everything being regarded, henceforth, as part of Brancifort. In 1845 the lands, buildings, and fruit trees of the ex-Mission were valued at less than $1000, and only about forty Indians were known to remain. The Mission has now entirely disappeared.

CHAPTER XVIII

LA SOLEDAD

THE Mission of " Our Lady of Solitude " has only brief record in written history; but the little that is known and the present condition of the ruins suggest much that has never been recorded.

Early in 1791 Padre Lasuen, who was searching for suitable locations for two new Missions, arrived at a point midway between San Antonio and Santa Clara. With quick perception he recognized the advantages of Soledad, known to the Indians as *Chuttusgelis*. The name of this region, bestowed by Crespí years previous, was suggestive of its solitude and dreariness; but the wide, vacant fields indicated good pasturage in seasons favored with much rain, and the possibility of securing water for irrigation promised crops from the arid lands. Lasuen immediately selected the most advantageous site for the new Mission, but several months elapsed before circumstances permitted the erection of the first rude structures.

On October 9 he returned, attended by Lieutenant Argüello and the guards, two priests, and a few Indians. It would not require a very vivid imagination to conceive that the inauguration ceremonies of ushering into existence the thirteenth Franciscan Mission were most impressive, — the little band assembled being the only visible occupants of thousands of acres, bare and brown, stretching away on every side in undisturbed silence. Little did the venerable padre dream of the pathetic scenes to be enacted in that quiet spot, or of the fragments that a century later would mark the place consecrated by him, as with placid face and

PLATE XXXII

a

b

RUINS OF LA SOLEDAD MISSION

hopeful heart he planted the Mission cross in the stillness of that peaceful day.

There were comparatively few Indians in that immediate region, and only eleven converts were reported as the result of the efforts of the first year. There was ample room for flocks and herds, and although the soil was not of the best and much irrigation was necessary to produce good crops, the padres with their persistent labors gradually increased their possessions and the number of their neophytes. At the close of the ninth year there were 512 Indians living at the Mission, and their property included a thousand cattle, several thousand sheep, and a good supply of horses. Five years later (in 1805) there were 727 neophytes, in spite of the fact that a severe epidemic a few years previous had reduced their numbers and caused many to flee from the Mission in fear. A new church was begun in 1808.

On the 24th of July, 1814, Governor Arrillaga, who had been taken seriously ill while on a tour of inspection, and had hurried to Soledad to be under the care of his old friend, Padre Ibañez, died there, and was buried, July 26, under the centre of the church.

Being inland, Soledad was named as the place of refuge during the alarm caused by the appearance of Bouchard; and while there is little of definite record, there is no doubt but that several bands of families from the different Missions did rendezvous here.

For about forty years priests and natives lived a quiet, peaceful life in this secluded valley, with an abundance of food and comfortable shelter. That they were blessed with plenty and prosperity is evidenced by the record that in 1829 they furnished $1150 to the Monterey presidio. At one time they possessed over 6000 cattle; and in 1821 the number of cattle, sheep, horses, and other animals was estimated at over 16,000. One writer credits them with having an aqueduct fifteen miles long, supplying water for irrigating thousands of acres; but I have not made careful enough examination to know whether this statement has any foundation in fact.

After the changes brought about by political administration the number of Indians rapidly decreased, and the property acquired by their united toil quickly dwindled away, until little was left but poverty and suffering.

At the time secularization was effected in 1835, according to the inventory made, the estate, aside from church property, was valued at $36,000. Six years after secular authorities took charge only about 70 Indians remained, with 45 cattle, 25 horses, and 865 sheep, — and a large debt had been incurred. On the 4th of June, 1846, the Soledad Mission was sold to Feliciano Soberanes for $800.

One of the pitiful cases that occurred during the decline of the Missions was the death of Padre Sarría, which took place at Soledad in 1835, or, as some authorities state, in 1838. This venerable priest had been very prominent in missionary labors, having occupied the position of *commisario prefecto* during many years. He was also the president for several years. As a loyal Spaniard he declined to take the oath of allegiance to the Mexican Republic, and was nominally under arrest for about five years, or subject to exile; but so greatly was he revered and trusted as a man of integrity and great ability as a business manager that the order of exile was never enforced. The last years of his life were spent at the Mission of Our Lady of Solitude. When devastation began and the temporal prosperity of the Mission quickly declined, this faithful pastor of a fast thinning flock refused to leave the few poverty-stricken Indians who still sought to prolong life in their old home. One Sunday morning, while saying mass in the little church, the enfeebled and aged padre fell before the altar and immediately expired. As it had been reported that he was " leading a hermit's life and destitute of means," it was commonly believed that this worthy and devoted missionary was exhausted from lack of proper food, and in reality died of starvation.

There were still a few Indians at Soledad in 1850, their scattered huts being all that remained of the once large rancherías that existed here.

The ruins of Soledad are about four miles from the station of the Southern Pacific of that name. The church itself is at the southwest corner of a mass of ruins. These are all of adobe, though the foundations are of rough rock. Flint pebbles have been mixed with the adobe of the church walls. They were originally about three feet thick, and plastered. A little of the plaster still remains.

In 1904 there was but one circular arch remaining in all the ruins; everything else has fallen in. The roof fell in thirty years ago. At the eastern end, where the arch is, there are three or four rotten beams still in place; and on the south side of the ruins, where one line of corridors ran, a few poles are still in place. Heaps of ruined tiles lie here and there, just as they fell when the supporting poles rotted and gave way.

It is claimed by the Soberanes family in Soledad that the present ruins of the church are of the building erected about 1850 by their grandfather. The family lived in a house just southwest of the Mission, and there this grandfather was born. He was baptized, confirmed, and married in the old church, and when, after secularization, the Mission property was offered for sale he purchased it. As the church — in the years of pitiful struggle for possession of its temporalities — had been allowed to go to ruin, this true son of the church erected the building, the ruins of which now bring sadness to the hearts of all who care.

Over the entrance is a niche in which a statue of Our Lady of Solitude — La Soledad — used to stand. Methinks that if the ghosts of things that were exist, surely a weeping ghost of the Lady of Solitude haunts these deserted and forlorn ruins.

Weep! weep! for the church of Our Lady of Solitude. It is entirely in ruins. The adobe walls are rapidly melting away. For years it has stood exposed to the weather, nothing whatever being done to preserve it. It is roofless and unprotected. The winds howl around it, the rains beat upon it, the fierce sun shines upon it, and all do their part to aid in its more speedy dissolution. It is not demolition; that could better be borne than this heartless abandonment, this careless indifference, this hateful casting aside of a once noble building, dedicated to high and blessed purposes, sanctified by the earnest labors of devoted men. It seems as if the building itself felt its desertion, though smiling fields of wheat and barley surround it. Nay, these evidences of material prosperity so close at hand only serve to accentuate the devastation of the old Mission.

The visitor to Soledad at the present day will find satisfaction in a few minutes spent at the parish church of the new railway town. In the sacristy the Rev. Andrew Garriga, the present priest, carefully treasures a chasuble said to be over a hundred years old, which was worn by the officiating padres at Old Soledad Mission. It is in perfect condition. Father Garriga also has a painting of Our Lady of Solitude that differs in spirit from any I have ever seen. As a rule, pictures of the Virgin Mother after her Son had ascended show her clad in mourning, with swords in her heart, the former symbolic of her desolation, and the latter of the sorrow that had pierced her soul. "But," says Father Garriga, "may it not be possible that this is an erroneous conception. Can it be thought possible that the Holy Virgin was not conscious of some of the wonderful meaning of the resurrection of her Divine Son? So, while she is alone, the Lady of Solitude, she is yet filled with unspeakable joy at the great work accomplished in her son; and that is just beginning for the human race." With these thoughts in mind he found an artist in a Mr. Downing, of San Francisco, who, in 1903, painted the picture that now hangs in the little chapel.

CHAPTER XIX

SAN JOSÉ DE GUADALUPE

THERE was a period of rest after the founding of Santa Cruz and La Soledad. Padre presidente Lasuen was making ready for a new and great effort. Hitherto the Mission establishments had been isolated units of civilization, each one alone in its work save for the occasional visits of governor, inspector, or presidente. Now they were to be linked together, by the founding of intermediate missions, into one great chain, near enough for mutual help and encouragement, the boundary of one practically the boundary of the next one, both north and south. The two new foundations of Santa Cruz and Soledad were a step in this direction, but now the plan was to be completed. With the Viceroy's approval Governor Borica authorized Lasuen to have the regions between the old Missions carefully explored for new sites. Accordingly the padres and their guards were sent out, and simultaneously a work of investigation began never before known. Reports were sent in, and finally after a careful study of the whole situation it was concluded that five new Missions could be established and a great annual saving thereby made in future yearly expenses. Governor Borica's idea was that the new Missions would convert all the gentile Indians west of the Coast Range. This done, the guards could be reduced at an annual saving of $15,000. This showing pleased the Viceroy, and he agreed to provide the $1000 needed for each new establishment on the condition that no added military force be called for. The guardian of San Fernando College was so notified August 19, 1796;

and on September 29 he in turn announced to the Viceroy that the required ten missionaries were ready, but begged that no reduction be made in the guards at the Missions already established. Lasuen felt that it would create large demands upon the old Missions to found so many new ones all at once, as they must help with cattle, horses, sheep, neophyte laborers, etc.; yet, to obtain the Missions, he was willing to do his very best, and felt sure his brave associates would further his efforts in every possible way. Thus it was that San José was founded, as before related, on June 11, 1797. The same day all returned to Santa Clara, and five days elapsed ere the guards and laborers were sent to begin work. Timbers were cut and water brought to the location, and soon the temporary buildings were ready for occupancy. By the end of the year there were 33 converts, and in 1800, 286. A wooden structure with a grass roof served as a church.

The mountain Indians near San José did not like the presence of the missionaries, consequently the padres were apprehensive of trouble from the very start. Yet nothing of a serious nature occurred until January, 1805. Then, Padre Cueva was called upon to visit some sick neophytes living in a ranchería some ten or fifteen miles to the east. He was escorted by Majordomo Higuera and two soldiers, as well as accompanied by a few neophytes. Either he was treacherously guided to the wrong ranchería, and was there attacked, or he was set on by hostiles on his return (the records are not clear), and Higuera killed, the padre struck in the face, a soldier badly wounded, three neophytes and all the horses killed. Though so badly demoralized, the remaining soldier fought on, killed a gentile, checked the pursuit, and managed to get back to the Mission. The news was forwarded to San Francisco, and immediately a force was sent out, augmented to 34 by settlers from San José, under Sergeant Peralta, who followed the now fleeing hostiles, killed eleven of them, and captured thirty, mostly women. Peralta made another raid in February, but found nothing but penitence and submission, one chieftain coming from as far as the San Joaquin River to assure the officer that he and his people had taken no part in the attack.

In April, 1806, Langsdorff visited Mission San José, where Padre Cueva hospitably received him, arranged an Indian dance for his entertainment (which he pictures), and generally made a holiday in his honor. His first attempt to reach the Mission by boat was unsuccessful; but on the second attempt, made a few days later, after perpetually going astray up wrong channels, he managed to find a landing ten miles away from the Mission. Of the Mission buildings, etc., he says:

"Although it is only eight years since they were begun, they are already of very considerable extent : the quantity of corn in the granaries far exceeded my expectations. . . . The kitchen garden is well laid out, and kept in very good order; the soil is everywhere rich and fertile, and yields ample returns. The fruit-trees are still very young, but their produce is as good as could be expected. A small rivulet runs through the garden, which preserves a constant moisture. Some vineyards have been planted within a few years, which yield excellent wine, sweet and resembling malaga.

"The situation of the Mission is admirably chosen, and according to the universal opinion, this Mission will in a few years be the richest and best in New California. The only disadvantage is, that there are no large trees very near. . . . To compensate this disadvantage, there are in the neighborhood of the mission chalk-hills, and excellent brick earth so that most of their buildings are of brick. The organization of the institution is entirely the same as at San Francisco. The habitations for the Indians, *las rancherías,* are not yet finished, so that at present they live chiefly in straw huts of a conical form."

In 1809, April 23, the new church was completed, and President Tapis came and blessed it. The following day he preached, and Padre Arroyo de la Cuesta said mass before a large congregation, including other priests, several of the military, and people from the pueblo and Santa Clara, and various neophytes. The following July the cemetery was blessed with the usual solemnities.

In 1811 Padre Fortuni accompanied Padre Abella on a journey of exploration to the Sacramento and San Joaquin valleys. They were gone fifteen days, found the Indians very timid, and thought the shores of the Sacramento offered a favorable site for a new Mission.

In 1817 Sergeant Soto, with one hundred San José neophytes, met twelve soldiers from San Francisco, and proceeded, by boat, to pursue some fugitives. They went up a river, possibly the San Joaquin, to a marshy island where, according to Soto's report, a thousand hostiles were assembled, who immediately fell upon their pursuers and fought them for three hours. So desperately did they fight, relying upon their superior numbers, that Soto was doubtful as to the result; but eventually they broke and fled, swimming to places of safety, leaving many dead and wounded but no captives. Only one neophyte warrior was killed.

In 1820 San José reported a population of 1754, with 6859 large stock, 859 horses, etc., and 12,000 sheep.

For twenty-seven years Padre Duran, who from 1825 to 1827 was also the padre presidente, served Mission San José. In 1824 it reached its maximum of population in 1806 souls. In everything it was prosperous, standing fourth on the list both as to crops and herds.

Owing to its situation, being the first Mission reached by trappers, etc., from the East, and also being the nearest to the valleys of the Sacramento and San Joaquin, which afforded good retreats for fugitives, San José had an exciting history. In 1826 there was an expedition against the Cosumnes, in which forty Indians were killed, a ranchería destroyed, and forty captives taken. In 1829 the famous campaign against Estanislas, who has given his name to both a river and county, took place. This Indian

15

was a neophyte of San José, and being of more than usual ability and smartness was made alcalde. In 1827 or early in 1828 he ran away, and with a companion, Cipriano, and a large following, soon made himself the terror of the rancheros of the neighborhood. One expedition sent against him resulted disastrously, owing to insufficient equipment, so a determined effort under M. G. Vallejo, who was now the commander-in-chief of the whole California army, was made. May 29 he and his forces crossed the San Joaquin river on rafts, and arrived the next day at the scene of the former battle. With taunts, yells of defiance, and a shower of arrows, Estanislas met the coming army, he and his forces hidden in the fancied security of an impenetrable forest. Vallejo at once set men to work in different directions to fire the wood, which brought some of the Indians to the edge, where they were slain. As evening came on twenty-five men and an officer entered the wood and fought until dusk, retiring with three men wounded. Next morning Vallejo, with thirty-seven soldiers, entered the wood, where he found pits, ditches, and barricades arranged with considerable skill. Nothing but fire could have dislodged the enemy. They had fled under cover of night. Vallejo set off in pursuit, and when two days later he surrounded them they declared they would die rather than surrender. A road was cut through the chaparral with axes, along which the field piece and muskets were pressed forward and discharged. The Indians retreated slowly, wounding eight soldiers. When the cannon was close to the enemies' intrenchments the ammunition gave out, and this fact and the heat of the burning thicket compelled retreat. During the night the Indians endeavored to escape, one by one, but most of them were killed by the watchful guards. The next day nothing but the dead and three living women were found. There were some accusations, later, that Vallejo summarily executed some captives; but he denied it, and claimed that the only justification for any such charge arose from the fact that one man and one woman had been killed, the latter wrongfully by a soldier, whom he advised be punished.

California in those days was not hospitably disposed to unknown and unaccredited foreigners, so when, in 1826, Jedediah Smith appeared in the province, having come from the Great Salt Lake, he was looked upon with suspicion. After various experiences with officials in the South, on working his way northward he finally reached Mission San José. Padre Duran afterwards accused him of enticing four hundred of his neophytes to run away, but investigation did not confirm the charge. Meeting with nothing but hostility, Smith crossed the Sierras, — the first known case on record, — and in twenty-eight days reached Salt Lake, having had to eat the horses that had succumbed to the rigors of the trip.

Later Smith returned, was vouched for by Captain Cooper at Monterey, and allowed to go back with full equipment of mules, horses, and provisions. He was killed in 1831 in New Mexico.

Up to the time of secularization the Mission continued to be one of the most prosperous. Jesus Vallejo was the administrator for secularization, and in 1837 he and Padre Gonzalez Rubio made an inventory which gave a total of over $155,000, when all debts were paid. Even now for awhile it seemed to prosper, and not until 1840 did the decline set in.

Captain Sutter of New Helvetia, one of the best known of the early California pioneers, had trouble in 1839 with a band of San José Indians, who came to him with a pass from the padres, entitling them to visit their relatives, the Ochumnes. Sutter permitted them certain privileges, but ere long they attacked a ranchería of Zalesumnes, many of whom, under Pulpulé, were working for Sutter. They killed seven of the men, and stole all the women and children. This treachery so incensed Sutter that he joined forces with Pulpulé, freed the captives, and finally shot ten of the aggressors, and delivered all the other San José neophytes he could catch to the authorities.

In accordance with Micheltorena's decree of March 29, 1843, San José was restored to the temporal control of the padres, who entered with good-will and zest into the labor of saving what they could out of the wreck. Under Pico's decree of 1845 the Mission was inventoried, but the document cannot now be found, nor a copy of it. The population was reported as 400 in 1842, and it is supposed that possibly 250 still lived at the Mission in 1845. On the 5th of May, 1846, Pico sold all the property to Andrés Pico and J. B. Alvarado for $12,000, but the sale never went into effect.

Mission San José de Guadalupe and the pueblo of the same name are not, as so many people, even residents of California, think, one and the same. The pueblo of San José is now the modern city of that name, the home of the State Normal School, and the starting-point for Mount Hamilton. But Mission San José is a small settlement, nearly twenty miles east and north, in the foothills overlooking the southeast end of San Francisco Bay. The Mission church has entirely disappeared, an earthquake in 1868 having completed the ruin begun by the spoliation at the time of secularization. A modern parish church has since been built upon the site. Nothing of the original Mission now remains except a portion of the monastery. The corridor is without arches, and is plain and unpretentious, the roof being composed of willows tied to the roughly hewn log rafters with rawhide. Behind this is a beautiful old alameda of olives, at the upper end of which a modern orphanage, conducted by the Dominican Sisters, has been erected. This avenue of olives is crossed by another one at right angles, and both were planted by the padres in the early days, as is evidenced by the age of the trees. Doubtless many a procession of Indian neophytes

PLATE XXXIII

PROCESSION OF SISTERS AND ORPHANS AT MISSION SAN JOSÉ

has walked up and down here, even as I saw a procession
of the orphans and their white-garbed guardians a short
time ago. The surrounding garden is kept up in as good
style under the care of the sisters as it was in early days
by the padres.

What a fine location it is! With beautiful rolling hills
behind, the Mission Peak to the south, the front view leading the eye over fertile meadows and pasture land to what
was once swamp land, — but now reclaimed and more productive than the dreams of the padres ever contemplated
for their best hilly soil, — beyond which is the placid and
silvery face of the bay. Even then the eye cannot rest,
for further still on the western shore are trees, foothills,
and the bold Santa Cruz range. During the rainy season
all this verdure and woods is washed clean, and everything
is rich, green, and beautiful. In the summer the green is
contrasted with the gold, and in the fall and winter new
tints come into the leaves about to fall.

The orphanage was erected in 1884 by Archbishop Alemany as a seminary for young men who wished to study
for the priesthood, but it was never very successful in this
work. For awhile it remained empty, then was offered
to the Dominican Sisters as a boarding-school. But as this
undertaking did not pay, in 1891 Archbishop Riordan
offered such terms as led the Mother General of the Dominican Sisters to purchase it as an orphanage, and as such it
is now most successfully conducted. There are at the present time about eighty children cared for by these sweet
and gentle sisters of our Lord.

The olive trees planted by the padres still bear plenti-
fully, and each February a large crop of rich, juicy olives
is gathered to be pressed for their oil, or put in large vats
and pickled for table use.

The Mission vines were still in existence until 1899,
when, becoming diseased, they were taken up and not re-
newed, the sisters feeling that wine-making was an industry

better suited to men than women, though for many years the wine made at San José had been used only for sacramental purposes.

Two of the old Mission bells are hung in the new church. On one of these is the inscription: " S. S. José.   Ano de 1826." And on the upper bell, " S. S. Joseph 1815, Ave María Purísima."

The old Mission baptismal font is also still in use.   It is of hammered copper, about three feet in diameter, surmounted by an iron cross about eight inches high.   The font stands upon a wooden base, painted, and is about four feet high.

CHAPTER XX

SAN JUAN, BAUTISTA

THE second of the "filling up the links of the chain" Missions was that of San Juan Bautista. Three days after the commandant of San Francisco had received his orders to furnish a guard for the founders of Mission San José, the commandant of Monterey received a like order for a guard for the founders of San Juan Bautista. This consisted of five men and Corporal Ballesteros. By June 17 this industrious officer had erected a church, missionary-house, granary, and guard-house, and a week later Lasuen, with the aid of two priests, duly founded the new Mission. The site was a good one, and by 1800 crops to the extent of 2700 bushels were raised. At the same time 516 neophytes were reported — not bad for two and a half years' work.

In 1798 the gentiles from the mountains twenty-five miles east of San Juan, the Ansayames, surrounded the Mission by night, but were prevailed upon to retire. Later some of the neophytes ran away and joined these hostiles, and then a force was sent to capture the runaways and administer punishment. In the ensuing fight a chief was killed and another wounded, and two gentiles brought in to be forcibly educated. Other rancherías were visited, fifty fugitives arrested, and a few floggings and many warnings given.

This did not prevent the Ansayames, however, from killing two Mutsunes at San Benito Creek, burning a house and some wheat fields, and seriously threatening the Mission.   Moraga, was sent against them and captured eighteen hostiles and the chiefs of the hostile rancherías.

Almost as bad as warlike Indians were the earthquakes of that year, several in number, which cracked all the adobe walls of the buildings and compelled everybody — friars and Indians — to sleep out of doors for safety.

In 1803 the Governor ordered the padres of San Juan to remove their stock from La Brea Rancho, which had been granted to Mariano Castro.   They refused on the grounds that the rancho properly belonged to the Mission and should not have been granted to Castro, and on appeal the Viceroy confirmed their contention.

In June of this year the corner-stone of a new church was laid.   Padre Viader conducted the ceremonies, aided by the resident priests.   Don José de la Guerra was the sponsor, and Captain Font and Surgeon Morelos assisted.

In June, 1809, the image of San Juan was placed on the high altar in the sacristy which served for purposes of worship until the completion of the church.

By the end of the decade the population had grown to 702, though the number of deaths was large, and it continued slowly to increase until in 1823 it reached its greatest population with 1248 souls.

The new church was completed and dedicated on June 23, 1812.   In 1818 a new altar was completed, and a painter named Chavez demanded six reals a day for decorating it.   As the Mission could not afford this, a Yankee, known as Felipe Santiago — properly Thomas Doak — undertook the work, aided by the neophytes.   In 1815 one of the ministers was Estéban Tapis, who afterwards became the presidente.

In 1836 San Juan was the scene of the preparations for hostility begun by José Castro and Alvarado against Governor Gutierrez.   Meetings were held at which excited speeches were made advocating revolutionary methods, and the fife and drum were soon heard by the peaceful inhabi-

Plate XXXIV

b. RUINS OF SAN JUAN CAPISTRANO MISSION

a. FACHADA OF SAN JUAN BAUTISTA MISSION

tants of the old Mission. Many of the whites joined in with Alvarado and Castro, and the affair ultimated in the forced exile of the Governor, and Castro taking his place until Alvarado was elected by the *diputacion*.

The regular statistics of San Juan cease in 1832, when there were 916 Indians registered. In 1835, according to the decree of secularization, 63 Indians were " emancipated." Possibly these were the heads of families. Among these were to be distributed land valued at $5120, livestock, including 41 horses, $1782, implements, effects, etc., $1467.

An inventory of 1835 gives the following: Buildings, $36,000; implements, goods, and furniture, $7774; church property (church, fully described, $36,000; ornaments, etc. $7740, library, $461, bells, $1060, choir furniture, $1643), $45,904; vineyards, lands, and buildings outside the Mission, $37,365; ranchos, probably including live-stock, $19,107; credits, $1040; cash, $222; total, $147,413; deducting amount distributed to Indians, $8439, and debt $250, balance, $138,723.

Alvarado says that secularization was a success here and at San Antonio, though nowhere else, the Indians being free and making tolerably good use of their freedom. After 1836 all traces of the community disappeared. The Indians were uncontrolled except by the regular laws of the province. A number of whites settled in the region, and the name of the new pueblo was San Juan de Castro. The outside gentile Indians caused a great deal of trouble for a number of years, but were ultimately wiped out of existence.

The summary of statistics from the founding of the Mission in 1797 to 1834 shows 4100 baptisms, 1028 marriages, 3027 deaths. The largest number of cattle owned was 11,000 in 1820, 1598 horses in 1806, 13,000 sheep in 1816.

In 1845, when Pico's decree was issued, San Juan was

considered a pueblo, and orders given for the sale of all property except a curate's house, the church, and a courthouse. The inventory gave a value of $8000. The population was now about 150, half of whom were whites and the other half Indians.

It will be remembered that it was at San Juan that Castro organized his forces to repel what he considered the invasion of Frémont in 1846. From Gavilan heights near by, the explorer looked down and saw the warlike preparations directed against him, and from there wrote his declaration: "I am making myself as strong as possible, in the intention that if we are unjustly attacked we will fight to extremity and refuse quarter, trusting to our country to avenge our death."

When Sloat made his memorable landing at Monterey, and California officially became a part of the United States, General Castro was at San Juan, and from there communicated with the conquerors; and it was rather humiliating to the California commander-in-chief that when the Stars and Stripes were eventually raised over the ex-Mission of San Juan it was done by Frémont and his forces.

Later, when Flores revolted in the South, Frémont organized his noted volunteer battalion at San Juan. Those were exciting times for the little town, for there were 475 mounted riflemen and 41 artillerymen, organized into ten companies. The force duly marched from here on the 29th of November, passing San Miguel to San Luis Obispo and thence over the Santa Inés range to Santa Barbara, finally to Cahuenga where the formal capitulation of the hostile forces took place.

In 1846 Pico sold all that remained of San Juan Bautista — the orchard — to O. Deleissèques for a debt, and though he did not obtain possession at the time, the United States courts finally confirmed his claim. This was the last act in the history of the once prosperous Mission.

Now the town is utterly deserted. When the Southern
Pacific railway was built San Juan was left out on one side.
Nothing to-day suggests the activity and excitement of
the Mission and revolutionary days. Grass grows in the
streets and sleepiness and laziness reign supreme.

As one steps into the plaza at San Juan Bautista he
observes that one whole side is occupied by the arched
corridors of the monastery. The church is in the corner
to the right, separated from the corridors by an ugly
modern wooden building, surmounted by the bell-tower which
was erected by Father Rubio in 1874. The *fachada* is
plain, simple, and unpretentious. It is merely the end of the
church building, divided by a cornice moulding into two
sections, the upper and lower. In the upper the only
features are a deeply embrasured square window, above
which is another simple cornice, which, however, is only a
little wider than the window. In the lower section there are
three arches, the centre being the main entrance and much
larger than the other two. It faces almost due east. The
appearance of the *fachada* is not improved by the four
cypress trees which have been trimmed to the shape of
four elongated barrels.

Where the plaster has fallen from the walls it reveals
that the bricks are of adobe, though on the side a repaired
place shows the use of large, flat, burned bricks as well as
adobe. The padres were brick-makers in the modern sense
of the word. Not only did they know how to make adobe,
or sun-dried bricks, but the roof and floor tiles and the
bricks used in their buildings are all properly burnt, showing a thorough knowledge of the art.

The monastery is of adobe, and the corridor floor is
brick-tiled. It is about 270 feet long, and 50 feet wide
(paced measurements). The corridor from the outside of
arch to the monastery wall is about twelve feet. The end
facing the street is built up with wood, and on it is a sign
which says: " Esta Mision fue cornenzada dia 24 Junio,

1797." The arches are evidently of flat burned brick, and are not of uniform size, a peculiarity I have elsewhere called attention to.

The entrance at San Juan Bautista seems more like that of a prison than a church. The Rev. Valentin Closa, of the Company of Jesus, who for many years had charge here, found that some visitors were so irresponsible that thefts were of almost daily occurrence. So he had a wooden barrier placed across the church from wall to wall, and floor to ceiling, through which a gate affords entrance, and this gate is kept padlocked with as constant watchfulness as is that of a prison. Passing this barrier the two objects that immediately catch one's eye are the semicircular arch dividing the church from the altar and the old wooden pulpit on the left.

The interior is different from most of the Missions in that the only windows are four square apertures on each side, almost at the top of the walls, just below which a cornice runs the whole length of the building. Around the church, about three feet from the floor, there is a kind of narrow seat let into the walls. These walls are divided into arches — seven on each side — evidencing the thought in the minds of the original builders. It was their expectation that the church would have to be enlarged into a three-aisled structure as soon as the enlarged attendance of the Indians demanded the extra space. The founder of San Juan had great visions and hopes for the future. The country was thickly populated with Indians, and the success of the Mission is shown in the large number of baptisms in so short a time. Doubtless had the original plans been carried out San Juan would have developed architecturally and have become a much more imposing building than it is.

Of the modern bell-tower it can only be said that it is a pity necessity seemed to compel the erection of such an abortion. The old padres seldom, if ever, failed in their architectural plans. However one may criticise their lesser work, such as the decorations, he is compelled to admire their *large* work; they were right, powerful, and dignified in their straightforward simplicity. And it is pathetic that in later days, when workmen and money were scarce, the modern priests did not see some way of overcoming obstacles that would have been more harmonious with the old plans than is evidenced in this tower and many other similar incongruities, such as the steel bell-tower at San Miguel.

To return to the interior. The sixth and seventh arches on the left open into a side chapel, in which is an altar to the virgin, and the confessional. The walls throughout are whitewashed, yet here and there a small patch of the original mural decorations may be seen, in brownish-red, green and light green, as on the further side of the seventh arch. There is a corresponding chapel in the sixth and seventh arches on the opposite side. In some places the plaster has fallen, revealing that the construction is of large flat bricks.

Inside the altar is a tombstone over the grave of Padre Estéban Tapis. The inscription is in Latin and records briefly his life-work. He was in America forty years, and in California thirty-five. He died the 3d of November, 1825.

From the side chapel a door leads into a small hall, lighted only by a triangle-shaped aperture in the wall. An adobe stairway leads from this hall into the old pulpit, which is octagonal, fastened to the wall, and rests on three four-inch joists scrolled at the end. It is of rude panelling in wood, recently painted a creamy pink.

At San Juan Bautista the old reredos remains, though the altar is new. The six figures of the saints are the original ones placed there when it was first erected. In the centre, at the top, is Our Lady of Guadalupe; to the left, San Antonio de Padua; to the right, San Isadore de

Madrid (the patron saint of all farmers) ; below, in the centre, is the saint of the Mission, San Juan Bautista, on his left, St. Francis, and on his right, San Buenaventura.

The baptistery is on the left, at the entrance. Over its old solid, heavy doors rises a half-circular arch. Inside are two bowls of heavy sandstone.

In the belfry are two bells, one of which is modern, cast in San Francisco. The other is the largest Mission bell, I believe, in California. It bears the inscription: " Ave María Purísima S. Fernando RVELAS me Fecit 1809."

There is a small collection of objects of interest connected with the old Mission preserved in one room of the monastery. Among other things are two of the chorals ; pieces of rawhide used for tying the beams, etc., in the original construction ; the head of a bass-viol that used to be played by one of the Indians ; a small mortar ; and quite a number of books. Perhaps the strangest thing in the whole collection is an old barrel-organ made by Benjamin Dobson, The Minories, London. It has several barrels and on one of them is the following list of its tunes : Go to the Devil ; Spanish Waltz ; College Hornpipe ; Lady Campbell's Reel. One can imagine with what feelings one of the sainted padres, after a peculiarly trying day with his aboriginal children, would put in this barrel, and while his lips said holy things, his hand instinctively grind out with vigor the first piece on the list.

CHAPTER XXI

SAN MIGUEL, ARCÁNGEL

L ASUEN'S third Mission, of 1797, was San Miguel, located near a large ranchería named *Sagshpileel*, and on the site called *Vahiá*. One reason for the selection of the location is given in the fact that there was plenty of water at Santa Isabel and San Marcos for the irrigation of three hundred fanegas of seed. To this day the springs of Santa Isabel are a joy and delight to all who know them, and the remains of the old irrigating canals and dams, dug and built by the padres, are still to be seen.

On the day of the founding Lasuen's heart was made glad by the presentation of fifteen children for baptism. At the end of 1800 there were 362 neophytes, 372 horses and cattle and 1582 smaller animals. The crop of 1800 was 1900 bushels.

Padre Antonio de la Concepción Horra, who was shortly after deported as insane, and who gave Presidente Lasuen considerable trouble by preferring serious charges against the Missions, was one of the first ministers.

In February of 1801 the two padres were attacked with violent pains in the stomach and they feared the neophytes had poisoned them, but they soon recovered. Padre Pujol, who came from Monterey to aid them, did not fare so well, for he was taken sick in a similar manner and died. Three Indians were arrested, but it was never decided whether poison had been used or not. The Indians escaped when being taken north to the presidio, and eventually the padres pleaded for their release, asking however that they be flogged in the presence of their families for having boasted that they had poisoned the padres.

In January, 1804, Padre Martin went with a soldier to Guchapa, chief of the Cholan ranchería, fourteen leagues away, to ask for some of his young men to make Christians of them. Guchapa refused, and in repulsing the friar and scorning his threats he said he was not afraid of the soldiers, for they died the same as other men. In order to modify the chief's ideas, thirteen soldiers were despatched to capture him; which they did, though he made a brave resistance. On his arrival at the Mission he was conciliated with presents, and persuaded into meeting the padre's ideas, finally departing leaving his son as a hostage for the fulfilment of his promises.

In August, 1806, a disastrous fire occurred, destroying all the manufacturing part of the establishment as well as a large quantity of wool, hides, cloth, and 6000 bushels of wheat. The roof of the church was also partially burned. At the end of the decade San Miguel had a population of 973, and in the number of its sheep it was excelled only by San Juan Capistrano.

In October, 1814, an expedition under Padre Juan Cabot left San Miguel for the exploration of the Tulare region. They must have travelled rapidly, for the next day they camped on the edge of a large lake where was a ranchería of seven hundred souls. Cabot baptized twenty-six of the old and sick and then pushed on to another ranchería — Sumtache — which was at enmity with the first. Misunderstanding the purport of the visit, the Sumtaches fought the Spaniards, killed two horses, and only ceased hostilities when one of their women was killed. Finally the region of King's River was reached, and, though trees were scarce, it was deemed that somewhere in this region a successful Mission could be established. In sending the report to Lasuen, Padre Martin urged the establishment of such a Mission, claiming that if it were not done

PLATE XXXV

INTERIOR OF SAN MIGUEL MISSION FROM THE CHOIR GALLERY

" Satan, war, and venereal disease would leave nobody to be converted."

In 1818 a new church was reported as ready for roofing, and this was possibly built to replace the one partially destroyed by fire in 1806. In 1814 the Mission registered its largest population in 1096 neophytes, and in live stock it showed satisfactory increase at the end of the decade, though in agriculture it had not been so successful.

Ten years later it had to report a great diminution in its flocks and herds and its neophytes. The soil and pasture were also found to be poor, though vines flourished and timber was plentiful. Robinson, who visited San Miguel, at this time, reports it as a poor establishment and tells a large story about the heat suffocating the fleas. Padre Martin died in 1824.

In 1834 there were but 599 neophytes on the register. In 1836 Ignacio Coronel took charge in order to carry out the order of secularization, and when the inventory was made it showed the existence of property, excluding everything pertaining to the church, of $82,000. In 1839 this amount was reduced to $75,000. This large valuation was owing to the fact that there were several ranches and buildings and two large vineyards belonging to the Mission. These latter were Santa Isabel and Aguage with 5500 vines, valued at $22,162.

The general statistics from the founding in 1797 to 1834 give 2588 baptisms, 2038 deaths; largest population was 1076 in 1814. The largest number of cattle was 10,558 in 1822, horses 1560 in 1822, mules 140 in 1817, sheep 14,000 in 1820.

In 1836 Padre Moreno reported that when Coronel came all the available property was distributed among the Indians, except the grain, and of that they carried off more than half. In 1838 the poor padre complained bitterly of his poverty and the disappearance of the Mission property. There is no doubt but that here as

16

elsewhere the Mission was plundered on every hand, and the officers appointed to guard its interests were among the plunderers.

In 1844 Presidente Duran reported that San Miguel had neither lands nor cattle, and that its neophytes were demoralized and scattered for want of a minister. Pico's 1845 decree warned the Indians that they must return within a month and occupy their lands, or they would be disposed of; and in 1846 Pico reported the Mission sold, though no consideration is named, to P. Rios and Wm. Reed. The purchasers took possession, but the courts later declared their title invalid. In 1848 Reed and his whole family were atrociously murdered. The murderers were pursued; one was fatally wounded, one jumped into the sea and was drowned, and the other three were caught and executed.

To-day San Miguel is desolate and forlorn. The present pastor is old and infirm, and would find life hard were it not for the kindness of a few of his people.

The register of baptisms at San Miguel begins July 25, 1797, and up to 1861 contains 2917 names. Between the years 1844 and 1851 there is a vacancy, and only one name occurs in the latter year. The title-page is signed by Fr. Fermin Franco de Lasuen, and the priests in charge are named as Fr. Buenaventura Sitjar and Fr. Antonio de la Concepción.

At the end of this book is a list of 43 children of the "gentes de razon" included in the general list, but here specialized for reference.

The register of deaths contains 2249 names up to 1841. The first entry is signed by Fr. Juan Martin and the next two by Fr. Sitjar.

The old marriage register of the Mission of San Miguel is now at San Luis Obispo. It has a title-page signed by Fr. Lasuen.

In 1888 some of the old bells of the Mission were sent

to San Francisco and there were recast into one large bell, weighing 2500 lbs. Until 1902 this stood on a rude wooden tower in front of the church, but in that year an incongruous steel tower took its place. Packed away in a box still remains one of the old bells, which has sounded its last call. A large hole is in one side of it. The inscription, as near as I can make out, reads " A. D. 1800, S. S. Gabriel."

In 1901 the outside of the church and monastery was restored with a coat of new plaster and cement. Inside nearly everything is as it was left by the robber hand of secularization, as is fully shown in the chapter on interior decorations.

On the walls are the ten oil paintings brought by the original founders. They are very indistinct in the dim light of the church, and little can be said of their artistic value without further examination.

There is also an old breviary with two heavy hand made clasps, dated Antwerp, 1735, and containing the autograph of Fr. Man. de Castañeda.

The arches at San Miguel are not all alike; indeed, careful observation shows that they are very irregular. Nearest to the church a wooden post is now doing service, then come two square pillars before the arches begin. The first arch is a small semicircular one, followed by four larger ones, and then two larger elliptical ones. These two form a centre, for on the other side are four large and one small semicircular arch as before.

Slightly to the right of the elliptical arch nearest the church is a chimney, which rises a little above the comb of the red-tiled roof. It is surmounted by six tiles, three on one side, sloping towards the three on the other side, these in turn capped with one tile laid flat over the ends of all six. It adds a picturesque though simple feature to the roof of the monastery.

There is a quadrangle at San Miguel 230 feet square,

and on one side of it a corridor corresponding to the one in front, for six pillars of burnt brick still remain.

At the rear of the church was the original church, used before the present one was built, and a number of remains of the old houses of the neophytes still stand, though in a very dilapidated condition.

San Miguel was always noted for its proximity to the Hot Springs and Sulphur Mud Baths of Paso Robles. Both Indians and Mission padres knew of their healthful and curative properties, and in the early days scores of thousands enjoyed their peculiar virtues. Little by little the " superior race " is learning that in natural therapeutics the Indian is a reasonably safe guide to follow; hence the present extensive use by the whites of the Mud and Sulphur Baths at Paso Robles. Methinks the Indians of a century ago, though doubtless astonished at the wonderful temple to the white man's God built at San Miguel, would wonder much more were they now to see the elaborate and splendid house being erected at Paso Robles for the purpose of giving to more white people the baths, the virtue of which they so well knew.

CHAPTER XXII

SAN FERNANDO, REY DE ESPAGNA

ON September 8, 1797, the seventeenth of the California Missions was founded by Padre Lasuen, in the Encino Valley where Francisco Reyes had a rancho in the Los Angeles jurisdiction. The natives called it *Achois Comihavit*. Reyes' house was appropriated as a temporary dwelling for the missionary. The Mission was dedicated to Fernando III, King of Spain. Lasuen came down from San Miguel to Santa Barbara, especially for the foundation, and from thence with Sergeant Olivera and a military escort. These, with Padre Francisco Dumetz, the priest chosen to have charge, and his assistant, Francisco Favier Uría, composed, with the large concourse of Indians, the witnesses of the solemn ceremonial.

On the 4th of October Olivera reported the guard-house and storehouse finished, two houses begun, and preparations already being made for the church.

From the baptismal register it is seen that ten children were baptized the first day, and thirteen adults were received early in October. By the end of 1797 there were fifty-five neophytes.

Three years after its founding 310 Indians were gathered in, and its year's crop was 1000 bushels of grain. The Missions of San Juan Capistrano, San Gabriel, San Buenaventura, and Santa Barbara had contributed live-stock, and now its herds had grown to 526 horses, mules, and cattle, and 600 sheep.

In December, 1806, an adobe church, with a tile roof, was consecrated, which on the 21st of December, 1812, was severely injured by the earthquake that did damage to almost all the Missions of the chain. Thirty new beams were needed to support the injured walls. A new chapel was built, which was completed in 1818.

By the end of 1810 neophytes had increased to 955, and the healthfulness of the location was proven by the fact that baptisms were twice as numerous as deaths.

San Fernando from the start seemed to be cramped for want of lands. In 1804 there was a strong protest made against granting the Camulos Rancho, and in 1816 Pico ordered the sheep away from his land at the Simí Rancho, as did also the proprietors of Refugio in 1817. Padre Ibarra, in 1821, had a hot correspondence with the Santa Barbara military authorities in reference to a proposed grant of the Pirú Rancho, on which he was pasturing the Mission herds. The protest kept it from Guerra, the proposed grantee, but did not save it to San Fernando, a fact which caused considerable irritation on both sides. The padre began to complain of the Santa Barbara presidio, of which De la Guerra was captain, declaring that his soldiers sold liquor, lent horses to, and generally demoralized his neophytes, even sheltering them when they ran away.

Already the Mission property had begun to decline, though from 1822 to 1827 the records show that the Santa Barbara presidio received supplies to the amount of $21,203. In 1826 Governor Echeandía declared San Fernando to be in the jurisdiction of Los Angeles instead of Santa Barbara.

In 1837 the Mission funds to the amount of $2000 were taken by the Los Angeles authorities into safe keeping, as Governor Alvarado was marching south to punish the southern people who had risen in rebellion against what they termed his unjust rule. At San Fernando, on January 16, a force of about 270 men under Rocha were massed to arrest Alvarado's march upon Los Angeles, and Alcalde

PLATE XXXVI

Copyright, 1903, by C. C. Pierce & Co.

a. SAN MIGUEL MISSION AND CORRIDORS

b. RESTORED MONASTERY AND MISSION CHURCH OF SAN FERNANDO

Sepúlveda issued an address calling upon the citizens to defend the honor of their beloved country against the Monterey usurper. After some fruitless negotiations Alvarado sent an ultimatum to Sepúlveda, that if San Fernando was not given up on the messenger's return he would take it by force. Though his force was much smaller, the order was obeyed at once. Rocha retired with his men to Los Angeles, and Alvarado occupied the Mission. Soon afterwards Alvarado entered Los Angeles, a council of the opposing forces was held, a compact made, and peace restored.

In 1834 Lieutenant Antonio del Valle was the comisionado appointed to secularize the Mission, and the next year he became majordomo and served until 1837. The inventory of 1837 gives credits, $14,293; buildings, $56,785; house utensils, $601; goods in storehouse, $5214; liquors, etc., $7175; live-stock, $53,854; San Francisco Rancho, $1925; grain, $618; tannery, $544; carpenter shop, $127; blacksmith shop, $789; soap works, $512; mills, $200; tools, $368; tallow works, $2540; church, $1500; ornaments, etc., $4348; library of fifty works. The debts were $1689. When Visitador Hartwell came in 1839 he found everything in excellent condition, with large herds for distribution among the Indians; but the next year things were far less satisfactory.

It was on his journey north, in 1842, to take hold of the governorship, that Micheltorena learned at San Fernando of Commodore Jones's raising of the American flag at Monterey. By his decree, also, in 1843, San Fernando was ordered returned to the control of the padres, which was done, though the next year Duran reported that there were but few cattle left, and two vineyards.

Micheltorena was destined again to appear at San Fernando, for when the Californians under Pio Pico and Castro rose to drive out the Mexicans, the Governor finally capitulated at the same place he had heard the bad news of the Americans' capture of Monterey. February 21,

1845, after a bloodless "battle" at Cahuenga, he "abdicated," and finally left the country and returned to Mexico.

In 1845 Juan Manso and Andrés Pico leased the Mission at a rental of $1120, the affairs having been fairly well administered by Padre Orday after its return to the control of the friars. A year later it was sold by Pio Pico, under the order of the assembly, for $14,000, to Eulogio Célis, whose title was afterwards confirmed by the courts. Orday remained as pastor until May, 1847, and was San Fernando's last minister.

In 1847 San Fernando again heard the alarm of war. Frémont and his battalion reached here in January, and remained until the signing of the treaty of Cahuenga, which closed all serious hostilities against the United States in its conquest of California.

Connected with the Mission of San Fernando is the first discovery of California gold. Eight years before the great days of '49 Francisco Lopez, the *mayordomo* of the Mission, was in the canyon of San Feliciano, which is about eight miles westerly from the present town of Newhall, and, according to Don Abel Stearns, "with a companion while in search of some stray horses, about midday stopped under some trees and tied their horses to feed. While resting in the shade, Lopez with his sheath knife dug up some wild onions, and in the dirt discovered a piece of gold. Searching further he found more. On his return to town he showed these pieces to his friends, who at once declared there must be a placer of gold there."

Then the rush began. As soon as the people in Los Angeles and Santa Barbara heard of it they flocked to the new "gold fields" in hundreds. And the first California gold dust ever coined at the government mint at Philadelphia came from these mines. It was taken around Cape Horn in a sailing vessel by Alfred Robinson, the translator of Boscana's "Indians of California," and consisted of 18.34 ounces, and made $344.75, or over $19 to the ounce.

Davis says that in the first two years after the discovery not less than from $80,000 to $100,000 was gathered. Don Antonio Coronel, with three Indian laborers, in 1842, took out $600 worth of dust in two months.

Water being scarce the methods of washing the gravel were both crude and wasteful. And it is interesting to note that the first gold " pans " were *bateas* or bowl-shaped Indian baskets.

In March, 1902, a San Fernando Mission Indian died, and was buried on the 22d by the side of his wife in the old cemetery back of the church. Rojerio Rocha by name, he was said to be one hundred and twelve years old at the time of his death. He was one of the noted blacksmiths and silversmiths of the Mission, in the days when it was famed for its excellent iron work. When the division of lands took place he was given about twelve acres, three miles east of the Mission; but later he was evicted, and thereafter felt nothing but scorn, contempt, and hatred for the Americans who dispossessed him. It was a cold, rainy night when he was carted away from his home, and his wife died from the exposure. He was quite familiar with the excitement at the time of the discovery of gold, and was one of the few neophytes who were allowed to visit the spot.

The church at San Fernando is in a completely ruined condition. It stands southwest to northeast. The entrance is at the southwest end and the altar at the northeast. There is also a side entrance at the east, with a half-circular arch, sloping into a larger arch inside, with a flat top and rounded upper corners. The thickness of the walls allows the working out of various styles in these outer and inner arches that is curious and interesting. They reveal the individuality of the builder, and as they are all structural and pleasing they afford a wonderful example of variety in adapting the arch to its necessary functions.

Four sets of pilasters on each side divide the walls into effective panels, in each of which is set a sunk-in arch.

Upon each pilaster rests a corbel. Additional corbels are placed between the pilasters, and on these the roof-beams rest.

Nine square recesses, as if for windows, are to be seen on both sides, but a few only are pierced through and used as windows.

The church walls throughout are built of adobe.

The sacristy is in the rear of the church, and it is evident that here, as in so many of the Missions, digging has been going on. Over the entrance is an arch, shell-like inside, built of burnt brick.

The choir loft is at the southwest end, over the main entrance, which is a rounded arch outside and a flat one inside.

The corridors of the inner court extended from this church to the monastery — the building recently restored by the Landmarks Club. Only one pillar now stands, all the rest having tumbled. They were built of large flat burned brick. Some of them were square, as at Purísima, others are ruins of rounded columns. These latter were made of square brick, and the rounding out was accomplished with cement.

The graveyard is on the northwest side of the church, and close by is the old olive orchard, where a number of fine trees are still growing. There are also two large palms, pictures of which are generally taken with the Mission in the background, and the mountains beyond. It is an exquisite subject. The remains of adobe walls still surround the orchard.

The doorway leading to the graveyard is of a half-circle inside, and slopes outward, where the arch is square.

There is a buttress of burnt brick to the southeast of the church, which appears as if it might have been an addition after the earthquake.

At the monastery the chief entrance is a simple but effective arched doorway, now plastered and whitewashed.

The double door frame projects pilaster-like, with a four-membered cornice above, from which rises an elliptical arch, with an elliptical cornice about a foot above.

From this monastery one looks out upon a court or plaza which is literally dotted with ruins, though they are mainly of surrounding walls. Immediately in the foreground is a fountain, the reservoir of which is built of brick covered with cement. A double bowl rests on the centre standard.

Further away in the court are the remnants of what may have been another fountain, the reservoir of which is made of brick, built into a singular geometrical figure. This is composed of eight semicircles, with V's connecting them, the apex of each V being on the outside. It appears like an attempt at creating a conventionalized flower in brick.

Two hundred yards or so away from the monastery is a square structure, the outside of boulders. Curiosity prompting, you climb up, and on looking in you find that inside this framework of boulders are two circular cisterns of brick, fully six feet in diameter across the top, decreasing in size to the bottom, which is perhaps four feet in diameter.

In March, 1905, considerable excitement was caused by the actions of the parish priest of San Fernando, a Frenchman named Le Bellegny, of venerable appearance and gentle manners. Not being acquainted with the *status quo* of the old Mission, he exhumed the bodies of the Franciscan friars who had been buried in the church and reburied them. He removed the baptismal font to his church, and unroofed some of the old buildings and took the tiles and timbers away. As soon as he understood the matter he ceased his operations, but, unfortunately, not before considerable damage was done.

CHAPTER XXIII

SAN LUIS, REY DE FRANCIA

THE last Mission of the century, the last of Lasuen's administration, and the last south of Santa Barbara, was that of San Luis Rey. Lasuen himself explored the region and determined the site. The Governor agreed to it, and on the 27th of February, 1798, ordered a guard to be furnished from San Diego who should obey Lasuen implicitly and help erect the necessary buildings for the new Mission. The founding took place on the 13th of June, in the presence of Captain Grajera and his guard, a few San Juan neophytes, and many gentiles, President Lasuen performing the ceremonies aided by Padres Peyri and Santiago. Fifty-four children were baptized at the same time, and from the very start the Mission was prosperous. No other missionary has left such a record as Padre Peyri. He was zealous, sensible, and energetic. He knew what he wanted and how to secure it. The Indians worked willingly for him, and by the 1st of July six thousand adobes were made for the church. By the end of 1800 there were 337 neophytes, 617 larger stock, and 1600 sheep.

The new church was completed in 1801–2, but Peyri was too energetic to stop at this. Buildings of all kinds were erected, and neophytes gathered in so that by 1810 its population was 1519, with the smallest death rate of any Mission. In 1811 Peyri petitioned the Governor to allow him to build a new and better church of adobes and bricks; but as consent was not forthcoming he went out to Pala,

PLATE XXXVII

a. SAN LUIS REY MISSION

b. SAN FRANCISCO SOLANO MISSION, AT SONOMA

and in 1816 established a branch establishment, built a
church, and the picturesque campanile now known all over
the world, and soon had a thousand converts tilling the
soil and attending the services of the church.

In 1826 San Luis Rey reached its maximum in population with 2869 neophytes. From now on began its decline,
though in material prosperity it was far ahead of any
other Mission. In 1828 it had 28,900 sheep, and the cattle
were also rapidly increasing. The average crop of grain
was 12,660 bushels.

Duhaut-Cilly left perhaps the best description extant of
San Luis in its palmy days. He visited it in 1827, and
says:

"At last we turned inland, and after a jaunt of an hour and a
half we found before us, on a piece of rising ground, the superb
buildings of Mission San Luis Rey, whose glittering whiteness
was flashed back to us by the first rays of the day. At that distance, and in the still uncertain light of dawn, this edifice, of
a very beautiful model, supported upon its numerous pillars
had the aspect of a palace. The architectural faults cannot be
grasped at this distance, and the eye is attracted only to the
elegant mass of this beautiful structure. . . . Instinctively I
stopped my horse to gaze alone, for a few minutes, on the beauty
of this sight."

Later he says, " The buildings were drawn on a large and
ample plan, wholly the idea of the Padre (Peyri) ; he directed
the execution of it, in which he was assisted by a very skilful
man, who had contributed also to the building of those at Santa
Barbara ; so, although these are much more sumptuous, at that
place may be recognized the same hand.

" This building forms a large square of five hundred feet on
each side. The main façade is a long peristyle borne on thirty-
two square pillars supporting round arches. The edifice is composed, indeed, of only a ground-floor, but its elevation, of fine
proportions, gives it as much grace as nobleness. It is covered
with a tiled roof, flattened, around which reaches, as much without as within the square, a terrace with an elegant balustrade
which stimulates still more the height. Within is seen a large

court, neat and levelled, around which pillars and arches similar to those of the peristyle support a long cloister, by which one communicates with all the dependencies of the Mission."

When Peyri saw that the republic was inevitable he became its enthusiastic friend and swore allegiance; but as the plans of the spoliators became more open, and the law of expulsion of all Spaniards was passed in 1829, he endeavored to obtain his passports, though unsuccessfully. When Governor Victoria was exiled he went from San Gabriel to rest and recruit awhile at San Luis Rey; and then the venerable padre decided that the time had come for him to leave the scene of over thirty years of arduous though congenial toil. Accordingly he went with Victoria to San Diego, where a vessel had been chartered. The story is told, and I do not question its material truth, that, knowing he could not comfortably take leave of his Indians, he fled in the night time, hoping to escape without their knowledge. Missing him, however, in the morning, they learned somehow that he had gone, so, mounting their ponies, a large number of them rode to San Diego, hoping to be able to bring him back. They arrived just as the ship was weighing anchor. Standing on the deck, with outstretched arms he blessed them amid their tears and cries. Some swam out after the ship, it is said. He had with him four neophyte boys, whom he took to Europe.

For many years the Indians left behind at San Luis Rey were in the habit of placing candles and flowers before the picture of Padre Peyri and offering prayers to him, pleading with him to return. Even after his death this was kept up, the simple-hearted Indians preferring to pray to a saint, whose goodness they had known and felt, rather than to those of whom they knew nothing but what they were told.

In his address before the assembly May 1, 1834, Figueroa stated that three pueblos had been organized out of

Mission communities, and that the one of Las Flores, by the neophytes of San Luis Rey was flourishing. How true this is there is no evidence in the records to show. By his decree of November 4 San Luis Rey was made a parish of the first class, and earlier, in October, he had issued a resolution of the assembly to the effect that Indian towns were no longer to be called Missions. They were towns of the republic, subject to the civil laws the same as other towns, and not under the control of the padres alone.

San Luis Rey was one of the Missions where a large number of cattle were slaughtered on account of the secularization decree. It is said that some 20,000 head were killed at the San Jacinto Rancho alone. The Indians were much stirred up over the granting of the ranchos, which they claimed were their own lands. Indeed they formed a plot to capture the Governor on one of his southern trips in order to protest to him against the granting of the Temécula Rancho.

The final secularization took place in November, 1834, with Captain Portilla as comisionado and Pio Pico as majordomo and administrator until 1840. There was trouble in apportioning the lands among the Indians, for Portilla called for fifteen or twenty men to aid him in quelling disturbances; and at Pala the majordomo was knocked down and left for dead by an Indian. The inventory showed property (including the church, valued at $30,000) worth $203,707, with debts of $93,000. The six ranchos were included as worth $40,437, the three most valuable being Pala, Santa Margarita, and San Jacinto.

Micheltorena's decree of 1843 restored San Luis Rey to priestly control, but by that time its spoliation was nearly complete. Padre Zalvidea was in his dotage, and the four hundred Indians had scarcely anything left to them. Two years later the majordomo, appointed by Zalvidea to act for him, turned over the property to his successor, and the inventory shows the frightful wreckage. Of all the vast herds and flocks, only 279 horses, 20 mules, 61 asses, 196 cattle, 27 yoke oxen, 700 sheep, and a few valueless implements remained. All the ranchos had passed into private ownership.

May 18, 1846, all that remained of the former king of Missions was sold by Pio Pico to Cot and José Pico for $2437. Frémont dispossessed their agent and they failed to gain repossession, the courts deciding that Pico had no right to sell. In 1847 the celebrated Mormon battalion, which Parkman so vividly describes in his Oregon and California Trail, were stationed at San Luis Rey for two months, and later on, a re-enlisted company was sent to take charge of it for a short time. On their departure Captain Hunter, as sub-Indian agent, took charge and found a large number of Indians, amenable to discipline and good workers.

The general statistics from the founding in 1798 to 1834 show 5591 baptisms, 1425 marriages, 2859 deaths. In 1832 there were 27,500 cattle, 2226 horses in 1828, 345 mules in the same year, 28,913 sheep in 1828, and 1300 goats in 1832.

In 1892 Father J. J. O'Keefe, who had done excellent work at Santa Barbara, was sent to San Luis Rey to repair the church and make it suitable for a missionary college of the Franciscan order. May 12, 1893, the rededication ceremonies of the restored building took place, the bishop of the diocese, the vicar-general of the Franciscan order and other dignitaries being present and aiding in the solemnities. Three old Indian women were also there who heard the mass said at the original dedication of the church in 1802. Since that time Father O'Keefe has raised and expended thousands of dollars in repairing, always keeping in mind the original plans. He now contemplates the restoration, or, rather, rebuilding — for all but the arches of the corridors are entirely gone — of the monastery.

San Luis Rey is now a college for the training of mis-

sionaries for the field, and Father J. J. O'Keefe, O. F. M.,
is working as rapidly as means will allow to reconstruct
some of the buildings and use them for the purposes of the
college. It is planned to erect over fifty rooms, which will
include kitchen, pantry, refectory, library, class-rooms,
recreation room, infirmary, and rooms for the " religious."
The building will occupy the site to the left of the old Mission, where the arches of the corridors still remain. It will
be a story and a half high, mainly of adobe, made on the
ground. The quadrangle will be restored on the old lines,
only smaller (about one fourth to one third the size of the
former one), and a wash-house or laundry, a bath-house,
new water tank, etc., are already built. The remaining
space, inside the quadrangle, will be utilized as a house
garden. Of course none of the standing arches will be disturbed. Those that are in the area will be utilized, as it is
planned to use the corridors for processions as in the old
days. The estimated cost is $20,000, exclusive of most of
the labor which will be done by the lay brothers of the college. The front wall will be 186 feet long and 14 feet high
to the ceilings, and the buildings will extend in wings, 174
feet, back to the end of the church, which is to the northwest. Much of this work is already accomplished, and,
possibly, by the time this book is issued the front portion
will be erected. But Father O'Keefe is compelled to go
slowly, owing to the scarcity of funds, and I can only suggest to my readers who desire to see San Luis Rey restored
to something of its former useful activity, that they willingly contribute to aid to that end. Letters with checks,
addressed to Father O'Keefe, San Luis Rey Mission, San
Diego Co., Calif., will receive grateful acknowledgment.

Of this plaza it is said that after the order of secularization had gone into effect it often saw the excitements
of the bull fight. Crowds of spectators used to assemble
on the roofs of the corridors, which afforded them an
excellent view and perfect safety. And rumor goes even

17

further, and asserts that Don Pio Pico himself, now and again, would assume the rôle of matador and engage the infuriated animal within, evidently enjoying the hearty applause of his audience.

On the *fachada* at San Luis Rey are two brackets at the foot of niches for statues. These are built of rounded courses of bevelled brick, moulded to the shape required, thus producing a pretty effect permanently. The pilasters or engaged columns also are of moulded brick to give the curved effects.

Immediately on entering the church one observes doorways to the right and left, — the one on the right bricked up. It is the door that used to lead into the Mortuary Chapel, later to be described.

A semicircular arch spans the whole church from side to side, about thirty feet, on which the original decorations still remain. These are in rude imitation of marble, as at Santa Barbara, in black and red, with bluish green lines. The wall colorings below are in imitation of black marble.

The holy-water vessels are both gone from their places in the wall, but the original decorations that surrounded them remain.

The main engaged columns, or pilasters, of which there are eight, — four on each side, — consist of a base, with a four-membered wainscot moulding, above which the column rises to within about two feet of the ceiling. Here, equally simple mouldings crown the pilaster. The decoration is imitation of marble. The bricks of which the pilasters are built are burnt, and the corner ones are specially moulded in a rounded device to add a pleasing effect.

Over each window the original distemper decorations remain, stretching out to the sides from a kind of mosaic star.

The choir gallery is over the main entrance, and there the great revolving music stand is still in use, with several of the large and interesting illuminated manuscript sing-

PLATE XXXVIII

a. SAN ANTONIO DE PADUA MISSION

b. GRAVEYARD AND REAR OF SANTA INÉS MISSION

ing-books of the early days. In Mission days it was generally the custom to have two chanters, who took care of the singing and the books. These, with all the other singers, stood around the revolving music-stand, on which the large manuscript chorals were placed.

The old byzantine pulpit still occupies its original position at San Luis Rey, but the sounding-board is gone — no one knows whither. This is of a type commonly found in continental churches, the corbel with its conical sides harmonizing with the ten panels and base-mouldings of the box proper. It is fastened to the pilaster which supports the arch above.

The original paint — a little of it — still remains. It appears to have been white panels, lined in red and blue.

It was entered from the side altar, through a doorway pierced through the wall. The steps leading up to it are of red burnt brick. Evidently it was a home product, and was possibly made by one of Padre Peyri's Indian carpenters, who was rapidly nearing graduation into the ranks of the skilled cabinet-makers.

The Mortuary Chapel, before referred to, is perhaps as fine a piece of work as any in the whole Mission chain. It is beautiful even now in its sad dilapidation. It was crowned with a domed roof of heavy cement. The entrance was by the door in the church to the right of the main entrance. The room is octagonal, with the altar in a recess, over which is a dome of brick, with a small lantern. At each point of the octagon there is an engaged column, built of circular-fronted brick which run to a point at the rear and are thus built into the wall. A three-membered cornice crowns each column, which supports arches that reach from one column to another. There are two windows, one to the southeast, the other northwest. The altar is at the northeast. There are two doorways, with stairways which lead to a small outlook over the altar and the whole interior. These were for the watchers of the dead, so that at a glance they might see that nothing was disturbed.

The altar and its recess are most interesting, the rear wall of the former being decorated in classic design.

The original altar table rested upon a vase-like base, built of brick and cement, now in ruins. On the occasion of my last visit, as I sat looking at the sage and other wild plants growing up on the chapel floor, the hens and chickens feeding and scratching, lizards and horned toads moving to and fro, with linnets, larks, and sparrows singing and chirping upon the walls above, I could not help the reflection that Nature pays no attention to the works of the past. She lives only for to-day. If the splendid achievements of architecture of man are neglected, they fall into ruins, and the lowest of the animals and insects come and take possession of them; the drifting seeds of the humblest weeds find lodgment and grow even in the places once held most sacred. There is no regretting, no mourning, no weeping. Only what is, is, and that must be utilized now.

Father O'Keefe assures me that this chapel is of the third order of St. Francis, the founder of the Franciscan Order. In the oval space over the arch which spans the entrance to the altar are the " arms " of the third order, consisting of the Cross and the five wounds (the stigmata) of Christ, which were conferred upon St. Francis as a special sign of divine favor.

CHAPTER XXIV

SANTA INÉS

"**B**EAUTIFUL for situation" was the spot selected for the only Mission founded during the first decade of the nineteenth century, — Santa Inés. Governor Borica, who called California " the most peaceful and quiet country on earth," and under whose orders Padre Lasuen had established the five Missions of 1796–97, had himself made explorations in the scenic mountainous regions of the coast, and recommended the location afterwards determined upon, called by the Indians *Alajulapu,* meaning *rincon,* or corner.

The native population was reported to number over a thousand, and the fact that they were frequently engaged in petty hostilities among themselves rendered it necessary to employ unusual care in initiating the new enterprise. Presidente Tapis therefore asked the Governor for a larger guard than was generally assigned for protecting the Missions, and a sergeant and nine men were ordered for that purpose.

The distance from Santa Barbara was about thirty-five miles, over a rough road, hardly more than a trail, winding in and out among the foothills, and gradually climbing up into the mountains in the midst of most charming and romantic scenery. The quaint procession, consisting of Padre presidente Tapis and three other priests, Commandant Carrillo, and the soldiers, and a large number of neophytes from Santa Barbara, slowly marched over this mountainous road, into the woody recesses where nestled the future home of the Mission of Santa Inés, and where the usual ceremonies of foundation took place September 17, 1804. Padres Calzada, Gutierrez, and Ciprès assisted President Tapis, and the two former remained as the missionaries in charge.

The first result of the founding of this Mission was the immediate baptism of twenty-seven children, a scene worthy of the canvas of a genius, could any modern painter conceive of the real picture, — the group of dusky little ones with sombre, wondering eyes, and the long-gowned priests, with the soldiers on guard and the watchful Indians in native costume in the background, — all in the temple of nature's creating.

This auspicious opening was not followed by uninterrupted prosperity. During the existence of the Mission, about thirty years, there was an annual average of forty-five baptisms, but also an annual average of forty-two deaths. The largest number of neophytes at any one time was in 1816, when there were 768; but many of these came from neighboring Missions. Although comparatively few in number, the results of their toil demonstrated the efficiency of padres and people. According to official reports, the total number of cattle, sheep, horses, mules, and swine possessed by them in 1821 was 12,368. They raised large crops of wheat, barley, corn, and beans, and accumulated stores of tallow, hides, wool, and soap. Between 1822 and 1827 they furnished supplies to the presidio at Santa Barbara valued at $10,767, — all the fruit of the labors of the neophytes, the so-called "lazy Indians," who received nothing in return for these contributions but "drafts" on the California treasury, that were never honored.

The first church erected was not elaborate, but it was roofed with tiles, and was ample in size for all needful purposes. In 1812 an earthquake caused a partial collapse of this structure. The corner of the church fell, roofs were ruined, walls cracked, and many buildings near

PLATE XXXIX

PADRE PEYRI, THE FOUNDER OF SAN LUIS REY

PLATE XL

GARDEN ENTRANCE AT SAN LUIS REY

domo to surprise the gentiles. The movement was a success from his standpoint, as twenty-one were killed, as many more wounded, and twenty made captives, some of these latter being women and children. When the matter was reported to Governor Figueroa he was exceedingly indignant, especially as the padre asked for reinforcements to " pacify " the rancherías. Mercado was suspended by his prefect, pending an investigation, while Vallejo, releasing the prisoners sent to San Francisco, also freed those in bonds at San Rafael, and then went among the rancherías, explaining the matter and doing his best to quiet the angry feelings aroused. In the middle of the following year Mercado was released and returned to San Rafael, two friars, who had been sent to report upon the matter, claiming he had nothing to do with the attack.

In 1834 Ignacio Martinez took charge as comisionado, and the inventory, September 31, shows values as follows: church, $192; ornaments, etc., $777; 75 volumes, $108; total, $1077. The Mission buildings, $1123; garden or orchard, $968; boats, etc., $500; live-stock, $4339; Nicasio Rancho, $7256; credits, $170; total, $18,474; debts, $3488; leaving a balance of $15,025.

In December there were distributed to 343 Indians, doubtless heads of families, 1291 sheep and 439 horses.

The statistics for the seventeen years of the Mission's history (1817–34) show 1873 baptisms, 543 marriages, 698 deaths.

The secularization decree ordered that San Rafael should become a parish of the first class, which class paid its curates $1500, as against $1000 to those of the second class.

In 1837 it was reported that the Indians were not using their liberty well; so, owing to the political troubles at the time, General Vallejo was authorized to collect everything and care for it under a promise to redistribute when conditions were better. In 1840 the Indians insisted upon this promise being kept, and in spite of the Governor's opposition Vallejo succeeded in obtaining an order for the distribution of the live-stock.

In 1845 Pico's order, demanding the return within one month of the Indians to the lands of San Rafael or they would be sold, was published, and the inventory taken thereupon showed a value of $17,000 in buildings, lands, and live-stock. In 1846 the sale was made to Antonio Suñol and A. M. Pico for $8000. The purchasers did not obtain possession, and their title was afterwards declared invalid.

In the distribution of the Mission stock Vallejo reserved a small band of horses for the purposes of national defence, and it was this band that was seized by the " Bear Flag " revolutionists at the opening of hostilities between the Americans and Mexicans. This act was followed almost immediately by the joining of the insurgents by Frémont, and the latter's marching to meet the Mexican forces, which were supposed to be at San Rafael. No force, however, was found there, so Frémont took possession of the Mission on June 26, 1846, and remained there for about a week, leaving there to chase up Torre, who had gone to join Castro.

When he finally left the region he took with him a number of cattle and horses, went to Sonoma, and on the 5th of July assumed active command of all the insurgent forces, which ultimated in the conquest of the State.

From this time the ex-Mission had no history. The buildings doubtless suffered much from Frémont's occupancy, and never being very elaborate easily fell a prey to the elements.

There is not a remnant of them now left, and the site is occupied by a modern, hideous, wooden building, used as an armory. Behind this are a few of the old pear trees planted by the padres, but little, if anything, else remains. Yet one feels the wisdom of the choice of even this spot.

Sheltered and secluded by surrounding hills, that are rounded and beautifully sloped, and then covered with richest verdure and a variety of trees in which song-birds nest and sing, and beneath which peaceful cattle and sheep graze, it must have been a place of rest, content, and retirement for the poor sick neophytes brought up from San Francisco.

CHAPTER XXVI

SAN FRANCISCO SOLANO

FIFTY-FOUR years after the founding of the first Franciscan Mission in California, the site was chosen for the twenty-first and last, San Francisco Solano. This Mission was established at Sonoma under conditions already narrated. The first ceremonies took place July 4, 1823, and nine months later the Mission church was dedicated. This structure was built of boards, but by the end of 1824 a large building had been completed, made of adobe with tiled roof and corridor, also a granary and eight houses for the use of the padres and soldiers. Thus in a year and a half from the time the location was selected the necessary Mission buildings had been erected, and a large number of fruit trees and vines were already growing. The neophytes numbered 693, but many of these were sent from San Francisco, San José and San Rafael. The Indians at this Mission represented thirty-five different tribes, according to the record, yet they worked together harmoniously, and in 1830 their possessions included more than 8000 cattle, sheep, and horses. Their crops averaged nearly 2000 bushels of grain per year.

The number of baptisms recorded during the twelve years before secularization was over 1300. Ten years later only about 200 Indians were left in that vicinity.

In 1834 the Mission was secularized by M. G. Vallejo, who appointed Ortega as majordomo. Vallejo quarrelled with Padre Quijas, who at once left and went to reside at San Rafael. The movable property was distributed

to the Indians, and they were allowed to live on their old
rancherías, though there is no record that they were formally allotted to them. By and by the Gentile Indians so
harassed the Mission Indians that the latter placed all their
stock under the charge of General Vallejo, asking him to
care for it on their behalf. The herds increased under his
control, the Indians had implicit confidence in him, and he
seems to have acted fairly and honestly by them.

The pueblo of Sonoma was organized as a part of the
secularization of San Francisco Solano, and also to afford
homes for the colonists brought to the country by Hijar
and Padrés. In this same year the soldiers of the presidio
of San Francisco de Asis were transferred to Sonoma,
to act as a protection of the frontier, to overawe the Russians, and check the incoming of Americans. This meant
the virtual abandonment of the post by the shores of the
bay. Vallejo supported the presidial company, mainly at
his own expense, and made friends with the native chief,
Solano, who aided him materially in keeping the Indians
peaceful.

The general statistics of the Mission for the eleven
years of its existence, 1823–34, are as follows: Baptisms
1315, marriages 278, deaths 651. The largest population
was 996 in 1832. The largest number of cattle was 4849
in 1833, 1148 horses and 7114 sheep in the same year.

In January, 1838, Tobias, the chief of the Guilucos,
and one of his men were brought to Sonoma and tried for
the murder of two Indian fishermen. The prosecutor asked
for five years in the chain-gang for the chief, and death
for his companion, but the records do not show what
punishment was awarded.

In August a band of fifty horse thieves crossed the
Sacramento with a number of tame horses for the purpose
of stampeding the Sonoma herds. Vallejo gave battle
and killed thirty-four of the robbers, the rest surrendered,
and the chief was shot at Sonoma. In October of the same

18

year Vallejo issued a circular stating that certain persons had made his friendly chief Solano drunk, and that many Indian children had been seized and sold into slavery. Solano was arrested, and forces sent after the children, all of whom were recovered and restored to their parents.

In 1838 he had worse troubles. Smallpox broke out and thousands of northern Indians were swept away by the dread disease. Vallejo estimated that fully 70,000 lost their lives. He claimed that the pestilence came from the English settlements by way of Fort Ross, and he urged that extra precautions be taken against it. Fortunately it did not spread south of the bay.

In 1845, when Pico's plan for selling and renting the Missions was formulated, Solano was declared without value, the secularization having been completely carried out, although there is an imperfect inventory of buildings, utensils, and church property. It was ignored in the final order. Of the capture of Sonoma by the Bear Flag revolutionists and the operations of Frémont, it is impossible here to treat. They are to be found in every good history of California.

In 1880 Bishop Alemany sold the Mission and grounds of San Francisco Solano to a German named Schocken for $3000. With that money a modern church was erected for the parish, which is still being used. For six months after the sale divine services were still held in the old Mission, and then Schocken used it as a place for storing wine and hay. In September, 1903, it was sold to the Hon. W. R. Hearst for $5000. The ground plot was 166 by 150 feet. It is said that the tower was built by General Vallejo in 1835 or thereabouts. The deeds have been transferred to the State of California and accepted by the Legislature. The intention is to preserve the Mission as a valuable historic landmark.

The church is about thirty-six feet long and sixteen feet wide. The vestibule is about fifteen feet square, and stairs

lead from it into the choir loft.   This vestibule is lathed
and plastered.   The front wall is about six feet thick, of
adobe faced with burnt red brick.   The side walls of the
church join the ceiling in a curve, instead of square, but
this effect, I believe, is produced by lath and plaster, and
is not a feature of the construction.   The interior condition
of the church can well be imagined after twenty-five years'
use as a hay barn.

The adjoining buildings are in even worse condition.
Unlike the church, which is roofed with shingles, these are
covered with tiles, but fully a fourth of them have fallen
in.   To protect the walls a temporary wooden roof has
been put up.   The building is divided longitudinally by
a thick wall of adobe, upon which poles rest supporting
the ridge poles.   The rafters are unhewn poles, and the
crosspieces are of rudely hewn planks, upon which bundles
of brush are placed, and, finally, the covering of red tiles.
The ceilings to the rooms are strongly constructed, the
beams being strong hewn logs with hewn planks laid across
them.   The marks of the adze or other tool are still clearly
to be seen on these logs and planks.   The attic was undoubtedly used for some purpose, possibly for the sleeping-
quarters of the Indian children, as at so many others of
the Missions.

This building is about ninety-five feet long, and the roof
overhangs on each side to cover the corridors, which are
constructed in the plainest, simplest fashion.   The corridor
roof is interesting, in that it is made of willows or other
brush laid across the roughly hewn rafters, then a strong
willow is laid at right angles, and the whole bound together
with rawhide thongs.

CHAPTER XXVII

THE MISSION CHAPELS OR ASISTENCIAS

THE Mission padres were the first circuit riders or pastors. It is generally supposed that the circuit rider is a device of the Methodist church, but history clearly reveals that long prior to the time of the sainted Wesley, and the denomination he founded, the padres were " riding the circuit," or walking, visiting the various rancherías which had no settled pastor.

Where buildings for worship were erected at these places they were called chapels, or asistencias. Some of these chapels still remain in use and the ruins of others are to be seen. The Mission of San Gabriel had four such chapels, viz., Los Angeles, Puente, San Antonio de Santa Ana, and San Bernardino. Of the first and the last we have considerable history.

LOS ANGELES CHAPEL

As I have elsewhere shown, it was the plan of the Spanish Crown not only to christianize and civilize the Indians of California, but also to colonize the country. In accordance with this plan the pueblo of San José was founded on the 29th of November, 1776. The second was that of Los Angeles in 1781. Rivera was sent to secure colonists in Sonora and Sinaloa for the new pueblo, and also for the establishments it was intended to found on the channel of Santa Barbara.

In due time colonists were secured, and a more mongrel lot it would be hard to conceive: Indian, Spanish, negro,

PLATE XLI

a. BRUSH CHURCH, BELLS, AND CROSS AT SANTA ISABEL

b. CAMPANILE AND CHAPEL, SAN ANTONIO DE PALA

Indian and Spanish, and Indian and negro bloods were represented, 42 souls in all. The blood which makes the better Spanish classes in Los Angeles to-day so proud represents those who came in much later.

There was nothing accidental in the founding of any Spanish colony. Everything was planned beforehand. The colonist obeyed orders as rigidly executed as if they were military commands. According to Professor Guinn:

" The area of a pueblo, under Spanish rule was four square leagues, or about 17,770 acres. The pueblo lands were divided into *solares* (house lots), *suertes*[1] (fields for planting), *dehesas* (outside pasture lands), *ejidos* (commons), *propios* (lands rented or leased), *realengas* (royal lands)."

On the arrival of the colonists in San Gabriel from Loreto on the 18th of August, 1781, Governor Neve issued instructions for founding Los Angeles on the 26th. The first requirement was to select a site for a dam, to provide water for domestic and irrigation purposes. Then to locate the plaza and the homes and fields of the colonists. Says Professor Guinn:

" The old plaza was a parallelogram 100 varas[2] in length by 75 in breadth. It was laid out with its corners facing the cardinal points of the compass, and with its streets running at right angles to each of its four sides, so that no street would be swept by the wind. Two streets, each 10 varas wide, opened out on the longer sides, and three on each of the shorter sides. Upon three sides of the plaza were the house lots 20 by 40 varas each, fronting on the square. One-half the remaining side was reserved for a guard-house, a town-house, and a public granary. Around the embryo town, a few years later, was built an adobe wall — not so much, perhaps, for protection from foreign invasion as from domestic intrusion. It was easier to wall in the town than to fence the cattle and goats that pastured outside."

[1] *Suerte.* This is colloquial. It really means " chance " or " haphazard." In other words it was the piece of ground that fell to the settler by " lot."

[2] A vara is the Spanish yard of 33 inches.

The government supplied each colonist with a pair each of oxen, mules, mares, sheep, goats, and cows, one calf, a burro, a horse, and the branding-irons which distinguished his animals from those of the other settlers. There were also certain tools furnished for the colony as a whole.

On the 14th of September of the same year the plaza was solemnly dedicated. A father from the San Gabriel Mission recited mass, a procession circled the plaza, bearing the Cross, the standard of Spain, and an image of " Our Lady," after which salvos of musketry were fired and general rejoicings indulged in. Of course the plaza was blessed and we are even told that Governor Neve made a speech.

As to when the first church was built in Los Angeles there seems to be some doubt. In 1811 authority was gained for the erection of a new chapel, but nowhere is there any account of a prior building. Doubtless some temporary structure had been used. There was no regular priest settled here, for in 1810 the citizens complained that the San Gabriel padres did not pay enough attention to their sick. In August of 1814 the corner-stone of the new chapel was laid by Padre Gil of San Gabriel, but nothing more than laying the foundation was done for four years. Then Governor Sola ordered that a higher site be chosen. The citizens subscribed five hundred cattle towards the fund, and Prefect Payeras made an appeal to the various friars which resulted in donations of seven barrels of brandy, worth $575. With these funds the work was done, José Antonio Ramirez being the architect, and his workers neophytes from San Gabriel and San Luis Rey, who were paid a real (twelve and a half cents) per day. Before 1821 the walls were raised to the window arches. The citizens, however, showed so little interest in the matter that it was not until Payeras made another appeal to his friars that *they* contributed enough to complete the work. Governor Sola gave a little, and the citizens a trifle. It is interesting to note what the contributions of the friars were. San Miguel offered 500 cattle, San Luis Obispo 200 cattle, Santa Barbara a barrel of brandy, San Diego two barrels of white wine, Purísima six mules and 200 cattle, San Fernando one barrel brandy, San Gabriel two barrels brandy, San Buenaventura said it would try to make up deficits or supply church furniture, etc. Thus Payeras's zeal and the willingness of the Los Angeleños to pay for wine and brandy, which they doubtless drank " to the success of the church," completed the structure, and December 8, 1822, it was formally dedicated. Auguste Wey writes:

" The oldest church in Los Angeles is known in local American parlance as ' The Plaza Church,' ' Our Lady,' ' Our Lady of Angels,' ' Church of Our Lady,' ' Church of the Angels,' ' Father Liébana's Church,' and ' The Adobe Church.' It is formally the church of Nuestra Señora, Reina de los Angeles — Our Lady, Queen of the Angels — from whom Los Angeles gets its name."

This latter statement is manifestly inaccurate, as the pueblo was named long before the church was even suggested.

The plaza was formally moved to its present site in 1835, May 23, when the government was changed from that of a pueblo to a city.

Concerning the name of the pueblo and river, Rev. Joachin Adam, Vicar General of the Diocese, in a paper read before the Historical Society of Southern California several years ago, said:

" The name Los Angeles is probably derived from the fact that the expedition by land, in search of the harbor of Monterey, passed through this place on the 2d of August, 1769, a day when the Franciscan missionaries celebrate the feast of Nuestra Señora de Los Angeles — Our Lady of the Angels. This expedition left San Diego July 14, 1769, and reached here on the first of August, when they killed for the first time some *berrendos,* or antelope. On the second, they saw a large stream with much good land, which they called Porciúncula on account of commencing on that day the jubilee called Porciúncula, granted to St. Francis while praying in the little church of Our Lady of the Angels, near Assisi, in Italy, commonly called Della Porciúncula from a hamlet of that name near by." This was the original name of the Los Angeles river.

The last two recorded burials within the walls of the Los Angeles chapel are those of the young wife of Nathaniel M. Pryor, " buried on the left-hand side facing the altar," and of Doña Eustaquia, mother of the Dons Andrés, Jesus, and Pio Rico, all intimately connected with the history of the later days of Mexican rule.

CHAPEL OF SAN MIGUEL

In 1803 a chapel was built at a ranchería called by the Indians *Mescaltitlan*, and the Spaniards San Miguel, six miles from Santa Barbara. It was of adobes, twenty-seven by sixty-six feet. In 1807 eighteen adobe dwellings were erected at the same place.

CHAPEL OF SAN MIGUELITO

One of the vistas of San Luis Obispo was a ranchería known as San Miguelito, and here in 1809 the Governor gave his approval that a chapel should be erected. San Luis had several such vistas, and I am told that the ruins of several chapels are still in existence in that region.

CHAPEL AT SANTA ISABEL (SAN DIEGO)

In 1816–19 the padres at San Diego urged the Governor to give them permission to erect a chapel at Santa Isabel, some forty miles away, where two hundred baptized Indians were living. The Governor did not approve, however, and nothing was done until after 1820. By

1822 the chapel was reported built, with several houses, a granary, and a graveyard. The population had increased to 450, and these materially aided San Diego in keeping the mountainous tribes, who were hostile, in check.

A recent article in a southern California magazine thus describes the ruins of the Mission of Santa Isabel:

" Levelled by time, and washed by winter rains, the adobe walls of the church have sunk into indistinguishable heaps of earth which vaguely define the outlines of the ancient edifice. The bells remain, hung no longer in a belfry, but on a rude framework of logs. A tall cross made of two saplings nailed in shape, marks the consecrated spot. Beyond it rise the walls of the brush building, *enramada,* woven of green wattled boughs, which does duty for a church on Sundays and on the rare occasions of a visit from the priest who makes a yearly pilgrimage to these outlying portions of his diocese. On Sundays, the General of the tribe acts as lay reader and recites the services. Then and on Saturday nights the bells are rung. An Indian boy has the office of bell-ringer, and crossing the ropes attached to the clappers he skilfully makes a solemn chime."

The graveyard at Santa Isabel is neglected and forlorn, and yet wears many evidences of the loving thoughtfulness of the loved ones who remain behind.

CHAPEL OF MESA GRANDE

Eleven miles or so from Santa Isabel, up a steep road, is the Indian village of Mesa Grande. The ranchería (as the old Spaniards would call it) occupies a narrow valley and sweep of barren hillside. On a level space at the foot of the mountain the little church is built. Santo Domingo is the patron saint.

A recent visitor thus describes it:

" The church was built like that of Santa Isabel, of green boughs, and the chancel was decorated with muslin draperies and ornaments of paper and ribbon, in whose preparation a faithful Indian woman had spent the greater part of five days. The altar was furnished with drawn-work cloths, and in a niche above it was a plaster image of Santo Domingo, one hand holding a book, the other outstretched in benediction. Upon the outstretched hand a rosary had been hung with appropriate effect. Some mystic letters appeared in the muslin that draped the ceiling, which, being interpreted, proved to be the initials of the solitary member of the altar guild, and of such of her family as she was pleased to commemorate."

CHAPEL OF SAN BERNARDINO

It must not be forgotten that one of the early methods of reaching California was inland. Travellers came from Mexico, by way of Sonora, then crossed the Colorado River and reached San Gabriel and Monterey in the north, over practically the same route as that followed to-day by the Southern Pacific Railway, viz., crossing the river at Yuma, over the Colorado desert, by way of the San Gorgonio Pass, and through the San Bernardino and San Gabriel valleys. It was in 1774 that Captain Juan Bautista de Anza of the presidio of Tubac in Arizona, was detailed by the Viceroy of New Spain to open this road. He made quite an expedition of it, — 240 men, women, and Indian scouts, and 1050 animals. They named the San Gorgonio Pass the Puerto de San Carlos, and the San Bernardino Valley the Valle de San José. Cucamonga they called the Arroyo de los Osos (Bear Ravine or Gulch).

As this road became frequented San Gabriel was the first stopping place where supplies could be obtained after crossing the desert. This was soon found to be too far away, and for years it was desired that a station nearer to the desert be established, but not until 1810 was the decisive step taken. Then Padre Dumetz of San Gabriel, with a band of soldiers and Indian neophytes, set out, early in May, to find a location and establish such a station. They found a populous Indian ranchería, in a region well

watered and luxuriant, and which bore a name significant
of its desirability. The valley was *Guachama*, " the place
of abundance of food and water," and the Indians had the
same name. A station was established near the place now
known as Bunker Hill, between Urbita Springs and Col-
ton, and a " Capilla " built, dedicated to San Bernardino,
because it was on May 20, San Bernardino's feast-day,
that Padre Dumetz entered the valley. The trustworthi-
ness of the Indians will be understood when it is recalled
that this chapel, station, and the large quantity of supplies
were left in their charge, under the command of one of
their number named Hipolito. Soon the station became
known, after this Indian, as Politana.

For two years prosperity smiled upon Politana. The
padres from San Gabriel visited it often, grain was planted
and good harvests reaped. Then came the sad year of the
earthquakes, " el año de los temblores." The hot springs
increased their temperature to such a degree that the Indians became alarmed; and the bursting out of a new hot
mud spring near Politana did not serve to quiet them. The
padres bade them cover up the spring with earth, but of
no avail. The " temblores " increased in power, the Indians' fears increased, their superstitions became more and
more aroused, and the soil of their minds was quickly prepared for the seed that was soon to be sown there. It can
readily be understood that the old Shamans (medicine men,
or native priests), of the Indians, had not viewed the destruction of their power by the padres with equanimity.
No man likes to feel his vocation taken from him by another, especially when that vocation is productive of wealth,
influence, and power. To be discredited and reduced to
poverty is enough to arouse in a civilized man a desire for
revenge. And thus it worked with the Indians. Now,
therefore, was their opportunity. Secretly they began to
work upon the newly aroused superstitious fears of their
fellows. These " temblores " were manifestations of the

dreadful anger of their gods, " Those Above " and " Those Below," because they had forsaken " the ways of the old," and had been led away into new and false paths by the " long gowns." These were only the beginnings. " Those Above and Below " had spoken to their earthly representatives; more evils were to come, — unless! Fear was now left to work and ferment awhile. Then the " unless " was explained, — " unless the long gowns and all renegade Indians were slain, stamped out, exterminated root and branch, and the accursed buildings erected for the more accursed worship were totally and completely destroyed. A few more " temblores " helped along the desire for vengeance, and at length, led by their medicine men, the now altogether aroused savages destroyed the buildings and slew most of the christianized Indians and later converts.

The destruction of Politana in 1810 was a source of great distress to the padres at San Gabriel, and they longed to rebuild. But the success of the attack of the unconverted Indians had reawakened the never long dormant predatory instincts of the desert Indians, and, for several years, these made frequent incursions into the valley, killing not only the whites, but such Indians as seemed to prefer the new faith to that of the old. But in 1819 the Guachamas sent a delegation to San Gabriel, requesting the padres to come again, rebuild the Mission chapel, and re-establish the supply station, and giving assurances of protection and good behavior. The padres gladly acceded to the requests made, and in 1820 solemn chants and earnest exhortations again resounded in the ears of the Guachamas in a new and larger building of adobe, erected some eight miles from Politana. The Indians soon settled around it, a resident priest was appointed from San Gabriel, a vineyard and olive orchard were planted, grain was extensively sown, herds of sheep and oxen covered the neighboring plains and foothills, a zanja was

built for conveying water for irrigation and domestic purposes, and an active and busy community was soon in full
operation.

For eleven years this peaceful life continued; and then,
in 1831, the desert Indians made another raid, destroying
the buildings and running off most of the stock. Fortunately no human lives were lost. And, as was their wont,
they resolutely set to work to rebuild, this time making
the chapel and residence buildings stronger than ever. A
foundation of cobblestones was put in, and walls of adobe
three feet thick crowned it to a height of 20 feet. The
structure was some 250 feet in length, and 125 feet in
width, and a corral added which extended nearly 100 feet
beyond the main building.

Scarcely had these new buildings become accustomed to
their occupants when the long-dreaded order of secularization was promulgated. Juan Bandini was appointed
to see that San Gabriel and all its dependencies were disposed of, according to the decree. This was in 1838–40.
But as early as October, 1834 (one year after the order
was issued), a band of Paiutis from over the Sierras, who
had been forced by famine to seek a new home for themselves, attacked the chapel of San Bernardino. The neophytes, led by a Christian Indian chief, named Perfecto,
defended themselves and their property with bravery and
courage. The invaders were repulsed again and again;
many lives were lost on both sides; and when, at last,
further resistance seemed hopeless, a sortie was made to
cause a diversion, while Perfecto gathered together all the
church vessels, vestments, and other valuable church property in three carretas, and started to San Gabriel. When
the Paiutis discovered the ruse they were infuriated, and
started in pursuit, but at Cucamonga were defeated, and,
consoling themselves with such stock as they had collected,
they beat a retreat into the mountains.

In December of the same year another attack was made;

but this time it was by two hundred native Indians, led by two war-chiefs who had once been neophytes at San Gabriel, but who felt they had real or fancied insults to avenge. As they marched to San Gabriel they stopped to anticipate their vengeance by destroying San Bernardino Chapel. The priest in charge, Padre Tomas Ellutario Estenaga, defended as well as he was able with his small band of neophytes, but the knowledge the attacking party had of the interior of the buildings and all their modes of defence materially nullified their efforts, and before long resistance was seen to be vain. The buildings were completely sacked and then set on fire. Padre Estenaga was captured and carried away to the mountains, where he undoubtedly would have been slain had it not been for the fear his captors entertained of him. They regarded him as a powerful medicine man, capable of working " strong medicine " to their undoing if they injured him, so he was finally released uninjured.

But never again was San Bernardino Chapel to resound to the sacred hymns and words of priests and dusky neophytes. Its work was accomplished. Now vandalism stepped in to finish with ruthless havoc the destruction the hatred of hostile Indians had begun. Many of the timbers used in the roof had been hewn in the mountains. These caught the eye of certain citizens of Los Angeles. Carretas were sent, and eleven loads were removed to be used in the construction of buildings in the newer city. Later on restitution was demanded of these respectable (?) vandals, and they paid three dollars per vara for the timber they had thus stolen. The adobes they took, however, were never accounted for. The bill for them is still outstanding; waiting for its final settlement when the Judge of all men shall ask of each an accounting for all the deeds done in the flesh.

There are a few ruined walls still standing of Bernardino at this time, but adobe rapidly disappears, and it will not be long before no smallest remnant will remain of this once prosperous and useful asistencia of the Mission of San Gabriel.

CHAPEL OF SANTA MARGARITA (SAN LUIS OBISPO)

One of the ranchos of San Luis Obispo was that of Santa Margarita on the north side of the Sierra Santa Lucia. As far as I know there is no record of the date when the chapel was built, yet it is a most interesting and important structure, even in its present utterly ruined and dilapidated condition. It is almost frontless, altogether roofless, and its interior has been wilfully destroyed within the last few years. And the work of destruction is now (May, 1904) going on, in order that it may be re-roofed and converted into a hay barn.

Situated on a knoll not far from the Santa Margarita river, a tiny stream which flows down from the Sierra Santa Lucia, it has the charm of close proximity to flowing water — a rarity in some parts of California. It is built northeast and southwest, with its front to the southwest. In order to get out the stones of which the interior division walls were made, and which have been deliberately pulled down, the front was recently almost entirely destroyed. So no picture can be presented of its *fachada*. It had an exquisite and rare outlook. Immediately before the doorway the grassy fields led the eye to the foothills and then the higher slopes of the Santa Lucia, where dense forests seem to exist. All around are live oaks, white and black oaks, sycamores and pines in abundance, and the flow of water could be utilized for irrigation and display in a fountain.

It originally consisted of a chapel about 40 feet long and 30 feet wide, and eight rooms. The chapel was at the southwest end. The whole building is 120 feet long and 20 feet wide. The walls are about three feet thick, and built of large pieces of rough sandstone and red bricks, all cemented strongly together with a white cement that is still hard and tenacious. It is possible there was no *fachada* to the chapel at the southwest end, for a well-built elliptical arched doorway still remains on the southeast side, which, most probably, was the main entrance. If this be so, then doubtless a window existed on the end, as the only other place pierced for a window is to the left of this doorway. Here the window-frame work still remains. It is of singular construction. Outside it appears to be square. Inside it is seen that this square part is a very thin portion of the wall, a kind of outer shell, the inside of which is beautifully arched and well built.

All the windows have this peculiar characteristic.

About midway in the remaining part of the building, on each side, is an elliptical arched doorway, and at the extreme southeastern corner is another, thus giving three doorway entrances to the residence portion of the structure. From the ruins of the partition walls it is easy to assume that there were eight rooms of about equal size, counting the halls as rooms. If this assumption be correct, then the windows would so tally as to give one window to a room, leaving out those that had a doorway entrance.

The question now arises: was this the only Mission building at Santa Margarita?

No! for near by are three old adobe houses, all recently renovated out of all resemblance to their original condition, and all roofed with red Mission tiles. These were built in the early days. The memory of the oldest Mexican inhabitants of the present-day Santa Margarita remembers them in childhood's happy years, so it is not unreasonable to assume that they were a part of the Mission buildings.

Here, then, is explanation enough for the assumption of a large Indian population on this ranch, which led the neighboring padres to establish a chapel for their christianization and civilization. Undoubtedly in its aboriginal

PLATE XLII

MAIN DOORWAY AT SANTA MARGARITA CHAPEL

days there was a large Indian population, for there were all the essentials in abundance. Game of every kind — deer, antelope, rabbits, squirrels, bear, ducks, geese, doves, and quail — yet abound; roots of every edible kind and more acorns than in any other equal area in the State. A never failing flow of mountain water and innumerable springs, as well as a climate at once warm and yet bracing, for here on the northern slopes of the Santa Lucia, frost is not uncommon.

What more natural, then, than that the padres should seek a closer contact with these large masses of unsaved souls, and diligently work to bring them into the bosom of the Church!

CHAPEL OF SANTA ISABEL (SAN MIGUEL)

I have elsewhere referred to the water supply of Santa Isabel as being used for irrigation connected with San Miguel Mission. There is every evidence that a large ranchería existed at Santa Isabel, and that for many years it was one of the valued rancheros of the Mission. Below the Hot Springs the remains of a large dam still exist, which we now know was built by the padres for irrigation purposes. A large tract of land below was watered by it, and we have a number of reports of the annual yield of grain, showing great fertility and productivity. Near the present ranch house at Santa Isabel are large adobe ruins, evidently used as a house for the majordomo and for the padre on his regular visitations to the ranchería. One of the larger rooms was doubtless a chapel where mass was said for the neophytes who cultivated the soil in this region.

CHAPEL OF SAN ANTONIO DE PALA

The chapel at Pala is perhaps the best known of all the asistencias on account of its picturesque campanile. It was built by the indefatigable Padre Peyri, in 1816, and is about twenty miles from San Luis Rey, to which it belonged. Within a year or two, by means of a resident padre, over a thousand converts were gathered, reciting their prayers and tilling the soil. A few buildings, beside the chapel, were erected, and the community, far removed from all political strife, must have been happy and contented in its mountain-valley home. The chapel is a long, narrow adobe structure, 144 by 27 feet, roofed with red tiles. The walls within were decorated in the primitive and singular fashion found at others of the Missions, and upon the altar were several statues which the Indians valued highly.

Pala is made peculiarly interesting as the present home of the evicted Palatingwa (Hot Springs) Indians of Warner's Ranch. Here these wretchedly treated " wards of the nation " are now struggling with the problem of life, with the fact ever before them, when they think, (as they often do, for several of them called my attention to the fact) that the former Indian population of Pala has totally disappeared. At the time of the secularization of San Luis Rey, Pala suffered with the rest; and when the Americans finally took possession it was abandoned to the tender mercies of the straying, seeking, searching, devouring homesteader. In due time it was " homesteaded." The chapel and graveyard were ultimately deeded back; and when the Landmarks Club took hold it was agreed that the ruins "revert to their proper ownership." The Club then took a lease on the property for the purpose of carrying out its intentions, which are elsewhere referred to.

Though all the original Indians were ousted long ago from their lands at Pala, those who lived anywhere within a dozen or a score miles still took great interest in the old buildings, the decorations of the church, and the statues of the saints. Whenever a priest came and held services a goodly congregation assembled, for a number of Mexicans, as well as Indians, live in the neighborhood.

That they loved the dear old asistencia was manifested by Americans, Mexicans, and Indians alike, for when the Landmarks Club visited it in December, 1901, and asked for assistance to put it in order, help was immediately volunteered to the extent of $217, if the work were paid for at the rate of $1.75 per day.

With a desire to promote the good feeling aimed at in recent dealings with the evicted Indians of Warner's Ranch, now located at Pala, the bishop of the diocese sent them a priest. He, however, was of an alien race, and unfamiliar with either the history of the chapel, its memories, or the feelings of the Indians; and to their intense indignation, they found that without consulting them, or his own superiors, he had destroyed all the interior decorations by covering them with a coating of whitewash.

CHAPTER XXVIII

THE PRESENT CONDITION OF THE MISSION INDIANS

THE disastrous effect of the order of secularization upon the Indians, as well as the Missions themselves, has been referred to in a special chapter. Here I wish to give, in brief, a clearer idea of the present condition of the Indians than was there possible. In the years 1833–1837 secularization actually was accomplished. The knowledge that it was coming had already done much injury. The Pious Fund, which then amounted to upwards of a half-million dollars, was confiscated — they called it "borrowed." This practically left the Indians to their own resources. A certain amount of land and stock were to be given to each head of a family, and tools were to be provided. Owing to the long distance between California and the City of Mexico, there was much confusion as to how the changes should be brought about. There have been many charges made, alleging that the fathers wilfully allowed the Mission property to go to ruin, when they were deprived of its control. This ruin would better be attributed to the general demoralization of the times than to any definite policy. For it must be remembered that the political conditions of Mexico at that time were most unsettled. None knew what a day or an hour might bring forth. All was confusion, uncertainty, irresponsibility. And in the *mêlée* Mission property and Mission Indians suffered.

What was to become of the Indians? Imagine the father of a family — that had no mother — suddenly snatched away, and all the property, garden, granary, mill, storehouse, orchards, cattle, placed in other hands. What would the children do?

So now the Indians, like bereft children, knew not what to do, and, naturally, they did what our own children would do. Led by want and hunger, some sought and found work and food, and others, alas, became thieves. The Mission establishment was the organized institution that had cared for them, and had provided the work that supported them. No longer able to go and live " wildly " as of old, they were driven to evil methods by necessity unless the new government directed their energies into right channels. Few attempted to do this ; hence the results that were foreseen by the padres followed.

July 7, 1846, saw the Mexican flag in California hauled down, and the Stars and Stripes raised in its place ; but as far as the Indian was concerned, the change was for the worse instead of the better. Indeed, it may truthfully be said that the policies of the three governments, Spanish, Mexican, and American, have shown three distinct phases, and that the last is by far the worst.

Our treatment of these Indians reads like a hideous nightmare. Absolutely no forceful and effective protest seems to have been made against the indescribable wrongs perpetrated. The gold discoveries of 1849 brought into the country a class of adventurers, gamblers, liquor sellers, and camp followers of the vilest description. The Indians became helpless victims in the hands of these infamous wretches, and even the authorities aided to make these Indians " good."

Bartlett, who visited the country in 1850 to 1853, tells of meeting with an old Indian at San Luis Rey who spoke glowingly of the good times they had when the padres were there, but " now, he said, they were scattered about, he knew not where, without a home or protectors, and were in a miserable, starving condition." Of the San Francisco Indians he says:

" They are a miserable, squalid-looking set, squatting or lying about the corners of the streets, without occupation. They have now no means of obtaining a living, as their lands are all taken from them; and the Missions for which they labored, and which provided after a sort for many thousands of them, are abolished. No care seems to be taken of them by the Americans; on the contrary, the effort seems to be to exterminate them as soon as possible."

According to the most conservative estimates there were over thirty thousand Indians under the control of the Missions at the time of secularization in 1833. To-day, how many are there? I have spent long days in the different Mission localities, arduously searching for Indians, but oftentimes only to fail of my purpose. In and about San Francisco, there is not one to be found. At San Carlos Borromeo, in both Monterey and the Carmelo Valley, except for a few half-breeds, no one of Indian blood can be discovered. It is the same at San Miguel, San Luis Obispo, and Santa Barbara. At Pala, that romantic chapel, where once the visiting priest from San Luis Rey found a congregation of several hundreds awaiting his ministrations, the land was recently purchased from white men, by the United States Indian Commission, as a new home for the evicted Palatingwa Indians of Warner's Ranch. These latter Indians, in recent interviews with me, have pertinently asked: " Where did the white men get this land, so they could sell it to the Government for us? Indians lived here many centuries before a white man had ever seen the ' land of the sundown sea.' When the ' long gowns ' first came here, there were many Indians at Pala. Now they are all gone. Where? And how do we know that before long we shall not be driven out, and be gone, as they were driven out and are gone? "

At San Luis Rey and San Diego, there are a few scattered families, but very few, and most of these have fled far back into the desert, or to the high mountains, as far as possible out of reach of the civilization that demoralizes and exterminates them.

A few scattered remnants are all that remain.

Let us seek for the real reason why.

The system of the padres was patriarchal, paternal. Certain it is that the Indians were largely treated as if they were children. No one questions or denies this statement. Few question that the Indians were happy under this system, and all will concede that they made wonderful progress in the so-called arts of civilization. From crude savagery they were lifted by the training of the fathers into usefulness and productiveness. They retained their health, vigor, and virility. They were, by necessity perhaps, but still undeniably, chaste, virtuous, temperate, honest, and reasonably truthful. They were good fathers and mothers, obedient sons and daughters, amenable to authority, and respectful to the counsels of old age.

All this and more may unreservedly be said for the Indians while they were under the control of the fathers. That there were occasionally individual cases of harsh treatment is possible. The most loving and indulgent parents are now and again ill-tempered, fretful, or nervous. The fathers were men subject to all the limitations of other men. Granting these limitations and making due allowance for human imperfection, the rule of the fathers must still be admired for its wisdom and commended for its immediate results.

Now comes the order of secularization, and a little later the domination of the Americans. Those opposed to the control of the fathers are to see the Indians free. They are to be " removed from under the irksome restraint of cold-blooded priests who have held them in bondage not far removed from slavery "!! They are to have unrestrained liberty, the broadest and fullest intercourse with the great American people, the white, Caucasian American, not the dark-skinned Mexican!!!

The authority of the priesthood being abolished, this beneficent intercourse begins!! Now see the rapid elevation in morals, honor, chastity, integrity, and all the virtues!! Gaze with amazement and delight upon the glorious blessings conferred upon the weak by the strong race!! Thank God, with uplifted eyes and hand, for all the mental and spiritual graces that begin to pour into the minds and souls of those benighted heathen, when they are removed from the benumbing influences of superstitious and ignorant Catholicism. Yes, indeed, let us sing pæans of joyous praises for the good that the aborigines now hold in free and absolute mastery.

Ah! hypocrites and vile! How I could wish for the power of Shakspere to show you in your true light. Richard of Gloster was not so vile a murderer, so ruthless a destroyer, so black-hearted a villain, so contemptible a plotter, so mean a layer of snares as the white race has been, whereby to trap, entangle, and exterminate the dusky race whose lands they coveted and determined to possess.

Had they been left in the hands of the Mission fathers, the Indians would slowly but surely have progressed to racial manhood. Given over to our own tender mercies, they have been hurried down an incline smeared by white men with every known form of slippery evil, in order that their destruction might be the more rapid and complete. Until we are able, nationally, to cleanse our own skirts from the blood of these trustful, weak, helpless aborigines, let us not insult the memory of the Mission fathers by asking, parrot-like: " For what end? "

The only real ground for criticism of the padres, to my mind, lies here. Their care of the Indians was too great, too fatherly. They treated their wards too much like children, instead of training them for the duties of citizenship. Hence they succumbed easily to the vices of civilization when the restraining influences were removed. I used to think this criticism a just one. It appeared to me that the kindness was a mistaken one; that greater freedom would have given greater responsibility, — especially had more time and attention been given to teaching them this responsibility. Yet, the more I think of it, the more puerile the criticism becomes. Peoples are not civilized in a day. Even our own sons and daughters, with all our training, now and again succumb to evil and go down as far as did these Indians, though we are constant and persistent in our efforts to save them.

Another difficulty in the way of rapid progress was the great distance from supplies and the lack of men. Communication with California was by water or land, and from far distant points. It was not an easy journey from Spain, via Mexico, to California. The overland trip from Mexico, whether by way of San Blas and then up the peninsula on horseback, or by way of Sonora and the deserts of Arizona and California was not a matter to be undertaken lightly. I should much like to start out a caravan of the critics of the padres, over either route, and in a modern air-ship (improved pattern) watch their performances. I am inclined to believe they would make a far worse mess of it than the padres did of educating and christianizing the Indians. It required *men* — men of stalwart conviction, men of courage, daring, and ability to undertake the journey, let alone the work when they arrived. And when the fact is recalled that, in the earlier days, some of these priests were left alone for months at a time at their respective stations, can we wonder that more than one of them went insane with the pressure of it. Solitariness is often a far harder burden to bear than actual physical pain or suffering; yet these devoted men faced even the dreaded solitariness rather than neglect the call, the voice they had heard.

With such training, therefore, they resented the interference of the politicians with their work. They saw the awful results that were sure to come. And in their resistance to the unjust encroachments of unprincipled men we have the secret of most of the criticism.

I think it can plainly be stated that the whole trouble arose from man's accursed greed for gold. It is well known that according to the rule of St. Francis every member of the order was pledged to certain things, one of which was perpetual poverty, another obedience. We have seen how, in the early days, those priests who came to California sacrificed all that men ordinarily hold dear. Little by little they built up their Missions in what had been a strange land, and they converted the savages into useful workers. Personally not one of them could own a dime's worth of property (unless, of course, he were a perjured scoundrel, and it is scarcely worth while to consider the prejudices of those who could regard any of the early padres as such), and if they did now and again enjoy the pleasures of the table, who shall cast a first stone at them for that? Their leaders were wise enough to see that when the influx of population came, as it was almost inevitable it should, the Indians would not be considered as having a first claim, unless they, as their guardians, protected them in their natural rights, — the rights of priority and nativity on the soil. Slowly they were christianizing and civilizing them. Of very necessity it was a slow process. The English, the French, the Germans, — aye, and the boasting Americans, — have been civilized none too rapidly. It does not need a very deep scratch to reveal the innate savagery of the best of us, and why should we expect these people to be civilized with such great speed.

The padres knew that secularization must come — sometime. They hoped it would not come too soon. In time they could have made their wards more independent, better developed mentally, more able to cope with " the world." When Mexico became the battle-field of adventurers, the coyote and vulture politicians began to assert themselves, and in the Missions they saw a good opportunity for the exercise of their peculiar functions. The padres withstood them, bravely, nobly, constantly, until the power brought to bear was too great to be longer resisted. What were they fighting for? Did it mean personal wealth to them? All they could possibly get out of it was their daily bread, as they were required by the law of their order to report constantly to their superiors as to the growth of flocks, herds, etc., and what became of them. The early reports of the padres were models of completeness; nothing was neglected; everything was accounted for. Who, then, can justly accuse them of selfishness in their stern resistance to the decrees of the politicians. They could have done no other without being recreant to the trust the helplessness of the Indians had imposed upon them. It was as if authorities of a hospital or an orphan asylum battled for the preservation of the institution that was essential to the care-taking of the helpless sick or young. Perhaps their pride in their organization had something to do with it, and I, for one, do not propose to find fault with them for that. It was a good organization for the work to be performed, and it did its work well; and it is no credit either to the republic of Mexico or, later, to the United States of America that more strenuous efforts were not made to preserve to the padres the right to continue their fatherly oversight over the Indians for a while longer.

An eye-witness, writing of events in the early fifties, thus recounts the Los Angeles method of *christianizing* the Mission Indians:

"These thousands of Indians had been held in the most rigid discipline by the Mission Fathers, and after their emancipation by the Supreme Government of Mexico, had been reasonably well governed by the local authorities, who found in them indispensable auxiliaries as farmers and harvesters, hewers of wood and drawers of water, and beside the best horse-breakers and herders in the world, necessary to the management of the great herds of the country. These Indians were Christians, docile even to servility, and excellent laborers. Then came the Americans, followed soon after by the discovery of, and the wild rush for, gold, and the relaxation for the time being of a healthy administration of the laws. The ruin of this once happy and useful people commenced. The cultivators of vineyards began to pay their Indian *peons* with *aguardiente*, a real 'firewater.' The consequence was that on receiving their wages on Saturday evening, the laborers habitually met in great gatherings and passed the night in gambling, drunkenness, and debauchery. On Sunday the streets were crowded from morning until night with Indians, — males and females of all ages, from the girl of ten or twelve to the old man and woman of seventy or eighty.

"By four o'clock on Sunday afternoon, Los Angeles Street, from Commercial to Nigger Alley, Aliso Street from Los Angeles to Alameda, and Nigger Alley, were crowded with a mass of drunken Indians, yelling and fighting: men and women, boys and girls using tooth and nail, and frequently knives, but always in a manner to strike the spectator with horror.

"At sundown, the pompous marshal, with his Indian special deputies, who had been confined in jail all day to keep them sober, would drive and drag the combatants to a great corral in the rear of the Downey Block, where they slept away their intoxication. The following morning they would be exposed for sale, as slaves for the week. Los Angeles had its slave-mart as well as New Orleans and Constantinople, — only the slaves at Los Angeles were sold fifty-two times a year, as long as they lived, a period which did not generally exceed one, two, or three years under the new dispensation. They were sold for a week, and bought up by vineyard men and others at prices ranging from one to three dollars, one-third of which was to be paid to the *peon* at the end of the week, which debt, due for well-performed labor, was invariably paid in *aguardiente*, and the Indian made happy, until the following Monday morning, he having passed through another Saturday night and Sunday's saturnalia of debauchery and bestiality. Those thousands of honest, useful people were absolutely destroyed in this way."

In reference to these statements of the sale of the Indians as slaves, it should be noted that the act was done under the cover of the law. The Indian was "fined" in a certain

sum for his drunkenness, and was then turned over to the
tender mercies of the employer who paid the fine. Thus
" justice " was perverted to the vile ends of the conscience-
less scoundrels who posed as " officers of the law."

To-day, the total Indian population of Southern California is reported by the agent as two thousand eight hundred fifty-five. It is not increasing, and it is good for the
race that it is not. Until the incumbency by W. A. Jones of
the Indian Commissionership in Washington, there seems to
have been little or no attempt at effective protection of the
Indians against the land and other thefts of the whites.
The facts are succinctly and powerfully stated by Helen
Hunt Jackson in her report to the government, and in
her " Glimpses of California and the Missions." The
indictment of churches, citizens, and the general government, for their crime of supineness in allowing our ac-
knowledged wards to be seduced, cheated, and corrupted,
should be read by every honest American; even though
it make his blood seethe with indignation and his nerves
quiver with shame.

Anno Domini 1903, the Indians of Warner's Ranch, by
a decree of the United States Supreme Court, affirming the
decisions of the highest State courts, were evicted from the
homes which they had occupied from time immemorial, and
which had been pledged to them and their successors by
General Kearney and others in authority, on behalf of the
United States government.

At this time, the Indian Department, under W. A. Jones,
then the commissioner, made the first honest and practical
attempt to come to the rescue of its wards. A hundred
thousand dollars was appropriated to find them a new
home, but some of this has been wasted by the incompetency
of self-constituted advisers and minor official stupidity and
incapacity. Let it suffice to say that to-day these Indians
are upon land where they cannot make a living, unless
large sums of money shall be expended in an irrigation-

scheme to convey water to their lands; they are "converted" from a self-sustaining, brave, and independent people to so many paupers looking to the government for rations; they regard every white man as a liar; one man who has especially posed as their friend they view with a hatred approaching a murderous sentiment, and, were they as warlike and strong numerically as the Sioux, the War Department would be confronted with another Indian war.

In other villages and tribes the same demoralization is apparent.

A short time ago I had a long, confidential interview with Marcos, once a chief of the Indian village at Palm Springs. Among other things, we discussed the morality of the women of his people. With a dejection in which there seemed to be no hope, the poor fellow stated that the burden of life was so hard for his people that he had long ceased to regard with anger the immorality of the women, young or old, married or single. " So long as they can get something to eat thereby, why should we care?" he sadly asked. " It is not easy to be good when the hunger is in the stomach and when one offers you a dollar to do that which is easy, though evil!"

This is one of the saddest proofs of the demoralization of this people. When the leaders have ceased to care; when the struggle has become so hard as to seem to be hopeless, then, indeed, are they in bad case.

To show the actual state of land matters among the Indians of Southern California, I present the subjoined table from the report of the agent for the " Mission-Tule" Consolidated Agency, which is dated September 25, 1903.

This is the official report of an agent whom not even his best friends acknowledge as being over fond of his Indian charges, or likely to be sentimental in his dealings with them. What does this report state? Of twenty-eight " reservations " — and some of these include several Indian villages — it announces that the lands of eight are

PLATE XLIII

a. FIGURE OF SAN JOSÉ

b. SAN ANTONIO DE PADUA,
SANTA BARBARA

c. SAN ANTONIO DE PADUA,
SAN CARLOS

d. SAN JUAN CAPISTRANO

yet " not patented." In other words, that the Indians are
living upon them " on sufferance." Therefore, if any cit-
izen of the United States, possessed of sufficient political
power, so desired, the lands could be restored to the public
domain. Then, not even the United States Supreme Court
could hold them for the future use and benefit of the
Indians.

On five of these reservations the land is " desert," and
in two cases, " subject to intense heat " (it might be said,
to 150 degrees, and even higher in the middle of summer) ;
in one case there is " little water for irrigation."

In four cases it is " poor land," with " no water," and in
another instance there are " worthless, dry hills ; " in still
another the soil is " almost worthless for lack of water! "

In one of the desert cases, where there are five villages,
the government has supplied " water in abundance for
irrigation and domestic use, from artesian wells." Yet the
land is not patented, and the Indians are helpless, if evicted
by resolute men.

At Cahuilla, with a population of one hundred fifty-five,
the report says, " mountain valley; stock land and little
water. Not patented."

At Santa Isabel, including Volcan, with a population of
two hundred eighty-four, the reservation of twenty-nine
thousand eight hundred forty-four acres is patented,
but the report says it is " mountainous; stock land; no
water."

At San Jacinto, with a population of one hundred forty-
three, the two thousand nine hundred sixty acres are
" mostly poor; very little water, and not patented."

San Manuel, with thirty-eight persons, has a patent for
six hundred forty acres of " worthless, dry hills."

Temecula, with one hundred eighty-one persons, has had
allotted to its members three thousand three hundred sixty
acres, which area, however, is " almost worthless for lack
of water."

Name of Reservation	Number of Acres	Population	Distance from Agency (Miles)	General Character of Land
Agua Caliente (Palm Springs)	3,844.00	31	50	Desert land, subject to intense heat; little water for irrigation. Patent.
Augustine	615.00	....	75	Desert; no water. Patent issued.
Torres (Alimo Bonito, Agua Dulce, Martinez, and Torres villages) and including Walters.	19,200.00	304	75	Desert land; intense heat; water in abundance for irrigation and domestic use from artesian wells furnished by the government. Not patented.
Cahuilla	18,240.00	155	35	Mountain valley; stock land; little water. Not patented.
Capitan Grande	10,253.00	118	118	Portion good; very little water. Patent issued.
Campo	280.00	14	170	Poor land; no water. Patent issued.
Cuaypipa	880.00	36	125	As above.
Cabazon	640.00	38	27	Desert; productive now, since government has furnished artesian water with reservoirs for irrigation and domestic use. Patent issued.
Injaya	280.00	42	100	Small amount of poor land. Patent issued.
Los Coyotes (San Ignacio and San Isidro villages).	22,640.00	106	85	Mountainous; very little farming land. Not patented.
Morongo	38,600.00	287	25	Fair land, with water. Not patented.
Mesa Grande	120.00	....	75	Small amount of farming land; little water; portion good; stock land. Patent issued.

Pala	3,598.00	258	40	Good land; water. Small portion allotted.
Pauma	250.00	67	50	Portion good land, with water. Not patented.
Potrero (La Jolla and La Piche)	8,329.12	203	75	Portion good: water on part. Allotted.
Rincon	2,552.81	175	65	Sandy; portion good, with water. Patented and allotted.
Syquan	640.00	42	110	Small amount of agricultural land. Patent issued and allotted.
Santa Isabel, including Volcan . .	29,844.96	284	80	Mountainous; stock land; no water. Patented.
San Felipe	. . . . . .	45	85	Will be moved to Pala.
San Jacinto	2,960.00	143	6	Mostly poor; very little water. Not patented.
San Manuel	640.00	38	55	Worthless; dry hills. Patent issued.
Santa Rosa	. . . . . .	52	. . . .	Unsurveyed.
Santa Inés . . .	a175.00	51	240	Land matter adjusted satisfactorily to the Indians. Splendid land, with abundance of water.
Tule River	45,000.00	146	450	Good reservation. Small amount farming land; mostly mountain grazing.
La Posta	238.88	. . . .	170	Poor land; no water. Not patented.
Manzanita	640.00	. . . .	170	As above.
Temecula	3,360.00	181	35	Almost worthless for lack of water, Allotted.
Twenty-nine Palms	160.21	36	190	Desert. Patent issued.
Agua Caliente No. I, Mataguay, Puerta La Cruz, San José.	. . . . . .	. . . .	. . . .	All known as Warner's ranch; moved to Pala and included in Pala statistics.

a Estimated.

Let us reflect upon these things! The poor Indian is exiled and expelled from the lands of his ancestors to worthless hills, sandy desert, grazing lands, mostly poor and mountainous land, while our powerful government stands by and professes its helplessness to prevent the evil. These discouraging facts are enough to make the just and good men who once guided the republic rise from their graves. Is there a remnant of honor, justice, or integrity, left among our politicians?

There is one thing this government should have done, could have done, and might have done, and it is to its discredit and disgrace that it did not do it; that is, when the treaty of Guadalupe-Hidalgo transferred the Indians from the domination of Mexico to that of the United States, this government " of, for, and by " the people, should have recognized the helplessness of its wards and not passed a law of which they could not by any possibility know, requiring them to file on their lands, but it should have appointed a competent guardian of their moral and legal rights taking it for granted that *occupancy of the lands of their forefathers would give them a legal title which would hold forever against all comers.*

In all the Spanish occupation of California it is doubtful whether one case ever occurred where an Indian was driven off his land.

In rendering a decision on the Warner's Ranch Case the United States Supreme Court had an opportunity offered it, once for all to settle the status of all American Indians. Had it familiarized itself with the laws of Spain, under which all Spanish grants were made, it would have found that the Indian was always considered first and foremost in all grants of lands made. He must be protected in his right; it was inalienable. He was helpless, and therefore the officers of the Crown were made responsible for his protection. If subordinate officers failed, then the more urgent the duty of superior officers. Therefore, even

PLATE XLIV

a. CHRIST DISPUTING IN THE TEMPLE

b. THE ARCHANGEL GABRIEL

c. THE ARCHANGEL MICHAEL

d. THE ARCHANGEL RAPHAEL

had a grant been made of Warner's Ranch in which the grantor purposely left out the recognition of the rights of the Indians, the higher Spanish courts would not have tolerated any such abuse of power. This was an axiom of Spanish rule, shown by a hundred, a thousand precedents. Hence it should have been recognized by the United States Supreme Court. It is good law, but better, it is good sense and common justice, and this is especially good when it protects the helpless and weak from the powerful and strong.

In our dealings with the Indians in our school system, we are making the mistake of being in too great a hurry. A race of aborigines is not raised into civilization in a night. It will be well if it is done in two or three generations.

Contrast our method with that followed by the padres. Is there any comparison? Yes! to our shame and disgrace. The padres kept fathers and mothers and children together, at least to a reasonable degree. Where there were families they lived — as a rule — in their own homes near the Missions. Thus there was no division of families. On the other hand, we have wilfully and deliberately, though perhaps without *malice aforethought* (although the effect has been exactly the same as if we had had malice), separated children from their parents and sent them a hundred, several hundred, often two or three *thousand* miles away from home, there to receive an education often entirely inappropriate and incompetent to meet their needs. And even this sending has not always been honorably done. *Vide* the U. S. Indian Commissioner's report for 1900. He says:

"These pupils are gathered from the cabin, the wickiup, and the tepee. *Partly by cajolery and partly by threats; partly by bribery and partly by fraud; partly by persuasion and partly by force,* they are induced to leave their homes and their kindred to enter these schools and take upon themselves the outward semblance of civilized life. They are chosen not on account of any particular merit of their own, not by reason of mental fitness, but solely because they have Indian blood in their veins. Without regard to their worldly condition; without any previous training; without any preparation whatever, they are transported to the schools — sometimes thousands of miles away — without the slightest expense or trouble to themselves or their people.

The Indian youth finds himself at once, as if by magic, translated from a state of poverty to one of affluence. He is well fed and clothed and lodged. Books and all the accessories of learning are given him and teachers provided to instruct him. He is educated in the industrial arts on the one hand, and not only in the rudiments but in the liberal arts on the other. Beyond the three r's he is instructed in geography, grammar, and history; he is taught drawing, algebra and geometry, music and astronomy and receives lessons in physiology, botany, and entomology. Matrons wait on him while he is well, and physicians and nurses attend him when he is sick. A steam laundry does his washing, and the latest modern appliances do his cooking. A library affords him relaxation for his leisure hours, athletic sports and the gymnasium furnish him exercise and recreation, while music entertains him in the evening. He has hot and cold baths, and steam heat and electric light, and all the modern conveniences. All the necessities of life are given him, and many of the luxuries. All of this without money and without price, or the contribution of a single effort of his own or of his people. His wants are all supplied almost for the wish. The child of the wigwam becomes a modern Aladdin, who has only to rub the government lamp to gratify his desires.

Here he remains until his education is finished, when he is returned to his home — which by contrast must seem squalid indeed — to the parents whom his education must make it difficult to honor, and left to make his way against the ignorance and bigotry of his tribe. Is it any wonder he fails? Is it surprising if he lapses into barbarism? Not having earned his education, it is not appreciated; having made no sacrifice to obtain it, it is not valued. It is looked upon as a right and not as a privilege; it is accepted as a favor to the government and not to the recipient, and the almost inevitable tendency is to encourage dependency, foster pride, and create a spirit of arrogance and selfishness.

The testimony on this point of those closely connected with the Indian employees of the service would, it is believed, be interesting."

So there the matter stands. Nothing of any great importance was really done to help the Indians except the conferences at Mohonk, N. Y., until, in 1902, the Sequoya League was organized, composed of many men and women of national prominence, with the avowed purpose " to make better Indians." In its first pronunciamento it declared:

" The first struggle will be not to arouse sympathy but to inform with slow patience and long wisdom the wide-spread sympathy which already exists. We cannot take the Indians out of the hands of the National Government; we cannot take the National Government into our own hands. Therefore we must work with the National Government in any large plan for the betterment of Indian conditions.

" The League means, in absolute good faith, not to fight, but to assist the Indian Bureau. It means to give the money of many and the time and brains and experience of more than a few to honest assistance to the Bureau in doing the work for which it has never had either enough money or enough disinterested and expert assistance to do in the best way the thing it and every American would like to see done."

CHAPTER XXIX

DISTINCTIVE FEATURES OF MISSION ARCHITECTURE

THE broader knowledge we gain of the Franciscan Mission structures, the greater becomes our respect for their architects and builders. Their boldness, originality, and diversity at once please and instruct us. It is not my purpose, in this chapter, to analyze all the varied forms of the Mission architecture, or to discuss technically the successes or the failures consequent upon their use. Purely as a layman, addressing himself to those sufficiently interested to allow one without technical knowledge to comment upon details which give marked individuality to these generally similar structures, I shall call attention to some general features, and then expatiate upon the details. As a rule, the Missions were built in the form of a hollow square: the church representing the *fachada*, with the priests' quarters and the houses for the Indians forming the wings. These quarters were generally colonnaded or cloistered, with a series of semicircular arches, and roofed with red tiles. (See Plate 25 a.) In the interior was the *patio* or court, which often contained a fountain and a garden. Upon this *patio* opened all the apartments: those of the fathers and of the majordomo, and the guest-rooms, as well as the workshops, schoolrooms and storehouses.

The Indians' quarters were generally the most secluded parts of the premises. The young girls were separated rigidly from the boys and youths; the first-named being under the guardianship of staid and trustworthy Indian women. The young charges were taught to weave, spin,

PLATE XLV

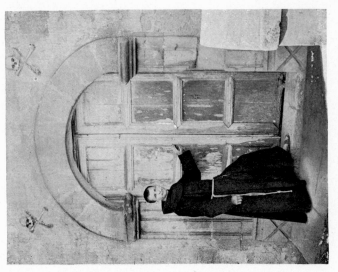

sew, embroider, make bread, cook, and to engage generally
in domestic tasks, and were not allowed to leave the " convent " until they married.

From Plate 31 b, showing the *fachada* of the Santa
Barbara Mission, a few details may be noted. Here the
engaged columns form a striking feature, there being six
of them, three on either side of the main entrance. The
capital here used is the Ionic volute. The entablature is
somewhat Grecian, the decoration being a variant of the
Greek fret. The pediment is simple, with heavy dentals
under the cornice. A niche containing a statue occupies
the centre.

The first story of the towers is a high, plain, solid wall
with a simply moulded cornice, composed of few, but heavy
and simple members, upon which rest the second and third
stories each receding about half the thickness of the walls
below. Each story is furnished with a cornice similar to
the one below, and the two upper stories are pierced with
semicircular arches for bells. The walls of the second
story are four feet three inches in thickness, and the lower
walls are sustained by massive buttresses at the sides.
Both towers are surmounted by semicircular domes of
masonry construction with cement finish, above which rests
the lantern surmounted by the cross. This lantern is a
marked feature of Mission construction. It is seen above
the domes at San Buenaventura, San Luis Rey, San Xavier
del Bac (Arizona), as well as on one or two of the old
churches at San Antonio, Texas.

Another Mission feature is the addition to the pediment.
This consists of a part of the main front wall raised above
the pediment in pedestal form, and tapering in small steps
to the centre, upon which rests a large iron cross. This
was undoubtedly a simple contrivance for effectively supporting and raising the Emblem of Salvation, in order
thereby more impressively to attract the attention of the
Indian beholder.

This illustration also shows the style of connecting the priests' quarters in the manner before described. There is a colonnade with fourteen semicircular arches, set back from the main *fachada*, and tiled, as are the roofs of all the buildings.

The careful observer may note another distinctive feature which is seldom absent from the Mission domes. This is the series of steps at each " corner " of the half-dome. Several eminent architects have told me that the purpose of these steps is unknown, but to my simple lay mind it is evident that they were placed there purposely by the clerical architects to afford easy access to the surmounting cross; so that any accident to this sacred symbol could be speedily remedied. It must be remembered that the fathers were skilled in reading some phases of the Indian mind. They knew that an accident to the Cross might work a complete revolution in the minds of the superstitious Indians whose conversion they sought. Hence common, practical sense demanded speedy and easy access to the cross in case such emergency arose.

Entirely different, yet clearly of the same school, is the Mission San Gabriel. The stone church elsewhere pictured was not completed until 1785. In this the striking feature is the campanile, from which that of the Glenwood Hotel, Riverside, was undoubtedly modelled. This construction consists of a solid wall, pierced at irregular intervals with arches built to correspond to the size of the bells which were to be hung within them. The bells being of varying sizes, there could be no regularity in the arrangement of the arches, yet the whole bell-tower is beautiful in outline and harmonious in general effect. On the left, the wall is stepped back irregularly up to the centre bell aperture, each step capped with a simple projecting moulded cornice, as at Santa Barbara. The upper aperture is crowned with a plain masonry elliptical arch, upon which rests a wrought iron finial in the form of a cross.

The walls of San Gabriel are supported by ten buttresses with pyramidal copings. (See Plate 5 a.) Projecting ledges divide the pyramids into three unequal portions. In some of these buttresses are niches, embellished with pilasters which support a complete entablature. At the base of these niches is a projecting sill, undoubtedly a device for the purpose of giving greater space or depth in which to place statues. On the concave surfaces of these niches and the entablatures it is possible that the architects designed to have distemper paintings, as such decoration is often found on both exterior and interior walls, although sometimes it has been covered by vandal whitewashers. In several of the Missions, the spandrels of the arches show evidence of having been decorated with paintings, fragments of which still remain.

Plate 37 a represents San Luis Rey, by many regarded as the king of California Mission structures. In this illustration will be seen one of the strongest features of this style, and one that has had a wide influence upon our modern architecture. This feature consists of the stepped and curved sides of the pediment.

I know no commonly received architectural term to designate this, yet it is found at San Luis Rey, San Antonio de Padua, Santa Inés, and at other places. At San Luis Rey, it is the dominant feature of the extension wall to the right of the *fachada* of the main building.

On this San Luis pediment occurs a lantern which architects regard as misplaced. Yet the fathers' motive for its presence is clear: that is, the uplifting of the Sign whereby the Indians could alone find salvation.

In the *fachada* at San Luis there are three niches for statues: one on either side of the doorway, and one in the centre of the pediment. It will be noticed that the *fachada* is divided into three unequal portions. The ends of the two outer walls of the main building are faced with pilasters which support the cornice of the pediment. Below the cornice and above the entablature is a circular window. The entablature is supported by engaged columns, upon which rests a heavily moulded cornice; the whole forming a pleasing architectural effect about the doorway, the semi-circular arch of which is especially fine.

It will be noticed by reference to Plate 31 b, that on the towers at Santa Barbara there is a chamfer at each corner. At San Luis Rey this detail is different, in that the chamfer is replaced by an entire flat surface. The tower thus becomes an irregular octagon, with four greater and four lesser sides. These smaller sides answer the same decorative purpose as the chamfer at Santa Barbara. The same idea is also worked out in the dome, which is not a hemisphere, but which prolongs the exaggerated chamfers of the stories below.

There is little doubt that the original design provided for a second tower to be erected at San Luis Rey, uniform with the existing one.

Santa Inés shown in Plates 2 and 38 b, presents pleasing features. Here the *fachada* is exceedingly simple; the bell-tower being a plain wall pierced as at San Gabriel. The same pyramidal feature, used here as an ornament for the four corners, and the curved pediment please the eye, and satisfy the desire for strength and grace. The rear view, 38 b, shows the massiveness of the walls and the extra reinforcement of them by means of the buttresses.

While simple and chaste, the two churches of San Carlos Borromeo — one in the ancient town of Monterey, and the other seven miles away in El Carmelo Valley — have a peculiar interest and fascination, since they were the home-churches of the saintly Serra himself. At the Valley church (Plate 3 b), lovingly called Carmelo by the neighboring people, Serra lived, worked, prayed, died, and was buried. By Padre Casanova it was restored some fifteen years ago, and the body of Serra was sought, identified, and recovered. Here the egg-shaped dome, surmounted by an ornament holding up the cross, is the principal architectural attraction, although the starred window of the *fachada*, under the semicircular cornice, and the ornamental doorway are also striking and pleasing features.

At Monterey (Plate 25 b) the *fachada* and tower are of entirely different character, although superficial observers remark upon the similarity of these features to those of the Valley church. The tiled pyramidal covering of the tower is especially pleasing, as is seen in Plate 8 a. At the four corners of the tower stand simple but effective finial ornaments, and in the centre of the front is a similar ornament, elevated upon a sloping base or pedestal.

This pyramidal tiled tower is a useful and structural device. It is perfectly adapted to its two purposes, viz., the uplifting of the bells and the cross: the former that, as the sound peals forth, it may reach further, and the latter that it may be seen at a long distance and also that it may surmount, crown, and dominate every other object of the building.

Even after this cursory survey, one cannot fail to observe the differences in *fachadas*, pediments, *campaniles* (bell-towers), columns, buttresses, door and window arches, etc., presented by Mission architecture. Some of these we shall now consider in detail.

1. *Fachadas.* Opinion is divided as to which is the most striking, pleasing, and architecturally correct of the Mission *fachadas*. Perhaps that of Santa Barbara (Plate 31 b) would receive the largest number of votes, were the question to be decided by such a test. Those whose tastes incline toward the more ornate Spanish styles, would choose between the two San Carlos buildings at Monterey. It will be easily conceded that in elaborateness of design the Monterey *fachada* leads all others. But elaborateness is not always the most pleasing quality, nor yet is it always

united with perfection.   The simple dignity of the Carmelo *fachada*, the doorway, the central star-window, with
the severely plain gable, broken only by the impressive
sweep of the semicircular arch, make a pleasing combination which is worthy of study.

That of San Luis Rey (Plate 37 a) is, perhaps, the most
distinctive of them all.   It contains all those features which
are recognized as typically " Mission " : such as the curved
and stepped pediment, the lantern crowning the same, and
the two-storied, pierced bell-tower, with chamfered corners
and lantern crown.

The *fachada* of San Francisco de Asís (Dolores), which
is presented in Plate 7 a, differs widely from any of the
others.   It has two stories, resting upon a solid, projecting double foundation, the front of which is cemented.
The lower story consists of four columns, two on either
side of the doorway, the arch of which is supported
by simple right-angled stone doorposts, crowned with a
half-round cornice.   The base consists of a double plinth
and a narrow fillet or cushion, upon which the plain shaft
rests.   Its cap is simple, being composed of two enlarged
sections of the shaft, divided by a fillet, and topped with a
plain abacus.

A double membered cornice now stretches across the
whole building and becomes the base for the upper portion
of the *fachada;* thus forming a kind of rude entablature.
Resting upon this cornice, yet retired somewhat behind
the lower columns, are six engaged columns ; the two outer
ones being but three or four feet high, the second pair
somewhat higher, and the inner pair from six to eight
feet in height.   In the central space between the two highest
columns, the wall is pierced by a rectangular void ; room
being thus afforded for a small bell.   In the two next outer
spaces, similar piercings occur, the tops of which are
arched, and in these hang two larger bells.   Each bell has
a wooden carriage to which it is fastened with rawhide

PLATE XLVI

b. AUXILIARY ARCH, SAN JUAN CAPISTRANO

a. DOORWAY AT SAN ANTONIO DE PADUA

thongs, the latter giving an excellent example of the toughness and durability of this material.

The use of rawhide instead of nails for the fastening together of building timbers, as well as for swinging bells, was often resorted to by the Mission builders. At San Fernando, San Antonio, San Miguel, San José and San Francisco, beams and rafters are thus fastened.

The remaining vestiges of the San Diego *fachada* (Plate 3 a), are similar in style to the central part of that of San Luis Rey (Plate 37 a), although it is less elaborate than its near northern and later-built neighbor.

San Gabriel is peculiar in construction, as it has no *fachada;* the side of the church, with its buttresses and stairway into the choir gallery forming the main front. Attached to this, at the left, stands the *campanile* (Plate 5 a), without which the entire structure would be dull and ineffective. Of a similar character, and yet quite different in detail is the *fachada* of Santa Inés (see Plate 2). Here the end of the church, with the addition of the *campanile*, serves as the *fachada;* since the wall at the right containing the bells is a solitary wall, as can be seen from an examination of Plate 38 b. It is the *campanile*, in each case attached to the church wall, which gives dignity and character to the *fachada* at San Gabriel and Santa Inés.

San Luis Obispo (Plate 5 b), San Juan Bautista (Plate 34 a), and San Miguel (Plate 36 a), make no pretence to imposing *fachadas*. The chief entrance is at the end of the main church building. Somewhat more elaborate, and made imposing with its massive tower at the right, and large hipped buttress at the left, is the *fachada* of San Buenaventura (Plate 7 b). Here, too, the arched and corniced doorway, with the simple pilasters, and the triangular entablature pierced by a square window aperture and a bracketed niche for a statue, break the monotony felt in the three previously named structures.

Santa Cruz much resembled San Buenaventura, as a

glance at Plate 31 a will show, although it will be noted
that there are but two buttresses; that there is no triangular entablature; and that the tower recedes, instead
of projecting along the right wall as at San Buenaventura.

San Rafael had a side entrance at one end of the church
building with twin star-windows, one above the other.

Most interesting and unique, perhaps, in this respect,
is San Antonio de Padua, imperfectly shown in Plate 38 a.
Here the *fachada* is built some ten or twelve feet in advance
of the front end of the church.   Then, the intervening
space is arched over to form a closed entrance.   This
fachada is of burnt brick, although the church is of adobe,
and, while the latter is in sad ruins, the former is almost
as perfect as when built.   At the bottom are three arched
entrances: all being semicircular, and the largest in the
centre.   The pediment is of the Mission order, and will be
later described.   Above the entrances are three piercings
for bells; the lateral ones contained in tower-like exten-
sions, which were formerly surmounted by crosses.   The
monotony of the plain brick-work is destroyed by a series
of dividing cornices, one of which reaches across from the
bases of the entrance arches.   The next higher cornice
stretches unbrokenly across from the bases of the two side
bell-towers, followed by a third, which extends from the
bases of the arches of the side towers, forming a base for
the central bell piercing.   There is still a fourth cornice
above this upper bell arch, and all the three bell spaces
are likewise divided by simple cornices.   The result is a
most pleasing whole.

2. *Pediments.*   At first one might believe that little or
no diversity could occur in the Mission pediments, yet
important variations may be observed.   If we take that of
San Luis Rey as the typical curved and stepped pediment,
we shall find that it stands absolutely alone.   Let us analyze it.   Beginning at the lantern, we find that this detail
rests upon a flat top, making a sharp downward curve to

the perpendicular and resting on a narrow horizontal platform; then, a concave and convex curve reaches another horizontal platform, followed by a final concave and convex curve to the supporting cornice.

Now compare this with five other existing pediments. That of San Gabriel has already been described. It is the pediment of the *campanile* (Plate 5 a). That of San Carlos at Monterey shows a long, sweeping, convex curve, with a flat termination at the bottom, and scrolls at the top connecting with a slight arch. It can scarcely be placed in the same class.

The pediment of San Diego (Plate 3 a) is in ruined condition, showing merely the double (concave and convex) curve; while that of Santa Inés (Plate 2) is a pediment to the *campanile*. Here we find a succession of convex curves; three in the series dropping down from the central arch on which the cross rests, make the pediment. The pediment of San Antonio (Plate 38 a) is again different. The bricks of the crown are stepped, there being eight or nine layers. Then follows a double brick cornice, the edges of the brick being moulded to the half-round. Next is a concave curve, a perpendicular step, resting on a flat platform, followed by two more concave curves of unequal length.

Here, then, we have the proof that of six Mission pediments no two are alike.

3. *Campaniles.* The bell-towers show almost equal diversity. There are eleven Missions which had (or have) distinct bell-towers, not including the quaint one at the Pala Asistencia. The points of similarity between San Gabriel and Santa Inés have been already indicated, and the uniqueness of that of San Antonio has been discussed. San Luis Obispo formerly had three pierced apertures in the main wall of the church above the doorway, shown in Plate 5 b; but when the restoration took place, this interesting feature was abolished by blocking up the apertures

and building an ugly, inharmonious, detached wooden tower. The same style of aperture characterizing San Luis, it will be remembered, is that which obtains at Dolores (San Francisco).

San Juan Capistrano has a unique *campanile*, since it is composed of a wall joining two buildings, and pierced with four apertures, as shown in Plate 30 a.

Of bell-towers proper, there are six; the best known being those of Santa Barbara and San Luis Rey. Between these two there are only slight differences, which already have been indicated. The bell-tower of San Buenaventura (Plate 7 b) is very similar except that it shows no chamfers, and that the corner finials are different. The tower of Santa Cruz has disappeared, but it belonged practically to the same class.

Entirely dissimilar, and also different from each other, are the towers of the two Missions at Monterey. The Mission in the Carmelo Valley, with the egg-shaped dome, and the Mission at Monterey with the pyramidal red-tiled roof, are well pictured in Plates 3 b and 25 b, although Plate 8 a accentuates the charm of the latter structure.

The Pala *campanile* (Plate 41 b) is unique, not only in California, but in the world. Built upon a pyramidal base, it is a peculiar pedimental structure standing alone. It is two stories high, each story being pierced with a bell aperture. There are two pediment curves, and three cornices which break the monotony of its face. It was undoubtedly built by the same hands that fashioned San Luis Rey.

4. *Columns.* Superficial observers have often condemned the use of certain columns in recent buildings, contending that they were not " Mission columns." But here, as in every other branch of architecture, the Mission builders enjoyed variety. A careful survey of the illustrations already published in this series will show more than one

kind of column. It will be observed that I shall use
the word in its broad, and not in its rigidly technical
sense.

Of engaged columns in imitation of the classical style,
two marked examples are found: at Santa Barbara
(Plate 31 b), and at San Luis Rey (Plate 9). In this
illustration it will be observed that the entablature of the
reredos of the mortuary chapel has four engaged columns
with Ionic capitals, like those at Santa Barbara, which
have been already described.

This mortuary chapel at San Luis Rey is most beautiful
even in its desolation. Octagonal in form, it was entered
from the church; the doorway occupying one side of the
figure, and the altar the opposite side. At each angle is
an engaged column built of brick, the front part of which
only is rounded. The rear part is rectangular and fits into
the ordinary brick of the wall, allowing the rounded surface to project. As will be seen from the picture, these
columns are capped with a three-membered cornice, also
of brick; and, springing from column to column, there is a
series of arches which serve to ornament the sides of the
octagon.

Plate 40 shows the ruined entrance to the San Luis Rey
garden, in which there occur two engaged columns which
have not yet lost all their original charm and beauty.

Columns, engaged and disengaged, are seen on the
fachada of the San Francisco de Asís (Dolores) Mission
(Plate 7 a).

The square piers for the colonnades of nearly all the
Missions are similar to those pictured in Plate 25 a and in
Plate 22. These square piers are built of brick and
plastered. At Santa Barbara, they have chamfered corners, and occasionally, as in the colonnade of the *patio*
at San Antonio de Padua, they are built of adobe; but
generally burnt bricks were used. At La Purísima Concepción, the nineteen remaining pillars are square, with

21

chamfered and fluted corners; some of them being brick, some of stone, and some of adobe, and all plastered.

The " gnawing tooth of time " wears away objects that are neglected much more quickly than those which are cherished. Here destruction proceeds in increasing ratio. The exposed brick-work of the piers of the colonnade at San Antonio is rapidly " eroding," and if nothing be done to arrest the decay, the masonry will soon crumble and fall.

5. *Pilasters.* Under this head two illustrations must suffice. Plate 66 a shows the side entrance of San Luis Rey. Here it will be seen that the supporting column of the entablature above the side entrance is of chamfered and fluted brick. Much of the Missioners' brick was thus moulded at San Luis and elsewhere: a point worthy of note. As it is difficult to make plaster adhere to adobe, in order to obtain an anchorage, the adobe walls, here and in other Mission buildings, were divided into lozenges, into which small pieces of brick were placed. These lozenges can be seen near the foot of the stairway in the picture and they are observable in many exposed portions of the walls throughout the whole line of the Missions.

At the side entrance to the church at San Buenaventura, a perfectly plain pilaster (except for the cornices) is used, and the general effect is good. (Plate 45 b.) This plain method was employed by the Mission builders in many places, for arches, door and window-frames, etc. The effect of this archway is most interesting, as showing how the Mission fathers brought with them and utilized memories of the old world. The arch is Moorish-Gothic, with renascence *motifs* in the entablature. The cross, as is evident, is a modern intrusion, to replace a lost, or stolen statue.

There is an ornate clustered column at San Carlos. It is the entrance to the chapel of the Sacred Heart of Jesus. Here is a distinct reminiscence of the Arch of the Two Sisters in the Alhambra. The arch is Moorish-Gothic, with distinctive renascence features in the columns and the entablature. It is, without question, the most ornate piece of architectural detail found on the long line of the Missions.

6. *Arches.* To treat the various Mission arches as the subject deserves would require many more pages than can be afforded. The variety, although nearly all of them are included within the limits of simplicity, is far greater than one might suppose.

Of prime interest, because it was probably the first arch built, and in any case, the principal arch of the first Mission established, is the main entrance at San Diego. (Plate 18 a.) The austere simplicity of this arch is most pleasing. It is structural and therefore satisfying; the more it is examined, the more it grows upon the observer. The simplicity of the device by which it is made to stand out should be observed. The bricks of which it is built are brought forward a few inches in advance of the main wall. Then, at the arch, the wall itself is recessed another inch or two, and arch and recess are crowned with a five-membered cornice; the members being plain flat brick, and each row set forward an inch or two beyond the row beneath.

Plate 18 b is interesting as showing a distributing arch of adobe at San Antonio. The arch proper is of brick, as is also the first distributing arch. Between the two are laid horizontal adobe bricks with above a second distributing arch, the latter of adobe bricks.

In Plate 15 is seen the square, plain arch in one of the doorways of the buildings at San Juan Capistrano. Here, except for the central decoration of the lintel, the whole frame is simple. In this picture, too, it is interesting to note the brick bases of the corridor seats.

At the same Mission, and now used as the entrance to the chapel, is one of the most ornate of the stone-work doorways found in the Missions of the Southwest. (Plate 26 a.) Indeed, the stone-work of the arches as a whole, at San

Juan, suggest that this Mission was the object of more care and work than any of the others. This fact is evident from the most cursory survey of Plates 26 a and 34 b. Here is cut stone-work done by master hands; all the piers and arches being of work that the best craftsmen of to-day would be proud to own.

The doorway here shown is of gray sandstone; the keystone, projecting several inches, being carved in a conventional eight-pointed floral design, from which a wide, deep fluting extends either side down the jambs and shows vase-like carving. Above there is an entablature, the main feature of which is a two-inch half-rounded fillet terminating in cross lines on each side. A heavy cornice crowns the whole.

In a number of instances both door and window arches are made square on one side and, owing to the thickness of the walls, they are recessed and rounded on the other, as in Plate 46 a, which shows the doorway to the church at San Antonio de Padua. The same effect is produced in stone at the Santa Margarita chapel (Plate 16), in which the arches of both doors and windows are deeply recessed.

But more striking, beautiful, and structural is another doorway at the same chapel, shown in Plate 42. Here, the curve of the ellipse of the outer side is greater than that of the inside. There are several double arches at La Purísima, as are those at Santa Margarita, but they are all built of adobe. A little to the southeast of the centre of the ruins is a beautiful arch. It opens into a shut-in room at the end of which is a piece of well executed brick-work ten feet in diameter.

Another effect, often found in the door and window arches, is pictured in Plate 6 a, which shows the square entrance on the church side at San Juan Bautista, and the pointed and curved effect within the recess on the sacristy side. With this curve as a *motif*, there are many changes played upon it in Mission door and window arches. An arch somewhat similar to the one here presented is seen in the window above the doorway leading into the graveyard at Santa Barbara, although the arch is much flatter.

At San Luis Rey, the curved *motif*, worked out differently and without the point, is shown in the arch leading from the church to the chapel of the Third Order of St. Francis, and pictured in Plate 6 b. Here three convex curves meet at a certain central convex curve, thus adding another pleasing variation to those already noted.

Plate 19 a presents the arch and entablature over the doorway leading from the altar to the sacristy at San Carlos Carmelo. Here the elliptical arch, with its corresponding elliptical cornice, is most effective and strong. The structural power of these simple arches, to my mind, contrasts most favorably with the effect of the more ornate ones in the Monterey church, one of which is shown in Plate 19 b. Here the direct influence of the Moorish-Gothic-Renascence is apparent. Indeed, no pretence is made that this is other than a copy of many similar doorways occurring in Spain. The arch, with the renascence scroll and the conventionalized design of the entablature, of which the egg-and-dart pattern is the chief feature, connect it closely with its European prototypes.

It is interesting here to note at the two Monterey churches, what is doubtless the direct influence of Padre Serra. In the archways, the columns, and the towers, there is an attempt at adornment of the more ornate character, which is not usually found in the other Missions. Four Missions, alone, of the earlier buildings, are prominent as expressions of architectural zeal and fervent affection. These are: I. San Luis Rey, in which Peyri's dominating mind revealed itself in a building which many consider the king, indeed, of all the Mission structures. It also revealed the builder's love and almost feminine tenderness in the exquisite quality of the octagonal chapel dedicated to the Third Order of St. Francis. II. San Juan Capistrano, in its pristine grandeur, surpassed, perhaps, all the others. Even the ruins speak eloquently of the love and devotion of its builders. The stone-work is more substantial and structural, and the ornamentation more artistic and pleasing than we find them in any other building. III. San Antonio de Padua, although built of brick and adobe, was a structure reared by affection. The *fachada* has been already discussed, and throughout the building, the lavish care and love of the priestly builder are evident. By reason of the short lives of these buildings, such indications of affection are intensely pathetic. What visions of centuries of power and influence must have cheered the faithful sons of Holy Church as they planned the structures destined so soon to crumble into ruin through the neglect of a ruthless people. But is love ever lost? Can affection ever be bestowed in vain? Only in the assurance that love is never really wasted, can we find comfort, as we stand in the presence of these eloquent ruins. IV. The fourth of these especially favored buildings is that of San Carlos Carmelo. Here Serra's power and love are felt, since this building was the object of his adoration. While the whole California field, in the wider sense, occupied his heart and energy, it was upon Carmelo that he expended his most immediate affection. This was his home, his special abiding-place; therefore tower, star-window, arches, columns, and walls evidence his influence.

Santa Barbara and Santa Inés came later, and they rightly belong to this same class of specially favored builders.

But to return to the details. At San Antonio, there are a number of recessed window arches; the frame being square, while the arch within is elliptical. One of these occurs in the wall of the monastery and affords a view of the wooded plain beyond, stretching away as far as the eye can reach; while, to the right, the live-oak clad hills lead up to the deep-blue California sky. We may here picture a monk of the olden days, sitting in meditation and transported in thought to a similar landscape in far-away Spain. We can imagine him thus meditating until his whole nature became saturated with the nostalgia that kills. Little by little his reason gave way, and he died while alive, as true a martyr as if he had been burned at the stake or pierced by a thousand arrows. Such a picture may seem a mere phantom of the imagination, but, alas! it had several proofs of truthfulness in the early days of the last century.

Plate 26 b shows the use at San Juan Capistrano of two elliptical arches of differing axes placed side by side, in the front corridor. It is not easy to explain this singularity, unless by assuming that as the wider elliptical arch is the later one, it was so constructed, either because a wider space was needed, or the builder regarded the variation as a pleasing one. Individual taste alone could decide such a question.

This peculiar feature of the difference in span of the arches occurs at several of the Missions and should be noted, for, as yet, I have seen no rational explanation of it. The rooms, too, are seldom perfect parallelograms and the pillars are often irregular. These latter imperfections are less noteworthy than the differences in the arches, though the same explanation is generally afforded for all alike, viz., that the work was done by the Indians, who had no idea of regularity. In the first place the assumption that they were incapable as to measurements is entirely gratuitous and fictitious, as the perfection of their work, mathematically considered, in shaping ollas, baskets, pottery, etc., demonstrates. And it is scarcely to be assumed, anyhow, that they erected these arches without direct supervision. So that I am led to believe, that possibly these irregularities, instead of being attributable to the Indians, were owing to the lack of care of the white artisans who were imported to instruct them.

Two other arches at San Juan Capistrano demand attention. Plate 24 is remarkable in that six arches are superposed one upon another in the perspective. The one in the foreground is an elliptical arch in the corridor. Next follows the arch in the wall of the *pteroma*,[1] a square bricked doorway. On the other side of the building is a semicircular arch over the doorway leading into the *patio*. Across on the other side of the court is another elliptical corridor-arch, behind which, dimly to be seen, are another elliptical arched doorway and a square arched gateway.

The quadrangle at San Juan was originally surrounded by corridors with picturesque semicircular and elliptical arches. At the northeast corner, where the *pteroma* made a right angle, an auxiliary arch was introduced with most picturesque effect. (Plate 46 b.) Such an arch is strongly structural, as a support to the corners of the two meeting lines of arches, and also to the roof covering the *pteroma*. The corner pier of the series thus becomes the resting-place of the bases of three arches, the other spandrel of the auxiliary arch resting upon a pier built triangularly into the wall. I do not know of a similar arch in any other of the Mission corridors.

Thirty-eight arches still remain on three sides of the *patio* at San Juan. There are none remaining on the western side.

Another glance at Plate 26 b will reveal the picturesque, although simple chimney at San Juan. A few hours' labor in placing the brick tiles produced a pleasing feature out of a necessity too often abandoned to extreme ugliness. It is suggestive in its possibilities for modern buildings.

In the same illustration and in Plate 24 the simple device

---

[1] Pteroma: the side or flank, hence, in modern usage, the space covered by the roof of a portico, and therefore including the columns and intercolumniations, although in general usage it applies only to the passage between the columns and the wall behind. — RUSSELL STURGIS.

PLATE XLVII

a. WOODEN STATUE AT SAN MIGUEL MISSION

b. CORBELS AND RAFTERS OF SAN MIGUEL MISSION

used for the ornamentation of the cornice of the corridor arches is clearly presented. The corners of thin flat brick tiles are placed obliquely on the top of the wall, then a heavier brick is set over these, square with the wall beneath.

Before concluding this chapter, I must refer to the heavy and massive buttresses found in nearly all the Mission buildings. Some of these are clearly seen in Plates 8 b, 7 b, 30 b, 32 b, and 38 b. Nearly all observers, on first seeing them, ask the reason of their massiveness. But when it is remembered that San Juan Capistrano, La Purísima, San Juan Bautista and others suffered severely from the shocks of earthquakes in the early part of the last century, the motive for these tremendous masses becomes apparent. They were made extra large and heavy as a precaution against future disaster.

Many more details might be presented with both interest and profit, but the ones chosen I regard as the most important. They at least suggest that, although the Mission architects and builders were dominated by one common style, they were, by no means, servile imitators of originals, or copyists of one another.

CHAPTER XXX

THE INTERIOR DECORATIONS OF THE MISSIONS

WE cannot to-day determine how the Franciscans of the southwest decorated the interiors of all their churches. Some of these buildings have disappeared entirely; while others have been restored or renovated beyond all semblance of their original condition. But enough are left to give us a satisfactory idea of the labors of the fathers and of their subject Indians. At the outset, it must be confessed that while the fathers understood well the principles of architecture and created a natural, spontaneous style, meeting all obstacles of time and place which presented themselves, they showed little skill in matters of interior decoration, possessing neither originality in design, the taste which would have enabled them to become good copyists, nor yet the slightest appreciation of color-harmony. In making this criticism, I do not overlook the difficulties in the way of the missionaries, or the insufficiency of materials at command. The priests were as much hampered in this work as they were in that of building. But, in the one case, they met with brilliant success; in the other they failed. The decorations have, therefore, a distinctly pathetic quality. They show a most earnest endeavor to beautify what to those who wrought them was the very home of God. Here mystically dwelt the very body, blood, and reality of the Object of Worship. Hence the desire to glorify the dwelling-place of their God, and their own temple. The great distance in this case between desire and performance is what makes the result pathetic. Instead of trusting to themselves, or reverting

PLATE XLVIII

a. OLD PULPIT AT SAN MIGUEL MISSION

b. JUNCTION OF CHOIR AND CHURCH ZONES OF DECORATION,
SAN MIGUEL MISSION

to first principles, as they did in architecture, the missionaries endeavored to reproduce from memory the ornaments with which they had been familiar in their early days in Spain. They remembered decorations in Catalonia, Cantabria, Mallorca, Burgos, Valencia, and sought to imitate them; having neither exactitude nor artistic qualities to fit them for their task. No amount of kindliness can soften this decision. The results are to be regretted; for I am satisfied that, had the fathers trusted to themselves, or sought for simple nature-inspirations, they would have given us decorations as admirable as their architecture. What I am anxious to emphasize in this criticism is the principle involved. Instead of originating or relying upon nature, they copied without intelligence. The rude brick, adobe, or rubble work, left in the rough, or plastered and whitewashed, would have been preferable to their unmeaning patches of color. In the one, there would have been rugged strength to admire; in the other there exists only pretence to condemn.

After this criticism was written I asked for the opinion of the learned and courteous Frays Glauber and Zephyrin, the former the guardian of Santa Barbara Mission, and the latter the Franciscan historian. In reply I received the following letter which so clearly gives another side to the matter that I am glad to quote it entire:

" I do not think your criticism from an artistic view is too severe; but it would have been more just to judge the decorations as you would the efforts of amateurs, and then to have made sure as to their authors.

" You assume that they were produced by the Padres themselves. This is hardly demonstrable. They probably gave directions, and some of them, in their efforts to make things plain to the crude mind of the Indians, may have tried their hands at work to which they were not trained any more than clerical candidates or university students are at the present time; but it is too much to assume that those decorations give evidence even of the taste of the Fathers.   In that matter, as in everything else that was not contrary to faith or morals, they adapted themselves to the taste of their wards, or very likely, too, to the humor of such stray "artists" as might happen upon the coast, or whom they might be able to import.   You must bear in mind that in all California down to 1854 there were no lay-brothers accompanying the Fathers to perform such work as is done by our lay-brothers now, who can very well compete with the best of secular artisans.   The church of St. Boniface, San Francisco, and the church of St. Joseph, Los Angeles, are proof of this.   Hence the Fathers were left to their own wits in giving general directions, and to the taste of white "artists," and allowed even Indians to suit themselves.   You will find this all through ancient Texas, New Mexico, and Arizona.   The Indians loved the gaudy, loud, grotesque, and as it was the main thing for the Fathers to gain the Indians in any lawful way possible, the taste of the latter was paramount.

"As your criticism stands, it cannot but throw a slur upon the poor missionaries, who after all did not put up these buildings and had them decorated as they did for the benefit of future critics, but for the instruction and pleasure of the natives.   Having been an Indian missionary myself, I acted just so.   I have found that the natives would not appreciate a work of art, whereas they prized the grotesque.   Well, as long as it drew them to prize the supernatural more, what difference did it make to the missionary?   You yourself refer to the unwise action of the Pala priest in not considering the taste and the affection of the Indians."

Another critic of my criticism insists that, "while the Indians, if left to themselves, possess harmony of color which seems never to fail, they always demand startling effects from us."   This, I am inclined to question.   The Indians' color-sense in their basketry is perfect, as also in their blankets, and I see no reason for the assumption that they should demand of us what is manifestly so contrary to their own natural and normal tastes.

It must, in justice to the padres, be confessed that, holding the common notions on decoration, it is often harder to decorate a house than it is to build it; but why decorate at all? The dull color of the natural adobe, or plaster, would have at least been true art in its simple dignity of architecture, whereas when covered with unmeaning designs in foolish colors even the architectural dignity is detracted from.

I am willing to allow my criticism to remain as I wrote it. It is no less a tribute to the great hold the work of the padres has on my heart that I am ready frankly to criticise it.

One writer says that the colors used in these interior decorations were mostly of vegetable origin and were sized with glue. The yellows were extracted from poppies, blues from nightshade, though the reds were gained from stones picked up from the beach. The glue was manufactured on the spot from the bones, etc., of the animals slaughtered for food.

As examples of interior decoration, the Missions of San Miguel Arcángel and Santa Inés are the only ones that afford opportunity for extended study. At Santa Clara, the decorations of the ceiling were restored as nearly like the original as possible, but with modern colors and workmanship. At Pala Chapel, within the last three or four months, the priest judged dead white preferable to the old decorations, and, greatly to the indignation of the Indians, whose wishes he did not consult, he has whitewashed the mural distemper paintings out of existence. A small patch remains at San Juan Bautista merely as an example; while a splashed and almost obliterated fragment is the only survival at San Carlos Carmelo.

At San Miguel, little has been done to disturb the interior, so that it is in practically the same condition as it was left by the padres themselves. Fr. Zephyrin informs me that these decorations were done by one Murros, a Spaniard, whose daughter, Mrs. McKee, at the age of over eighty, is still alive at Monterey. She told him that the work was done in 1820 or 1821. He copied the designs out of books, she says, and none but Indians assisted him in the actual work, though the padres were fully consulted as it progressed.

Plate 35 shows the interior of the church. As its arrangement is not unlike many of the others, and the decorations, necessarily, are dependent upon the various functions performed in different parts of the building, I shall take the privilege of describing San Miguel interior in detail, with a chief eye, however, upon the mural decorations. Five distinct divisions deserve attention. These are: I. the reredos and its ornaments; II. the ceiling; III. the walls; IV. the old pulpit; V. the ancient confessional.

I. *The Reredos.* This occupies the entire western end of the church, reaching from the floor to the ceiling. (Plate 35.) The altar now in use is modern; with the remainder just as it came from the hands of the fathers. The reredos consists of three panels; the central one containing the wooden statue of San Miguel, and the side panels showing other saints. The San Miguel, representing the patron of the Mission, is a striking statue, about six feet in height, and much larger than the side statues. In his right hand he holds the scales and in his left a sword, on which is inscribed a Latin motto. The bracket upon which he stands is the original one cut and painted by the fathers. It is rude, heavy, and composed of simple members: namely, a slightly rounded base supporting a thick block with quarter-round, square, and round moulding.

The statue at the left of the altar is clothed in the garb of the Franciscan, with beard, tonsured head, outstretched hands, and one foot upon a skull.

Plate 47 a shows the figure to the right. It is tonsured, shaven, and wears the Franciscan garb. The panels are divided from one another by coupled columns; those supporting the pediment of the centre panel standing out about two feet in front of the others, and having two flat

PLATE XLIX

b. DOORWAY LEADING INTO SACRISTY AT SANTA INÉS

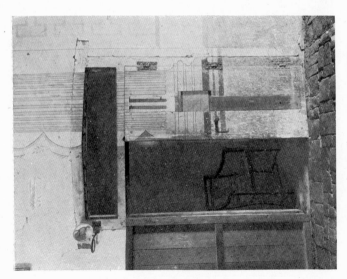

a. OLD CONFESSIONAL AT SAN MIGUEL

engaged columns at their back. The bases of these columns are simple, half-rounded mouldings, the shaft is a plain cylinder, and the capital a dual leaf, as if in rude imitation of the Corinthian. The entablature is simple and effective, its centre bearing a large All-Seeing Eye, radiating beams of light. Above this and over each side panel is a bracket sustaining an ornament in the shape of a chalice, each connected with the other across the whole face of the altar by clusters of grapes and leaves. These chalices have each a cover and two handles. The rays issuing from the centre piece bear evidences of having afforded a resting-place for owls and other night birds during the days when the Mission was abandoned. Even now, as I sit writing, I hear the cooing of many doves that nest under the open eaves, through which feathers come floating into the sacred edifice.

The pillars are mottled in imitation of marble, and the altar and mural decorations are in colors, chief of which are blue, green, red, pink, and pale-green. The base of the panellings is pink.

On the left, above the statue, is an oval panel painted with the two crossed hands of the Christ, showing the nail-holes of the cross. On the other side is a similar oval panel, decorated with symbolic figures.

There are two side altars, the one at the right sacred to the Holy Mother; and the other to Saint Joseph and the Holy Child. The figure of the Madonna is modern, but the painting is old and well illustrates the artistic ideas of the fathers. A similar painted canopy covers the old figure of San José.

II. *The Ceiling.* This can be studied in Plate 35. There are twenty-eight rafters upholding the roof, and extending completely across the church. Each rafter rests upon a corbel which can be seen a little more distinctly in Plate 47 b. Both rafters and corbels are rough-hewn from the solid trees and they have sustained unimpaired to the present day the heavy weight of the roof. This is estimated to be not less than two hundred thousand pounds. The rafters are each ten by twelve inches in the square, and fully forty feet long. They were cut in the mountains at Cambria, forty miles away, and carried by the Indians to their destination. These rafters protrude some twelve inches or so through the wall, to which they are fastened or keyed with large wooden spikes.

Over the altar, the corbels are tinted a light green, and the ceiling and rafters pink. Other colors used in the mural decorations, are blue and white. Over the altar, there is also a further decoration of the ceiling in a leafy design in blue, by which special honor is given to the most sacred portion of the church.

III. *The Walls.* These are executed in three zones: that of the altar, and those of the church and choir. These decorations are generally called frescoes, but, as I believe, erroneously. They are in reality distemper paintings on plaster. A true fresco is executed with mineral or earthy pigments upon a newly laid stucco ground of lime or gypsum; so that the colors sinking in become as durable as the stucco itself. This, it appears to me, is not the case with the San Miguel decorations. As a general criticism I may say that, although crude and inharmonious, they are exceedingly interesting, as they are so evidently a work of love and devotion. The desire to beautify the sacred house is there manifest, although the power adequately to accomplish the purpose was wanting. To the Mission fathers the completed church was dear, beautiful, and sacred, because beautified to the best of their ability, and raised with the ardor of their whole souls to the glory of God.

In the altar space the mural decorations on the sides consist of thirteen bands, alternating green and brown; the green being a design of pomegranate leaf, sprig, and fruit; the brown a conventional design of leaves arranged

PLATE L

a. WALL DECORATION, SANTA INÉS

b. WALL DECORATION, SAN JUAN CAPISTRANO

in a lozenge pattern. On each side a painted panel is introduced for an altar, as before described. In Plate 48 a can also be seen, above the perpendicular bands, a horizontal band about three feet wide, the design being of small squares set with a conventional pattern. There is a fringe or border, painted in blue to represent lace with tassels, both above and below this band. Still another horizontal band, about three feet wide, in gray and pink, with a painted cornice connecting the wall decorations with the moulded cornice above, complete the mural adornments in the altar zone.

Beginning at the altar, there is a zone of decoration extending on each side of the church, about eighteen feet. This might be termed the pulpit zone, for in it, on the right side, the pulpit is located, as seen in Plate 48 a. This decoration comprises a series of bands in pink and shades of green, radiating fan-shaped from a green base, situated between three and four feet above the floor. This fan design is enclosed in a painted panel, outlined by fluted columns, in blue. These columns continue, at a distance of about twelve feet apart, along the body of the church to the choir zone, at which point an entirely different design is introduced. The columns are further decorated by a conventional leaf-and-fern pattern, as seen in Plate 48 b, which also shows the frieze and the painted balustrade, both of these extending from the altar zone to that of the choir. Above and below the choir loft, the design is the Greek key.

IV. *The Old Pulpit*. A peculiar fascination pertains to this little structure, with its quaint sounding-board and crown-like cover, the whole resembling a bird-nest fastened upon the right wall. It is reached by a flight of eight steps from the inside of the altar rail, and is octagonal in form, three of the eight sides being occupied by the door and the point of attachment to the wall. It is decorated as follows: the inner panel is deep blue, with a band of

22

greenish yellow; the outer panel being in dark green enclosed by a moulding in blue, red, and gray. The under scallop is in red, with a band above of greenish yellow. The sounding-board is shaped like a crown surmounted with a ball, on which rests a cross. The crown is painted green, gold, black, and silver, with the scalloped edge in red.

V. *The Old Confessional.* The confessional shown in Plate 49 a is built into the solid adobe wall, with two swinging doors opening from it. One of these has been replaced by new material, as seen in the picture; the other, except for the insertion of a new panel of redwood, is as the fathers left it. The old iron hinges, three pairs of which remain, are originals, and good examples of the iron handiwork of the time. The decoration of the old door is the continuation of one of the fluted columns before described.

At Santa Inés the original decorations of the altar zone still remain. Elsewhere they have been destroyed with the all-covering whitewash. In this church the ceiling beams are painted with red, yellow, and green, into a portion of a circle with pendants at each point, and with a leaf design inside each arc. On the bottom of each beam is a conventionalized trailing vine.

The decorations of the side wall are of black and green around the window, and a rude imitation of marble in panels at each side. In each panel hangs a wooden bracket, painted in water-color, and supporting oil paintings. About three feet from the base is a border of yellow, green, and red of a large conventionalized leaf, alternating with a chalice, or vase.

The reredos is pretentious and inharmonious. Indeed, were it not for the sacred furnishings, statues, and altar beneath, it would suggest a rude stage-setting hastily prepared for an emergency, rather than its sacred function. It is a series of marbleized panels, enclosed in columns, with bases and cornices. The archway leading from the sanctuary into the sacristy is somewhat elaborately, although rudely decorated, as shown in Plate 49 b. This figure, also, gives some detail of the dadoes of the reredos, with its marble panelling and conventional figures in diamonds of differing size.

The most striking and pleasing mural decoration of the whole building is found in the seclusion of the sacristy. It is done in blues, reds, and yellows, and is pictured in Plate 50 a. The flower (rose?) and leaf below the Greek key, and the conventional flower and leaf above are the most artistic decorations that I have yet seen in the California Missions.

At San Luis Rey some of the old mural decorations remain, as seen in the marbleizing of the engaged columns, the dadoes at their base, the wavy line extending about the lower part of the walls, and the designs in the doorways and arches (Plate 51 a). On the reredos of the side altar, also, there are remnants of decoration in distemper.

The winged angels, carrying the crown, constitute a fair example of the ability of the fathers in this branch of decorative art; the columnar design on the right and the left of the reredos, as well as the decoration of the lower wall on the right, deserve to be examined.

Plate 51 b shows the interior wall decorations of the Pala Chapel, a dependency of the San Luis Rey Mission. The adobe walls were plastered and whitewashed; then the rude columns and arches were colored in distemper to a reddish brown. When the Palatingwa Indians were removed from Warner's Ranch to Pala, they were told that this chapel would be theirs, and that a priest would be sent regularly to minister to them. Imagine their chagrin to find it leased to the Landmarks Club of Los Angeles. Bishop Conaty of Los Angeles arranged that services should be conducted with regularity, sending a priest to reside among them. This latter, with a zeal for cleanliness and for making all things under his control conform to his own ideas, neglectful or unobservant of the irritated condition of the Indians under his charge, and without consulting them (so I am informed), ordered the walls to be whitewashed. The indignation of the Indians was intense; and were it not that high feeling had been common to them of late, they would have practically resented this desecration of the time-honored wall decorations. To an unsympathetic stranger their anger might appear unreasonable and absurd; but when it is remembered that all the Indians of this region are responsive to the memories and traditions of Padre Peyri and other early workers at the Missions of San Diego and San Luis Rey, their feelings appear natural and almost proper.

At Santa Barbara all that remains of the old decorations are found in the reredos, the marbleizing of the engaged columns on each wall and the entrance and side arches, as shown in Plate 29. This marble effect is exceedingly crude, and does not represent the color of any known marble.

Here and there on the walls at San Juan Bautista are a few remnants of the old distemper paintings. On the further side of the seventh arch on the left is a conventional leaf design in brownish red.

In the old building of San Francisco the rafters of the ceiling have been allowed to retain their ancient decorations. These consist of rhomboidal figures placed conventionally from end to end of the building.

At Santa Clara, when the church was restored in 1861–62, and again in 1885, the original decorations on walls and ceiling were necessarily destroyed or injured. But where possible they were kept intact; where injured, retouched; and where destroyed, replaced as near the original as the artist could accomplish. In some cases the original work was on canvas, and some on wood. Where this could be removed and replaced it was done. The re-

PLATE LI

a. REREDOS AND SIDE ALTAR, SAN LUIS REY

b. MURAL DECORATIONS AT PALA CHAPEL

touching was done by an Italian artist who came down from San Francisco.

On the walls, the wainscot line is set off with the sinuous body of the serpent, which not only lends itself well to such a purpose of ornamentation, but was a symbolic reminder to the Indians of that old serpent, the devil, the father of lies and evil, who beguiled our first parents in the Garden of Eden.

In the ruins of the San Fernando church faint traces of the decorations of the altar can still be seen in two simple rounded columns, with cornices above.

At San Juan Capistrano, on the east side of the quadrangle, in the northeast corner, is a small room; and in one corner of this is a niche for a statue, the original decorations therein still remaining. It is weather-stained, and the rain has washed the adobe in streaks over some of it; yet it is interesting. It consists of a rude checkerboard design, or, rather, of a diagonal lozenge pattern in reds and yellows (see Plate 50 b).

There are also a few remnants of the mural distemper paintings in the altar zone of the ruined church.

CHAPTER XXXI

THE FURNITURE AND OTHER WOOD-WORK OF THE MISSIONS

WITHIN the past few years, the term " Mission Furniture " has become current. But it has been accepted too freely, and without having been subjected to proper investigation. If by the use of that name the idea is conveyed that it is modelled after the furniture made and used in the old California Missions it is clearly unjustified, since the Spanish fathers who established the California Missions failed to create a style of furniture as distinctive as their architecture.

In the erection of the buildings themselves the padres seemed to reach the limit of their artistic capacity. This result was inevitable. The Mission houses were the property of one of the two great brotherhoods founded early in the thirteenth century in the effort to preserve the religious unity of the world. Everything tending to assure the life, to strengthen the power of the fraternity, was to be undertaken without fear and executed at all risks. As a consequence, the claims of the individual were reduced to nothing, or rather absorbed in the general scheme. The vow of the Franciscan involved personal poverty, chastity, and obedience. Daily he was reminded of his vow by the scourging of the three knots of his rope girdle, and constantly he found the results of his solemn promises in the most frugal of fare, hard labor, and the absolute bareness of his cell.

From these facts it is clear that everything which approached the idea of individual belongings, ease, or luxury was strictly eliminated from the life of the California mis-

PLATE LII

a. MISSION BENCH AT LOS ANGELES CHAPEL

b. CONFESSIONAL AT SAN JUAN CAPISTRANO

sionaries, as fatal to the interests of their order. They provided their cells, their refectories, their chapels with such movables only as served their strictest necessities. To have done otherwise would have been to attack the foundations of their brotherhood, to have provided for the comfort of their bodies, which they were taught to abase and mortify. It was as impossible as it was unsought on their part for them to create any types whatsoever of domestic art. Their movables were collected by chance, or, when made by them, were constructed upon primitive models. Their chairs, tables, and benches were such as fell into their possession, or else were fashioned from such upright and horizontal timbers as might have been used by the first cabinet maker.

Thus, obedient to their conception of the religious life, furthermore, not possessing a racial art-instinct like certain other divisions of the Latin peoples, these Spanish monks accepted whatever material objects were most easily obtainable, and held themselves aloof from their influence. It cannot be too much emphasized that, regarding life as a mere passage, as a series of painful tests and proofs, they rejected upon principle whatever might attach them to it.

Therefore, from argument, and equally from evidence existing in the objects themselves, it is apparent that there is no " Mission Style," except that which pertains to architecture. And as the latter has been illustrated in the present pages by its most notable examples, so now the movable objects used or constructed by the missionaries for domestic or ecclesiastical purposes are here shown in a representative collection. These objects may be divided into two classes, one of which comprises such things as were copied more or less accurately from typical originals, as they were remembered, or else such as were brought from the mother country. These especially are the pulpits, confessionals, lecterns, and candelabra. It is proper to designate them as objects *found* in the Missions. The other class consists, for the most part, of objects for domestic use. They originated in the Missions, without, however, constituting a distinctive style, since they show nothing but the simplest provisions to meet bare necessities. They prove that no " Mission Style " of furniture ever existed, and place the term where it rightly belongs; that is, among those names which, first applied for commercial purposes, are generally accepted, in obedience to that love of mystery and romance which invades even the most prosaic lives.

In order, then, to afford a basis of judgment between the types of the new style and the objects from which they received their name, the accompanying illustrations have been selected from those Missions of the entire California chain which offer the best examples; and, as already it has been said, the collection has been arranged with the direct purpose to show that the furnishings of these religious houses, being indiscriminately gathered, can present no thorough principles upon which to base a system of constructive art. In this collection there is included, it is believed, a specimen of every important variety, excepting the altar chairs at San Carlos, Monterey, and one chair formerly at San Diego; all of which, plainly of Oriental origin, were probably brought by one of the ships trading with the Philippines in the early days of Spanish supremacy.

The series of illustrations may well begin with the benches which are among the most direct models serving for the new " Mission Style." Plate 52 a is a seat of this character, preserved at Los Angeles. We observe in this a piece of good form, constructed of rough uprights and horizontals crudely put together by an unskilled joiner, the back-rest and the seat front board even suggesting the work of Indians. It is interesting to note that the priest sitting on this bench is the Reverend Father Adam, widely

PLATE LIII

a. CHAIR IN RELIC-ROOM,
SANTA CLARA

c. CHAIR IN RELIC-ROOM,
SANTA BARBARA

b. CHAIR AT SAN JUAN BAUTISTA

d. CHAIR AT SAN BUENAVENTURA

known and greatly esteemed, whose departure for Spain a few years since was much regretted in California, where he had been one of the most zealous workers of the Catholic Church. Father Adam is here seen holding in his hand one of the old registers of the San Juan Capistrano Mission, bound in the soft leather peculiar to the conventual books of the period.

A similar simple and well-constructed piece, displaying on the seat front board carvings which are not ungraceful, exists in the relic-room at Santa Barbara.

Plate 53 a is one of two old chairs of the sanctuary, now preserved in the relic-room at Santa Clara. They are heavy, solid, and crude in workmanship and ornamentation. The legs of one of the chairs are strongly curved and carved. The seats of both are much too narrow, and eloquently speak of the compulsion they laid upon their users to sit bolt upright. The arms of one are slightly hollowed for the elbows, and the ends are scrolled. The top of the head-rest has a slight pretence of ornamentation in the crude scalloped work. The other chair is absolutely plain except for the scalloping, which it is evident was laboriously done by hand. Hand-made nails and wooden pegs were used to hold the pieces together.

Plate 53 b, a dilapidated chair at San Juan Bautista, is of a type often seen in Spain. Although quite simple, the chair, as judged by its structure and lathe-work, proceeded from the hand of a well-skilled cabinet-maker.

Plate 53 c, from the relic-room at Santa Barbara, mingles the Dutch with the Spanish type, an occurrence not infrequent in art and handicraft work, owing to the close political and social connections once existing between the peoples of these two widely different races.

Plate 53 d, a chair, at San Buenaventura, is built upon sound structural principles, although in a crude fashion. It is mortised and tenoned, and there is an attempt at ornamentation in the front stretcher, the rounding of the arms, and the terminations of the posts.

Plate 54 a is a cupboard at San Juan Bautista, still bearing the rude hinges of the early Mission forge, and carved with the utmost skill of the early fathers; the work on this piece being much superior to that which is generally seen on similar pieces. The ornament is here significant of the use fulfilled by the cabinet, which is a receptacle for ecclesiastical vessels. The monstrance and the chalice appear surmounted by a design which may be a variant of the "Tree of Life," so frequently seen in old Italian, Spanish, and Flemish wood-carvings; while the cockle-shell of the cornice is the symbol of Saint James the Elder, or Santiago, the traveller among the Apostles and the patron of Spain.

Plate 54 b shows brackets, shelf, and a cupboard, the work of the Indians at Santa Barbara, and dating from 1824.

Leaving now the furniture proper, let us pass on to examine other wood-work found in the Missions. The first specimen chosen is a door, and it may be observed that in producing work of this character the Mission fathers kept within the limits of their capabilities, no delicate handling being required in order to attain satisfactory results. The entrance door at San Luis Obispo is shown in Plate 56 b. At this Mission the entire church has been " restored " out of all resemblance to its original state. But fortunately, although the framework seen in this picture is new, the door itself dates from the days of the early fathers. It has sustained the attack of time and weather better than most modern work will do, and some of its original hinges are still in use. It is ornamented by two rosette-like panels with terrace-bevelled edges, fastened upon each of the two divisions; these being impaled with heavy spikes, the heads of which form star-like bosses, while other similar bosses are disposed symmetrically throughout the body of the

Plate LIV

a. RECEPTACLE FOR ECCLESIASTICAL
VESSELS, SAN JUAN BAUTISTA

b. BRACKETS, SHELF, AND CUPBOARD,
MADE BY INDIANS, SANTA BARBARA

c. CONFESSIONAL, SAN BUENAVENTURA

d. PULPIT, SAN LUIS REY

door. Regarded as ornament, both panels and bosses are trivial, but, serving to strengthen the door, they are admissible as a constructive feature.

Plate 56 a is chosen from San Miguel. Here, also, the frame is new, the door only being original. This, as occurs elsewhere, is a device of a door within a door, the construction of which may be better understood by reference to the illustration than through an explanation in words. It may be noted that here some of the original hinges are still in use, being as firmly riveted as when first attached. Of these there are three pairs fully a foot in length, together with three smaller pairs for the use of the smaller doors.

Plate 54 c shows a confessional at San Buenaventura, and in Plate 28 a is seen a pulpit of similar workmanship, both of which were brought from Spain through Mexico, or else were made in the latter country by a superior workman. Unfortunately, like the church in which it stands, the confessional has been subjected to a " restoration " which has greatly marred its original character. The pulpit has totally disappeared, or, at least, so stated the present priest when recently questioned.

Plate 55 a shows a pulpit, being the original construction still in use at San Juan Bautista. It is in no wise distinctive, and might be found in any Roman Catholic country, just as the reredos or the side altars might as well be located in France or in Lower Canada, for aught that is revealed in their structure. The pulpit, however, attains importance from the fact that from it, seventy-five years since, a devoted missionary, Father Arroya, preached the gospel to the Indians in thirteen of their native dialects.

Another pulpit (Plate 54 d) is of a type commonly found in continental churches, and calls for no special comment, except that the corbel with its conical sides harmonizes with the panels and base-moulding of the box proper. This model, so frequently seen, loses nothing by familiarity, and is always grateful to the eye by reason of its symmetrical proportions.

Plate 28 b is a picture which no lover of the old Missions can look upon without being sensible of its pathos. It represents the interior of San Antonio, as it stood some twenty years ago; and when it is compared with the present state of the place it awakens deep regret. A number of interesting features have disappeared. The wooden ceiling, the altar rails, the benches, the confessional, the pulpit have been taken away or destroyed by ruthless hands. Other objects of interest would have shared the same fate had they not been seized and preserved by Mr. G. C. Dutton of Jolon, who, holding them in trust, has now arranged to deliver them to the Landmarks Club of San Francisco, which has undertaken to preserve what remains of the buildings at San Antonio.

Plate 56 c is a Paschal candlestick now in use at Santa Barbara, showing the undisguised constructive lines which the new " Mission Style " takes as its basis. On the other hand, the Paschal candlestick of the Santa Clara Mission is quite elaborate, carved in a very conventional and ornate manner, and then painted and gilded. It is nearly six feet high, and is composed of three parts, — the base, the supporting column, and the candleholder. There appear in Plate 57 a two other light-holders, placed on either side of a large crucifix. The former are evidently of domestic make, but are pleasing by their obelisk-like outlines and the lamps at the apex, which accentuate the artistic idea. The crucifix is notable in having the feet of the suffering Christ crossed and pierced by a single nail. It once served on the high altar, and it shows over all its surface the assiduous work of " the worm, our busy brother."

Plate 56 d represents the music desk, or lectern, at San Juan Bautista, which once held the ponderous psalter-book, while the brothers stood about it chanting the service. The pages of the book were kept in place by small wooden pegs

PLATE LV

b. CONFESSIONAL, SANTA INÉS

a. PULPIT, SAN JUAN BAUTISTA

inserted into holes, and the pegs were hung upon the desk by means of fine, braided catgut.

In the missal-stand for use on the high altar, shown in Plate 57 c, and contained in the relic-case at Santa Clara, we have an ingeniously constructed piece of wood-work. It is formed of what appears to be two pieces of inch-board which open and shut without hinges. The two pieces of board are themselves hinged in the shoulder, so that the piece closes up tightly, or can be opened at the angle permitted. It was made from a two-inch board sawed down to the upper part of the shoulder from above, and up to the lower part of the shoulder from below. Five vertical cuts or slits were made in the shoulder for the hinges and then the curves of the shoulder itself, on both upper and lower sides, were cut with a sharp instrument. The result displays much inventive faculty, and the repetition of the device at several of the Missions proves that its merit was appreciated.

At Santa Barbara there is preserved among the relics an old processional wooden cross, having the floriated terminals familiar in examples of the Holy Symbol, dating from the crusading period. This piece is shown in Plate 57 b, while Plate 57 d represents the old font for holy water, still in use, at the entrance to the Mission of San Miguel. This is made from the bole of a tree, and is about three feet in height, fluted and fitted to contain a basin.

At San Juan Capistrano and Santa Barbara rude movable wooden belfries formerly served on occasions when it was not advisable to ring the larger bells. The one seen in Plate 58 a is now preserved in the relic-room at Santa Barbara. It is a rude wheel of wood, to the circumference of which the bells are fastened; the whole revolving on an iron pin, held in the sockets of the supporting posts and operated by an iron handle.

Plate 58 b pictures the *matraca* (clapper or rattle) used at the Mission from Holy Thursday to Easter Sunday, a period when the bells of the *campanario* are never rung, and are said to have " gone to Rome."

At San Juan Capistrano the baptismal font is capped with a wooden cover represented in Plate 58 c. It is an interesting although crude piece of workmanship, provided with old iron hinges made in the Mission shops. Three sections of the carved circular frame have disappeared, but the remaining portion testifies to the taste and the rudimentary skill of the one who fashioned it. The pouring shell seen at the front is of silver, and was probably brought from Mexico.

Plate 58 d is of a chandelier made by the Indians, and long used in the Santa Barbara Mission.

Almost hidden in an obscure corner of the relic-room at Santa Barbara is an interesting decorative fragment. It is the crown-piece of the ancient altar tabernacle, and is ornamented with the Sacred Hearts of Jesus and Mary, and the instruments of the Passion. The piece is furthermore notable as affording the first instance, as far as is known, of the use of the iridescent abalone shell, which is now employed so frequently and effectively in the modern handicraft of California.

There remain many other uses of wood and many other wooden objects which might be described, such as the wooden bells once hanging as " dummies " in the *campanile* at San Buenaventura; the old pulpit at Santa Clara (which has been restored according to the original scheme); the reliquary case used in processions by Father Junipero Serra; the altar rail in the practically new Mission church at Santa Clara, made from the original redwood beams which spanned the old Mission structures.

CHAPTER XXXII

THE SILVER AND BRASS WARE OF THE MISSIONS

I T is impossible in a brief chapter to present pictures and descriptions of all the silver and brass ware found at the Missions, but it will be interesting and instructive to see a few examples. Much of this ware was brought by the padres from Mexico. Of much of it we have Padre Palou's lists, made ere the things were shipped from Lower California. As we have elsewhere seen, many of them were contributed — willingly or otherwise — by the Missions there. Hence all these pieces have a peculiar and romantic interest. Some came from Spain to Vera Cruz. They were then packed on mules across the hundreds of miles to the City of Mexico. From thence they were transported on mule-back to the coast, and then in vessels across the Gulf of California to the Jesuit Missions. Here for years they were the objects of respect and veneration of the rude savages of the Peninsula; then they came into the hands of the Franciscans, were gathered together, and either transported by vessel to San Diego, or on mule-back up the dreary roads and over the frightful mountain passes of the Peninsula to the new Missions of Alta California; so that each article has condensed within it a wide range of romance, and should be religiously guarded and preserved because of what it enshrines.

From the technical standpoint, they are also interesting as showing a wonderful difference in artistic conception and workmanship. Some of them are pathetic in their makeshift grasp of essentials, and the rudeness of their make; others are grandiose, almost bombastic in their portrayal of half-forgotten splendors. Some bring the memory of the land of the dignified Arab, with his orientalism and desert abandon; others the careful touch of classical origin, and of a culture that has departed or become changed out of all its original character. In all the pieces, however, there is a frankness that wins us, and that adds a page to the note-book of the enthusiast, bringing us into closer sympathy with the people who made and who used them, who, while their thoughts seem in the nebulous clouds to us, yet kept one foot on the earth in their childlike wholesomeness and honest intent. The fire needed for their forge and furnace was kindled from the sparks of love and reverence, — love for the supreme goodness of God and reverence for his power; and their hands were guided by thoughts of conceptions above this earth, — conceptions of the mysteries of the hereafter.

The processional cross that used to be borne before the sainted Serra is now at the old presidio church at Monterey. (Plate 59 a.) It is of silver, with a maker's stamp, " Ton," upon it, and is chased with a neat and appropriate design. The Christ is of brass, evidently modern, and used to replace the original, which was probably lost or stolen during the dark days of the secularization period. The reverse side of the cross (Plate 59 b) is most beautifully chased.

There are also two pairs of altar candlesticks, beautifully ornamented in olive-leaf design.

The processional cross of San Miguel stands neglected and forgotten in the sacristy. It is of brass. The cross itself is a foot and a half high, and is hand-carved, rather rudely. Above the figure of the Christ are the letters in capitals, " I N R I," and an aureola around the figure.

There is a close similarity between this cross and the one at San Buenaventura. While the design is somewhat different, the workmanship suggests that it might have been done by the same hand. (Plate 59 c and d.) The

PLATE LVI

ENTRANCE DOORS, SAN MIGUEL   b. ENTRANCE DOORS, SAN LUIS OBISPO

c. PASCHAL CANDLESTICK,   d. MUSIC DESK, SAN JUAN BAUTISTA
        SANTA BARBARA

PLATE LVII

a. WOODEN CANDLESTICKS AND
CRUCIFIX, SANTA INÉS

c. MISSAL STAND FOR ALTAR USE,
SANTA CLARA

b. WOODEN PROCESSIONAL CROSS,
SANTA BARBARA

d. FONT FOR HOLY WATER,
SAN MIGUEL

detail of this cross is both interesting and unusual from
the quaint use of decoration of Persian-Moorish character.
The rose centre, the floriated detail at crossing and at the
foot of the cross show much thought, while the addition of
a cross in the lower panel on the reverse side is pathetic
and exceptional.

There are two processional candlesticks of plain silver
at Santa Inés, and a processional cross, which is finely
carved and chased. (Plate 21 c.) The base and standard are plain. (Plate 21 d.) There is a lace-like quality in the contriving of these narrow bands with rosette
centres which is very ingenious in that the ornament ties
the cross to the standard and increases its apparent length.

The processional candlesticks of the old presidio church
at Monterey were brought from Carmelo. (Plate 60 a.)
They are of superior workmanship. They afford an excellent lesson in values. Note in each one the relation of the
decorative fluting and chasing to the plain moulding at
top and to the staff. They are a strong, bold piece of
composition.

There are also six other silver candlesticks at Monterey
which came from Carmelo. (Plate 60 b.) They are em-
bossed and chased, or engraved in a manner that reminds
one somewhat of the work of the Navaho silversmiths,
though the design is a little more elaborate than any attempted by these nomad Indians of the plains. These
candlesticks are of a type always associated with Spanish
metal-work and of considerable value. The turning and
the ingenious arrangement of detail, in that it is well-bal-
anced, are added elements of charm. Note the increasing
strength given by the use of upright lines and movement.

Equally beautiful, though of different style, are two
fine silver altar candlesticks, still used at San Juan Capistrano, one of which is shown in Plate 60 c. These are
somewhat unusual in that the shaft is interrupted by the
introduction of a square motif, rosetted. The base is

23

square, hollowed in plan, with corners removed. The feet are quaint and of grand design, riveted from face. The interest of the whole is much enhanced by this method of simple outline. They illustrate considerable thought and understanding of proportion.

Another style of candlestick, in brass, is shown in Plate 60 d. This is at the presidio church at Monterey. Variations of this same type are shown in the two pairs (Plate 62 a and b), which are at San Luis Obispo. The singular delicacy of these candlesticks is well worthy of note. The mouldings are " under cut," finely turned, and full of delightful charm. The work shows considerable thought and artistic taste. The method of attaching the feet by a system of overlapping the lower moulding is both quaint and curious.

With a somewhat different base are two of several at San Juan Capistrano, shown in Plate 62 c. These have balustered stems, turned in sections with delicate mouldings. They stand on three-sided bases, — significant and curious, — with splayed projecting moulding to top edge. The feet have strangely shaped claws.

Plate 61 a shows two silver incense-burners, an incense-holder, etc., from San Luis Obispo. The pierced portion of these incense-burners speaks eloquently of the craftsman's knowledge of grotesque rococo scrolls, while the concave and convex ornament, alternating and overlapping, is curious and interesting. All this is distinctly Spanish in character and workmanship.

Plate 61 b is a fine silver piece of beautiful workmanship for holding the elements used in the sacrament of baptism. This is in use at San Luis Obispo. It is of late design, and a singular expression of indifference to the relation of things; convenience, rather than artistic result, being the thing sought. Note the ends to the arms of the cross.

There is an incense cup of silver at Santa Inés, from

PLATE LVIII

a. MOVABLE WOODEN BELFRY,
SANTA BARBARA

c. CARVED TOP OF BAPTISMAL FONT,
SAN JUAN CAPISTRANO

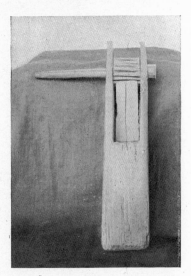

b. MATRACA, OR CLAPPER,
SANTA BARBARA

d. WOODEN CHANDELIER,
SANTA BARBARA

La Purísima, and a silver incense-burner from San Miguel. It is pleasant thus to think of the older Missions contributing to the equipment of the younger one; as of big brothers and sisters caring for a smaller and newer member of the family. Let us hope it was done with more willing tenderness than was felt when the Missions of Peninsula California were called upon to contribute for the establishments in Alta California.

Three aspergers must suffice to represent these vessels. Plate 63 a shows the influence of Moorish design. The handle is cast and turned. The base is hammered from the back in primitive fashion, the whole portraying the quaint workmanship of a simple people.

More ornate and elaborate in its chasing is Plate 63 b, from San Carlos, Carmelo, and now in use at Monterey. The handle, with its interlacing moons and ring, and the arabesque ornament through body and base, — all show the distinct influence of Moorish conception, though it is clearly Spanish in execution.

That at San Juan Bautista (Plate 63 c) is beautiful and artistic. The only ornament is a silver band, which is worked into a simple design for a handle. This is undoubtedly of Moorish character, and the very unusual method of attachment to so large and plain a body is a striking proof of ability in design, far beyond the average. The ring and its system of riveting is well worth the study of both craftsman and artist. The flat lip also adds a small note to the charm of the whole.

At San Luis Obispo is a baptismal font of hammered copper, as shown in Plate 63 d. It is a rude and simple piece of work, and was undoubtedly made either there or at one of the other Missions, as, for instance, San Fernando, which had a great reputation for its copper work. The stand upon which it rests is of wood, painted in a rude design. As one looks at this piece, the blows of the hammer can be heard, and the eyes of the worker glowing with affection and pride. Each blow leaves its mark and tells its own story. The overlapping seam, the big projection of the edge, the hinging of the cover, its fastenings, — all lend intense and appealing interest to the piece. There are more of these copper fonts at others of the Missions, but that of San Luis Rey has a history peculiarly its own. After secularization the Indians stole it and sold it, and for many years it was used for "base purposes." But ultimately it was located and claimed, and is now back at San Luis; but its travels and experiences away from home have so injured it that it needs considerable repairs. At present, therefore, a temporary font is being used, with an abalone shell as the pourer. In all Catholic churches water is poured over the head of the child or adult to be baptized by means of a small vessel, generally a silver shell, as pictured elsewhere in these pages. This necessitates a font, for the holding of the consecrated water and oil, and then a waste bowl, over which the neophyte holds his head. In the more elaborate fonts the two bowls are in one. At San Luis the waste bowl is of fine soapstone, probably gained from the Indians of Santa Catalina Island. It stands about four feet high.

PLATE LIX

a. PROCESSIONAL CROSS (FRONT),
PRESIDIO CHURCH, MONTEREY

b. PROCESSIONAL CROSS (REVERSE),
PRESIDIO CHURCH, MONTEREY

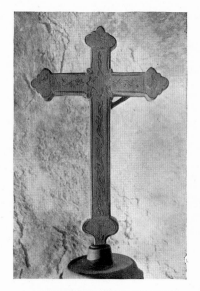

c. PROCESSIONAL CROSS (FRONT),
SAN BUENAVENTURA

d PROCESSIONAL CROSS (REVERSE),
SAN BUENAVENTURA

CHAPTER XXXIII

A CHAPTER OF SAINTS

IT is instinctive in the ordinary human being to look up to some one above himself. Carlyle was not the first hero-worshipper, nor is he the last. In this matter the Catholic Church has proven herself wise in recognizing this universal propensity to select from among her members men and women conspicuous for their blameless and heroic Christian lives, and to whom it believed that Heaven had borne indubitable testimony, — sometimes by the power to work miracles, — and raise them to the honors of her altars by the solemn decree of canonization. Longfellow beautifully enunciated the principle upon which they acted when, in his " Psalm of Life," he reminded us that " Lives of great men all remind us we can make our lives sublime."

It is not my purpose to expatiate upon the lives of the saints, but, as many, otherwise interested in the old Missions, are perhaps not so familiar with the saints, I thought it would be well, in showing some of the pictures of the wooden figures of the saints that are to be found at the Missions, to make some brief mention of their lives.

The Viceroy Galvez placed the first sea expedition for the missionizing and colonization of Alta California, under the patronage of San José (Saint Joseph). This saint, as the foster father of our Lord, was necessarily the provider of all his needs, and also of those of the Virgin, his mother. Hence he is made the patron saint of the temporalities of all institutions. There are several statues of San José found in the Missions, one (Plate 43 a) being in the relic-room at Santa Barbara.

In the sacristy at the old presidio church at Monterey, is a rudely carved statue of the Blessed Virgin. (Plate 64 b.) Its place, in art, is among that class of figures intended by the artificer for draping, as it was thus rendered more in touch with the every-day life of the Indians it was intended to impress. To this class also pertain the various Child-Jesus statuettes, a typical case being the Infant Jesus of Prague, commonly known as " The Holy Child." It is possible that this statue of Our Lady was carved by the Indian neophytes under the direction of the padres. Statues that were imported were generally carved throughout and could be placed in position without draping. The " Saint Clare " of the Santa Clara Mission belongs to the former class. This statue of the Monterey sacristy stands about four feet high and wears a very modern tinsel halo and garments.

Almost every Mission has, or had, its figures of the Virgin and Holy Child, and it would be a wonderful study in expression if all of these could be gathered together for comparative study. In Plate 20 a Our Lady is represented crowned, as the Queen of Heaven, the Child Jesus in her arms. But in Plate 20 b there is a sweet, gentle, and maternal look that wins and captivates the soul.

In Plate 44 a is a conception of the Holy Child when he was disputing with the elders in the Temple. It is neither pleasing nor artistic, and the enlarged head and the strained attitude make a grotesque effect rather than the deep impression its maker doubtless intended. Yet it never must be forgotten that all these figures were designed to impress the childlike Indians and the devout, to whom everything of this nature was too serious and solemn to be looked at critically.

At the San Diego school (which is close to the old Mis-

PLATE LX

a. PROCESSIONAL
CANDLESTICK
AT MONTEREY

b. ALTAR CANDLESTICK,
MONTEREY

c. ALTAR CANDLESTICK,
SAN JUAN CAPISTRANO

d. ALTAR CANDLESTICK,
MONTEREY

sion) are two small wooden figures of Christ: one in the Garden of Gethsemane (Plate 12 a), and the other after the scourging, when the soldiers mockingly put on him the scarlet robe. (Plate 12 b.) The cloak is of canvas, painted red, but so well put on that at first sight the red canvas appears to be part and parcel of the carved wood. The shading from one kind of material into the other is very ingeniously done.

These statuettes are about a foot and a half high, and have a wooden base which is so worm-eaten as to be slowly crumbling away. It looks almost like cork, so completely have the tiny creatures cut their way through it.

Two valued treasures of the Dominican Sisters Orphanage at Mission San José are the statues of Ecce Homo (Plate 4) and San Buenaventura (Plate 64 a), which used to belong to the old Mission. That of the Ecce Homo is in the convent precincts, and a special dispensation had to be produced ere I was permitted to photograph it. To me it is one of the most wonderful statues in the whole of the Missions; the sad, tender austerity of the face, the pain and woe thereon depicted. Only the face, hands, and feet are carved; the body is unshapen, so that it was necessary to clothe the figure. The rich silk gown and the Franciscan girdle, therefore, are real, and were undoubtedly put on when the statue was first made, and this accounts for its present forlorn and dilapidated condition. It stands about three feet high, and is on a bracket at the end of the corridor where the young sisters sleep. Some of them are avowedly afraid of it, for, especially in the twilight, standing there under the skylight with a full view of the whole corridor, it is easy to imagine it some austere and stern monk looking even into the very depths of the heart of those who come within its ken.

The San Buenaventura is of the more ordinary type, the dress being composed of leather moulded to the required form, then stiffened and painted.

San Buenaventura was originally Giovanni di Fidanza. He was born at Bagnarea in Tuscany in 1221. St. Francis of Assisi, meeting him one day and being charmed with the attractive power of his personality, and foreseeing his future greatness, exclaimed "O buona ventura!" and this appellative — Buenaventura in Spanish (Good Fortune in English) — clung to him. Because of his great skill as a writer and teacher of mystic theology he was called the seraphic doctor. He was in turn bishop, minister-general of the Franciscan Order, and Cardinal. He died in 1274. His day is July 14.

At Santa Barbara are three figures which represent the three archangels, Gabriel, Miguel, and Rafael. It will be remembered that San Gabriel announced to Mary the mystery of the incarnation, hence he is intimately connected with that great dispensation. His place in christian symbolism is largely determined thereby. His day is March 18. In Plate 44 b he appears, robed in vesture bedight with shimmering stars and silver moon. Just as the arrows in the talons of the American eagle on the national shield symbolize the nation's defenders ready at their country's call, so the stars and moon of San Gabriel are worn by him as the messenger of the Holy Virgin, as explained in Rev. xii. 1.

San Miguel is presented in Plate 44 c. With crossed lines on breast, and fingers pointing upwards, this statue presents the saint as breastplated, uttering his cry to the angelic hosts: Mi-cha-el Quis-ut-Deus — Who-as-God? thus calling upon them to decide under whom they would muster. His day is September 29, but there is a subsidiary festival of his on May 8.

Plate 44 d is of San Rafael. The fish under his feet symbolizes him as the specially assigned heavenly guardian of the young Tobias. (See Tobias vi. 2, 3, 4.) San Rafael's day is October 24.

At Santa Barbara also is the statue of San Antonio de

PLATE LXI

b. SILVER VESSELS FOR BAPTISMAL ELEMENTS, SAN LUIS OBISPO

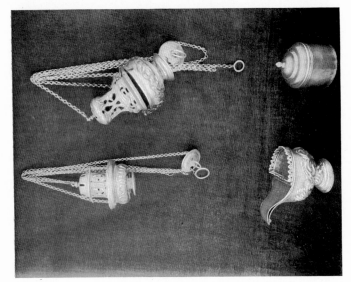

a. ALTAR VESSELS, SAN LUIS OBISPO

Padua (Plate 43 b). He was born in Lisbon in 1195, and died in Padua in 1231, and was canonized in 1232.   He was a famous preacher, and a zealous Franciscan.   He is invariably represented with the Infant Jesus in his arms. In tradition the reason of this is that his devotion was so intense, and his love for the Blessed Babe so sincere, that the Holy Mother, to give him a signal proof of appreciation of his devotion, yielded to the importunate look and outstretched arms of her Child and gave the Infant into the saint's embrace.   Thus, with the ever-abiding benison of the Child whom he had held for a time in his arms, he went forth to more zealous and powerful service for the honor and glory of God and the propagation of the faith. His day is June 13.   The Santa Barbara figure is singularly pleasing, and the expression upon the face is of a deeply thoughtful, spiritual, tender nature.

Of an entirely different character is the face of the St. Anthony shown in Plate 43 c.   This is at San Carlos, Carmelo.   There is neither dignity nor tenderness in this face; instead, a kind of weak simpering that is effeminate and displeasing.

Plate 21 a is of St. John the Evangelist, as shown by the book he has in his hands.   Here are dignity, benignity, and sweetness, a true and artistic portrayal of the wondrous " Seer of Patmos."

Plate 21 b is probably of St. Stephen, the Protomartyr.   Both this and Figure 21 a are in the collection room at Santa Clara.   The main reason of doubt as to the identity of this statue — or, in other words, that it was really meant to represent St. Stephen, is in the dress, which is rather mediæval than archaic enough to coincide with the martyr's period — the Jerusalem of Our Lord.   But the eyes turned heavenward and the martyr's palm, taken together, make it probable that it is for St. Stephen.

Saint Louis, Bishop of Toulouse (Plate 64 c) (1274– 1297, A. D.), son of Charles II, surnamed the Lame, King of Naples and Sicily, was canonized in 1317. His day is August 19.

The figure within the church, which represents San Luis, is young and fair and pleasing. He became a Franciscan in 1296, in his twenty-third year, and, as he died four years later, he must have been one of the youngest bishops of the church; and thus also he is a junior among the saints.

It used to be the fashion to observe the Saint's Day at San Luis Obispo, as elsewhere, with a special fiesta. One observer, present in the later days of the last century, has given us a vivid picture of this fiesta, part of which is worth extended quoting:

" We turned from the inspection of things sacred and curious to follow the gathering multitude through the narrow street to the *plaza* where we might see the bull-baiting. . . . The small town was alive with people. Matrons and maidens crowded the sidewalk, while their husbands, brothers and lovers, in all the bravery of Mexican saddles, jangling spurs, and coiled reatas, charged up and down the one crooked street upon their favorite mustangs in the most reckless manner. The outer fringe of the motley gathering was composed of curious spectators, — a fair and rather mixed contingent composed of French, Germans, and Americans.

Undaunted by the heat and glare of the August midday, we waited for the fight. Arrived at the place which had been enclosed for the sport, we found that seats had been prepared for the ladies. The men were generally mounted, and so well did they sit and ride that horse and rider seemed one creature. The managers of the performance were gay and distinguishable in red and yellow scarfs. The hum of voices in many unfamiliar tongues disturbed the stillness, while the expectant throng waited and simmered.

At last, after we had ceased to care for the promised ' show,' there was an uproar of trumpets, tambourines, and voices, and the Toro victim, with his tormentors, entered the enclosure. The skilled horseman whose duty it was to provoke the animals was armed with spears and barbed darts, with tiny flags attached. These were thrown at the bull to improve his temper, and it im-

PLATE LXII

c. ALTAR CANDLESTICKS, SAN JUAN CAPISTRANO

b. ALTAR CANDLESTICK, SAN LUIS OBISPO

a. ALTAR CANDLESTICK, SAN LUIS OBISPO

proved with each admonitory sting. A few footmen were in the enclosure, armed with dark-colored blankets. It was their part to divert the maddened creature and throw the blanket over his head in case of danger. One at a time, some twenty bulls were brought into the corral. Some ignored the hostility of the enemy, and others accepted the challenge and fought until exhausted."

In the account from which the foregoing was quoted, the impression was given throughout that the bull fight was part of the honors to the saint. A scholarly Catholic priest at one of the old Missions protests against this idea, asserting that " the Catholic Church never counselled, much less introduced, bull fights. At most she simply tolerated them as a fond mother's concession to her little ones, that they might not deem her rule too hard."

San Juan Capistrano was born at the town of the same name in the kingdom of Naples in 1385. He was educated as a lawyer, became a judge, and in 1415 entered the Franciscan Order. He became noted for his austerity, his zeal for the preservation of the true faith, and his diplomacy, travelling extensively in Europe on business of the Pope. He was one of the high officials of the Inquisition, and also preached to the Crusaders while they were on their arduous marches. With the cross in hand which he had received from the Pope, he animated the Christian forces before Belgrade and was present when they entered the town in 1456. He died in October of that year, and was canonized in 1690. His day is the 23d of October. As an author of ecclesiastical works he is also worthy of note. The figure of San Juan (Plate 43 d) shows him with a book in his left hand, and outstretched right hand, as if arguing or disputing on some matter of importance, as he is said to have done against the Hussites.

Plate 20 c is of Santa Lucia in an attitude of devotion. Her name is borne by the range of mountains that separates the region of San Luis Obispo from the Valley of the Salinas.

At Santa Inés, the chief figure in the centre of the reredos is that of the patron saint. She was martyred by beheading in Rome in the year 304. Bancroft says this occurred when Agnes was but thirteen years of age, which agrees with the authority of Alban Butler's "Lives of the Saints," vol. i., under January 21. Butler cites St. Ambrose and St. Austin for thirteen.

At that age, the son of Sempronius, prefect of Rome at the time, desired to marry her, but she answered him, as well as all other suitors, that she had consecrated her virginity to a heavenly spouse, who could not be beheld by mortal eyes. Sempronius, the father, enraged at her resolution and constancy, ruthlessly delivered her up to profligates, all of whom, however, save one, were so awed by coming in sight of the saint at her prayers, that they durst not approach. But that foolish youth, attempting to be rude to her, was instantly struck blind from Heaven. But the good Agnes, compassionating his misfortune, by prayer restored him to his sight and health.

The figure at Santa Inés is certainly of a person much older than thirteen years of age, but this is doubtless an anachronism of art. Over four feet in height, the statue is quite heavy, and when the kindly lay brother at the Mission aided me in lifting it from its elevated position, he could not help commenting on its weight; and then, as if he had somehow said that which would be displeasing to the dear saint, he caressed the figure with his hands and a soft and pleading voice whispered "Santa Inés Hermosa" — Beautiful Saint Agnes. No doubt the sweet-spirited saint heard and forgave him for any pain his recognition of her great weight may have given her. In her right hand she holds what evidently represents the feather palm symbol of martyrdom, a feather being the best temporary substitute at hand. In her left hand she bears a lamb, symbol of her name, Agnes in Latin, and also of her virginal purity and innocence. These are added to the figure (Plate 20 d) when it occupies its elevated position. The feast of St. Agnes occurs on January 21. Both the Roman Breviary and the Bollandists' " Acte Sanctorum " confirm thirteen as the age at which she was martyred.

San Francisco Solano, the missionary to the Indians, was born at Monsilia, in Andalucía, March, 1549. In his youth he studied with the Jesuits, but when twenty years of age he joined the Franciscan Order in his native town. He requested to be sent as a missionary to Peru. A fearful storm arose, and the vessel was driven upon a rocky shore. The captain wanted Francis to come into his life-boat, but the devoted priest refused to leave some pagans who were on board. He instructed them as well as circumstances would allow, baptized them hurriedly in the midst of the storm, and thus prepared them for death. However, by the efficacy of his prayers they weathered the storm and were saved. Francis labored long thereafter for the aborigines in Peru, until his death which occurred July 14, 1610. He was canonized in 1726. His festival takes place July 24. An extended life of St. Francis Solano is given in " The Bollandists," vol. 5, of the month of July, under July 24.

San Carlos Borromeo was the son of Gilbert Borromeo, Count of Arona. He was a nephew of Pope Pius IV, and was born at Arona, near Milan, Italy, in 1538; was appointed Archbishop of Milan in 1560, and not long after created Cardinal. He died in 1584, and was canonized in 1610 by Pope Paul V. His day is November 4.

San Diego de Alcalá (St. James of Alcalá) was an Andalusian Franciscan, who lived from 1400 to 1463, and was canonized in 1588 by Pope Sixtus V, for his saintly and heroic life, and confirmed by miracles wrought through him before and after his death. His day is November 13. The saint's surname, Alcalá, was seldom attached to the name of his Mission in popular usage.

Santa Barbara was the daughter of Dioscorus, who lived in Asia Minor. Being an idolater and hating the new religion, he gave his daughter, who had become a Christian, to the torture, and then beheaded her with his own hand, angered at her steady adherence to the new faith. The unfortunate man soon paid the penalty of his cruel act for immediately thereafter he was struck by lightning. The protection of Santa Barbara, therefore, is often invoked by sailors as a safeguard against the fury of lightning during the storms to which they are so frequently exposed on the high seas. Santa Barbara's day is December 4. Her martyrdom occurred at Nicomedia, about the year 240.

Of St. Francis (San Francisco de Asís) one would enjoy writing a whole chapter. He is worthy of note, not only because he founded the religious order which bears his name, but also because, as it were, he has lived his beautiful life over and over again in the lives of the many great and worthy men who have been members of his illustrious order. Francis was born at Assisi, in Umbria, Italy, in 1182, in a stable, his pious mother having thus, by divine monition, secured a safe delivery. On his right shoulder was a birth mark of a cross, which the faithful deem was placed there by an angel at the time of his birth.

After a somewhat vain and frivolous life, which, however, never found vent in unrestrained waywardness, he was taken prisoner in a local war. The captivity which followed, and a prolonged illness, tempered and subdued his spirit to a better mood, and it was then that his future vocation was revealed to him in a dream. Thus divinely enlightened and changed to a better self, he began to carry out his formed plan of a more worthy and christian life. His father, on this account, endeavored to have him adjudged insane. He on his part, gladly gave up all claim to the paternal inheritance, and, retiring to the convent of Portiúncula, near Assisi, laid the foundations for his great order, which, approved by the Pope in 1209, 1210, and 1221, in a few years numbered many thousands of members.

In 1219, Francis, accompanied by Blessed Illuminatús of Reate, and other companions from Ancona, set sail for Egypt and there joined, as missionaries, the Sixth Crusade, which was then besieging Babylon on the Nile, the modern Grand Cairo. Fearless in the cause of Christ, Francis passed into the Saracen camp to preach the gospel to the heathen his brethren were fighting; and the Sultan, admiring his intrepid zeal, would not allow him to be injured. Many miracles are recorded as having been worked by and through him. But by far the most remarkable was the reception, while in a state of ecstasy, through the medium of an angel, of the stigmata of Jesus, — the sacred wounds of the nails and spear. These are painted, it will be remembered, upon the mortuary chapel at San Luis Rey. Though St. Francis was in feeble health after he returned from Egypt, he still kept on preaching until his death on October 4, 1226. Two years later, 1228, he was canonized by Pope Gregory IX. His festival is celebrated October 4.

The 16th of April is the day of the profession of St. Francis; so on that day all members of the order renew their vows. It is also a day celebrated in the Franciscan Order, in honor of the Holy Archangel San Rafael, as the patron of travellers, though his principal day is October 24.

Santa Clara was a native of the same town as St. Francis. She was born in 1193, of noble parents, and lived the ordinary frivolous life of her class, until, when about 19 years old, she was converted by the example and preaching of St. Francis. Retiring at once to the convent of Portiúncula, whither her example drew both her mother and her sister, she soon became as famous for her austerity and piety as before she had been for her wit and beauty. In conjunction with her saintly neighbor, she founded the second order of St. Francis, namely a sisterhood bearing her name, and often known as "The Poor Clares." She died in 1253 and was canonized in 1255. Her day is the 12th of August.

The first order of St. Francis is that to which all the Franciscan priests belong. They take the vow of perpetual chastity, poverty, and obedience, and are banded together in brotherhoods.

The second order is that of St. Clare (Santa Clara) and is of women who take the same vows as the men, and are banded together in sisterhoods.

The third order is of laymen, living in the world and carrying on their regular work, but who have taken the same vows as the priests.

Neustra Señora de la Soledad — Our Lady of Solitude — is the name given to the Holy Virgin in her period of solitude. While Christ was going through the stages of the Passion she was "Our Lady of Sorrows" — Dolores — but during the three days from Friday until the Sunday morning of the resurrection, when he arose from the dead, she was in "loneliness," and so she became Our Lady of Solitude. La Soledad Mission is named for her, and her day, under this special title, is commemorated in some places on Good Friday in Holy Week, and in others on Holy Saturday of the same week.

Roman Catholics also have Holy Days dedicated to personages and mysteries, and also to sacred objects as well as to saints. Among such festivals, as has been shown, are the days of the Holy Archangels Gabriel, Miguel (Michael) and Rafael. Another sacred day is that of December 8, dedicated to the holy mystery of the Immaculate Conception — La Purísima Concepción — and a Mission bearing this name was established in the California chain.

Belonging to this same class are the two festivals in honor of the Santa Cruz — the Holy Cross — of Christ, for which another Mission was named. One of these festivals, the " Invention," or the finding of the Cross by the Empress Sant Helena, mother of Constantine the Great, at Jerusalem, in the year 326, occurs on May 3, and the other, that of the " Exaltation " of the Holy Cross, on September 14.

San Juan Bautista — St. John Baptist — scarcely needs any comment, his history in the New Testament being so well known. His day is June 24.

San Fernando, Rey de Espagna, — St. Ferdinand was the third king of Spain of that name. He reigned from 1217 to 1252, and under his reign the crowns of Castile and Leon were united. He was canonized in 1671 by Pope Clement X. His day is May 30.

Another king is Saint Louis IX of France, whose name, San Luis Rey, is given to the noble pile second in the Mission chain. San Luis reigned from 1226 to 1270, and earned his reputation for piety both at home and abroad in the Crusades. He was canonized by Pope Boniface VIII, in 1297, in the reign of his grandson, Philip the Fair. His day is August 25.

24

CHAPTER XXXIV

THE PIOUS FUND OF CALIFORNIA

IT is singular how hidden things come to light. Nothing more clearly exemplifies this than the history of the " Pious Fund " of California. The personage who brought the history of this fund to light is John T. Doyle, a fine old American gentleman, now residing at Menlo Park, Cal. It was a personal joy when he kindly consented to outline the story of the original founding of the fund; its various vicissitudes up to its confiscation by Santa Anna, the Mexican dictator; the modern discovery of the claim the Catholic Church of California had upon it; the presentation of that claim; the various obstacles met in furthering it; the award by Sir Edward Thornton, the umpire appointed to decide the case; the payment of over $900,000 by Mexico in consequence of that award. Then the failure of Mexico to pay the annual instalments of interest implied in that award; the various efforts made to secure diplomatic action upon it in Mexico by our State department; the final submission of the case to the Hague tribunal through the efforts of Secretary John Hay; and the final award. Here, indeed, was history at first hand.

Though I should much like to present the whole story *in extenso* the limits of this book will prevent more than a brief synopsis.

That such a fund existed was well known generally to many old Californians in the early days of American occupation of the Golden State, and in 1851 the State Senate endeavored to find out something definite about it.

These legislators, however, were ignorant of the exist-

PLATE LXIII

a. ASPERGER OF MOORISH DESIGN

c. ASPERGER AT SAN JUAN BAUTISTA

b. ASPERGER AT MONTEREY

d. FONT AT SAN LUIS OBISPO

ence of Palou's and Gigedo's and Ramirez's reports, and of the letters and reports of Galvez, all of which later research has made familiar to all students. The result of their ignorance was a discouraging report, though there seemed to be no doubt as to the existence of the fund.

Late in 1853 Mr. Doyle was associated with Hon. Eugene Casserly in prosecuting before the U. S. Land Commission a petition of the Rt. Rev. Joseph A. Alemany, Bishop of Monterey, for the confirmation of the title of the Catholic Church of California to the Church edifices, cemeteries, Mission buildings, orchards, vineyards, etc., of the old Missions. Now I let Mr. Doyle tell his own story:

" One day he brought to me a small package of papers he had found in one of the church's safes, saying that they appeared to relate to the missing Pious Fund. He desired me to look them over carefully and see if there was any justification or basis for a claim against the United States for the recovery of any of that fund.

" The papers turned out to be correspondence in a cramped, crabbed hand on flimsy paper and considerably dilapidated, being fastened together, woman fashion, with a needle and thread. On careful examination I found them to be correspondence between Don Pedro Ramirez, the commissioner who held the funds in trust at the time they were confiscated by the government. He was evidently a conservative and business-like man, for he had made out a complete list of all the property and funds transferred, and had required a receipt from the government official to whom he relinquished his charge. These papers led me to give the Bishop my opinion that there was no claim against the United States, but that there might be some against Mexico.

" The matter then dropped. In 1857, in April, I had purchased my steamer ticket for New York. I was going back East, indeed had about made up my mind to leave California for good, when the Archbishop, in company with Bishop Amat, called on me and asked if I would undertake the case against the Mexican government.

" I consulted with my partner, Eugene Casserly, and gave

him an outline of the case and said I was willing if he was, and that if, after due consideration, he thought it well to go ahead, he might make the suggested contract and sign my name to it.

"This was eventually done. In the meantime I went East and remained there five years. As soon as I learned of the signing of the contract I began to read everything on Mexican Mission history I could lay my hand on in order to find out what I could as to the founding of the fund, what it originally consisted of, how it was used, when and how it was diverted, etc., and it was astonishing what I did find. A little here, and little there, — one thing suggesting another, one clue leading to a further and more important one, I soon gathered a good deal.

"Once on the right track I followed its history until I had it clear enough to lay before any responsible tribunal. I found that it was owing to the endeavors of the Jesuit padres Kino and Salvatierra, to establish missions in Lower California that the fund was contributed by the faithful. By means of this fund the missions were established and largely supported. When, after many years of administration the Jesuits were inhumanly expelled from all the provinces of Spain, the missions in Lower California were placed under the control of the Franciscans, and the Spanish king's Visitador General, Galvez, arranged with the new president of the missions, Junipero Serra, to establish new missions in Alta or Upper California. For that purpose he drew largely on the Pious Fund. On February 12, 1772, Padre Francisco Palou reported to the Superior of the Convent San Fernando in the city of Mexico, Fray Juan Roman de Mora, the financial status of the Pious Fund as follows:

"Copy of the pious works founded by the different individuals for the purpose of the spiritual conquest of the Californias:

YEAR

1698. Don Juan Caballero founded the first mission, and for this
purpose gave $10,000
1699. the same founded the second 10,000
1700. Don Nicolas Artega founded the third, and furnished the
same amount 10,000
1702. different individuals through Father José Vidal, Jesuit,
the fourth 7,000
1704. the Marquis de Villapuente founded the fifth in the sum of 10,000
1709. the same founded the sixth in 10,000
1713. the same founded the seventh in 10,000

Year

1718. His Excellency, Don Juan Ruiz de Velasco founded the
eighth in $10,000
1719. The Marquis de Villapuente founded the ninth in . . . 10,000
1725. the Jesuit, Father Juan Maria Luyando, founded the
tenth in 10,000
1731. Doña Maria Rosa de la Peña donated to one of the missions
of Villapuente 10,000
1746. the Marquis de Villapuente founded the eleventh in . . 10,000
1747. The Most Excellent Doña Maria de Boya, Duchess of
Gaudia, instituted the missions of California as her
heirs, but they have only received 62,000
Total of donations $179,000

Balances found at the time of the Expulsion of the Jesuits:

In cash found in the Atty Genl's office of California at
the expulsion $92,000.00
Value of merchandise found in the same office 27,255.75
Value of merchandise in warehouse of Loretto 79,377.37½
Total balances $199.733.12½

Loans made by the Attorney General's office of California of the capitals
of said missions as appears by the corresponding instruments —

To the College of San Idlefonso in city of Puebla, at 3½
per cent $22,000
To the College of San Ignacio in the city of Puebla, at 4
per cent 5,000
To the College of San Pedro and San Pablo in the city of
Mexico without int. 29,000
To the College of San Idlefonso in the city of Puebla at 3
per cent 23,000
To the College of San Geronimo in the city of Mexico, at 3
per cent 38,500
To the College of San Idlefonso in the city of Puebla, at 3
per cent 9,000
Total loans $126,600

Recapitulation :

Total of donations $179,000.00
Total of balances on hand 199,033.12½
Total of loans 126,600.00
Grand total $504,633.12½

"This report was made on account of another royal order to
the effect that the Dominicans were to take charge of one-half
of the missions formerly controlled by the Jesuits. Accordingly
the Franciscans and Dominicans made an agreement by which
the latter were to assume charge of the missions of Lower Cali-

fornia, and the Franciscans proceeded to the establishment of new ones in Alta California. The income and product of the Pious Fund was thereafter appropriated to the missions of both orders.

" In 1793, April 12, the great viceroy, Gigedo, reported upon the Funds and pays a high tribute to the fidelity with which the Jesuits administered them. He says : ' After they were managed by outsiders they began to decrease. Viceroy Flores [Gigedo's predecessor] had placed them in the hands of the two magistrates of the royal treasury, but this measure far from producing any good, was fast precipitating the funds to utter ruin, and that they could be saved only by an active, intelligent, and zealous general manager, who should frequently inspect the estates and be capable of developing their resources and disposing at a fair price of the products ; and who also should keep watch over the conduct of the subaltern administrators.' He also reported that : ' The landed properties of the special funds are valued at \$527,500 ; its capitals loaned out on interest amount to \$188,000 ; therefore the total is the large sum of \$715,500, whose yearly interest at the rate of five per cent, should be \$35,575. The missionaries receive every year a little above \$22,000 ; consequently a balance should remain of \$12,000 to \$13,000 to be used for the establishment of new missions, traveling expenses and transportation of the missionaries by land and water.' Gigedo also clearly avows that the Pious Fund was collected by the priests.

" These missions were founded and maintained at the expense of the capitals which the zeal and apostolic labors of the aforementioned fathers of the Society of Jesus had acquired for the purpose of effecting the spiritual conquest of the California Indians. The principal benefactors and founders of these special funds were the Marquis de Villapuente and the Marchioness de las Torres de Rada."

Of the establishment of the California Missions by Serra, all detail may be left out of Mr. Doyle's narrative. The following is his history of the fund.

" After Mexico declared her independence of Spain, the fund was taken in trust by the new government and when in 1836, Sept. 19, it passed an act attaching an endowment of \$6,000 per

PLATE LXIV

c. SAN LUIS OBISPO

b. OUR LADY OF SORROWS, PRESIDIO CHURCH, MONTEREY

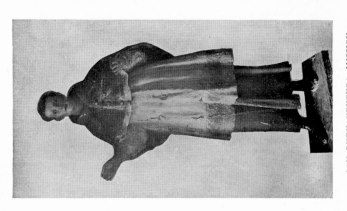

a. SAN BUENAVENTURA, MISSION SAN JOSÉ

year to a new bishopric, which it prayed the Holy Father to establish for Upper and Lower California, it also conceded to the new bishop when appointed, and his successors, the administration and disposal of the Pious Fund. Accordingly García Diego was made bishop and the Fund was administered by him, until Feb. 8, 1842, Santa Anna, then President of the Republic of Mexico, withdrew the management from the bishop, and on Oct. 24 of the same year ordered the property to be sold, the proceeds turned into the public treasury, from which he pledged to pay to the church *annually* the sum of six per cent of the sum so contributed.

" In accordance with this decree the property was sold for a sum approximating two millions of dollars. When, by the treaty of Guadalupe Hidalgo, Upper California became a part of the United States of America the interest on this fund still inhered to the church in Upper California, and, inasmuch as what arrears were due up to the time of that treaty were due to the Catholic Church of California as a Mexican province, and, therefore, not subject to the interference of the United States, after that treaty they were due to the Church of California as a part of the United States and, therefore, were eminently subject to such interference.

" Here you have practically the whole of my case and its argument for the Catholic Church in all the subsequent proceedings.

" In 1859 I presented the matter to the Hon. Lewis Cass, then Secretary of State, requesting the interposition of the United States to aid my clients in obtaining justice from Mexico, and as the object was rather to put the claim on file in the department than the expectation of any immediate result, I made my claim in very general terms, not undertaking to define what specific redress was asked for. Mr. Cass rather thought the claim released by the treaty of Guadalupe Hidalgo, and I promised to submit to him at a future time an argument to show that was not so. Thus the case stood open until 1870. In the meantime I continued to read every Mexican publication that I could obtain until I had at last found out pretty much all about the Pious Fund, and was enabled to write its history as fully as needed for the instruction of any tribunal that might be called on to pass on our claim.

In 1863 circumstances again called me to California where I resumed practice. In 1868 Mr. Casserly was elected to the Senate and took his seat in that body March 4th, 1869. Down to that time I had been accustomed at the close of each session to look through the treaties published with the acts of Congress for any possible claims convention with Mexico, but on the election of my associate to the Senate my vigilance relaxed, and the convention of 1868 was concluded and commissioners under it were appointed without my knowledge. My associate, however, was retained in some cases before the commission, and in them engaged the assistance of Mr. Nathaniel Wilson, then recently admitted to the bar in Washington. He took no action in the Pious Fund case, for which reason I am led to believe that he had forgotten all about our retainer in it.

"And now here occurs a remarkable event. On Sunday, March 27, 1870, I picked up a New York paper and accidentally saw a paragraph to the effect that Wednesday, March 30, would be the last day that claims could be presented before the American and Mexican Commission then sitting in Washington. It gave me quite a shock! What commission? I did not even know that a commission had been appointed. I was here at Menlo Park and could get no conveyance to take me to San Francisco, so had to wait impatiently until Monday. As soon as I arrived I hunted up a copy of the Convention of July 4, 1868, between the two governments, and saw that, according to its terms, a demand for the restoration of the fund as a whole could never be maintained. The claim must be framed otherwise. Both my clients were away in Europe; there was no one to consult with on this new phase of the case, and I had to decide my course on my own responsibility.

"Many complications arose from my associate in Washington, — who had not given an iota of the time to the study of the case that I had, — altering one of the chief points, indeed the main one, of my pleading not only without consulting, but actually without apprising me. But even with these complications the cause was so clear that when it finally came to the umpire — owing to the differences in opinion of the commissioners — he awarded us finally $904,070 in Mexican gold dollars. This sum was duly paid by Mexico in accordance with the terms of the convention. This may be called the end of the first battle.

"In 1882, 1883 and 1884 Archbishop Alemany informed me that, while this award had been paid, Mexico had avoided the payment of any further annual interest, which this first award clearly implied as a perpetual charge. He asked me to undertake the case again and press it to a conclusion, but owing to a variety of causes practically over twenty years elapsed and nothing was done except in a diplomatic way to seek the enforcement of payment, and only slight progress was made; enough, however, to keep the question alive between the two countries. Then came the foundation of the Hague tribunal, and here, at once, I saw a chance for its final adjudication. I proposed to the Archbishop that we submit the case to that tribunal. He agreed. I wrote to Secretary Hay, and it must be confessed that his exceeding cleverness in presenting the matter won us that long deferred interest. He got the Mexican government to agree to a submission of the case and that neither Mexicans nor Americans should be on the jury. That one clause satisfied me that we should win. I was absolutely certain that no jury of impartial outsiders but would decide in our favor.

"As you know, the case was formally presented. The arbitrators named by the United States were Sir Edward Fry of England and Professor F. de Martens of Russia. Those nominated by Mexico were Messrs. J. M. C. Asser and F. de Savornin Lohman, both of Holland, and these gentlemen promptly agreed on Professor Henry Matzen of Denmark as their President and Umpire. The case on the part of Mexico was managed by Señor Don Emilio Pardo, an eminent jurisconsult of the Mexican capital, who was accredited to Her Majesty the Queen of Holland as Minister Plenipotentiary of his country. He associated with himself as counsel Messrs. Beerwaert and Delacroix, local counsel of distinction, and Archbishop Riordan retained Mr. Descamps, also of the local bar.

"The court with little delay, and unanimously, decided that the whole controversy was controlled by the former decision, under the governing principle of *res judica*, and consequently awarded us our whole demand of $1,420,682.67, being thirty-three annual instalments of interest of $43,050.99 then in arrear, and adjudged that the last named amount be paid to us annually thereafter in perpetuity."

In a letter received from the Coadjutor Archbishop of San Francisco, George Montgomery, he reports that the annuity has thus far been paid regularly. " This payment, as the others were, is made to the Roman Catholic Archbishop of San Francisco, acting for the other bishops, by power of attorney. The same use is made of these moneys as of the others, in accordance with the purposes for which the original donors made the bequests."

CHAPTER XXXV

THE CAMINO REAL

IT is generally taken for granted that the original plan of Padre Serra was to establish a chain of Missions in California a day's journey apart. The number of the Indians and their location seemed peculiarly adapted to this plan. In travelling to and fro, prior to, and during their establishment, a trail, and eventually a road, would necessarily be made. It is claimed by Don Antonio Coronel that this road or highway became the " recognized highway of official travel," and that it commenced in Guatemala and ended first in Monterey; then, as the Missions reached San Francisco and Sonoma, it was extended thither. He says: " it was called either the *Camino del Rey* or the *Camino Real* in our Spanish," which being interpreted is " the King's Highway." It was never much of a road from the road-maker's standpoint, but to the historian, the romancer, the artist, it is one of the most fascinating highways in the world. It did not always stick exactly to the same narrow boundaries; when a tree fell across it, a slight detour was made; when rain fell and made a large puddle it branched off to right or left. Occasionally some one discovered a " short cut," and then a new road took the place of the old; but, in the main, it remained a king's highway, connecting the Missions one with another, and linking together the little picturesque settlements of Spanish and Indians that clustered around them.

When the Americans came it was necessarily their main line of travel; and though slight changes have been made in it by the rectangular system of denoting farm and other boundaries, here and there compelling it to a more strait and rigid plan, it is still the Camino Real of the Mission days.

And what a history it has had. Though less than a century and a half old, what changes it has seen. First the crude trail, doubtless, of the original aborigines, who, in their skin costumes, with their simple gifts slung by means of rawhide bands from their foreheads went on errands of friendship to neighboring rancherías. Now and again a band of deer or antelope would course upon it, having discovered that they were in danger from hunters. Occasionally a mountain lion, a black bear, or a grizzly, and often a coyote, a fox, a badger, or that beautifully furred small animal with the name that suggests everything but agreeableness in its odor, would stroll leisurely on this man-made path, each and all sniffing significantly at the footprints of the upright animal whose " scent " so often meant danger to them.

Then came the padres, with their military escort. Aye, but prior to that, perhaps, in spots, this that was ultimately to be the Camino Real had felt the pressure of the feet of Cabrillo or Viscaino or Drake or Cavendish, — so that these new feet were not the first of white men to walk upon its length. But they soon became the most familiar. Serra, Crespí, Portolá, Fages, Rivera, — what a list of names of the earliest travellers, the real explorers who gave our California to the world.

Then some of those earlier scenes; how they come back. After San Diego and San Carlos and San Antonio had been established, and Fages had been appointed governor, and his autocratic conduct had led to two desertions from the San Diego garrison, one of ten, the other of five men, this road saw Fages follow the five, and saw them intrenched, and heard their declaration that they would never be taken back alive. What did that mean? Had tyranny already begun in this to-be-land-of-the-free? Then it saw

PLATE LXV

a. REAR OF SAN GABRIEL MISSION

b. CORRIDORS AT SAN FERNANDO

the good Father Dumetz come sadly yet eagerly along, pleading with both governor and deserters that there be no bloodshed, and finally prevailing upon the five to return, after Fages had promised not to punish them.

From the beginning of its real history, over this King's Highway, again and again, back and forth, happily or wearily, according as his extensive plans prospered or dragged, walked the sainted Serra. Here he sang aloud; there he sank upon his knees in prayer; yonder he wept in anguish as the news of some delay in his beloved work, or some Indian outburst reached him.

This road saw the coming of the colonists from Mexico; heard their openly expressed hopes, fears, expectations. As the years rolled on it heard the squeak and rattle of the lumbering carreta as elderly señoras rode, accompanied by gay *caballeros* clad in zarape and sombrero, riding on saddles of price, carved in exquisite design and skilfully inlaid with silver. And the señoritas, did they stay at home? No! the historic road saw them ride also, always, of course, accompanied by their duennas, but by no means the less happy and joyous, though perhaps somewhat less exuberant.

Indeed to know the history of the Camino Real is to know the history of the California of those days. Don Antonio Coronel might well say he had a separate legend of this highway for every day in the year.

For several years Augustus Wey (Miss Picher of Pasadena) has agitated the rehabilitation of the Camino Real. With far-sighted wisdom she saw that it was not only good from the historic and picturesque standpoint, but good from the business standpoint. The thousands of visitors that come to California annually are ready to be interested in everything that really appeals to their intelligent sympathies; and the more foci of interests there are, the more they enjoy their visits to the State. Later, Charles F. Lummis, in "Out West," intelligently presenting the claims of the Missions, saw that this was an allied project, and he has earnestly and consistently worked for it ever since. At last the automobilists and politicians were interested, and then the matter was more widely agitated. It became a State affair. An association was effected in 1904, with efficient officers and a State secretary, to push the organizing of local branches of the State Camino Real Association, so that a definite plan could be presented to the legislature. This was done; the act passed, and it would have become law had the funds in the State treasury justified the expenditure called for.

The State and local organizations are still in existence, and are working more or less energetically, so that it is reasonable to hope that ultimately its aims will be crowned with complete success, to the honor, comfort, and pleasure both of the citizens of the State and its visitors.

CHAPTER XXXVI

THE PRESERVATION OF THE MISSIONS

THERE is a vast difference between " restoration " and " preservation " of architectural landmarks. I do not know whether William Morris ever used the word " accursed " when speaking of restorations. He certainly felt it. It is not given to the builders of one generation to " restore " the architecture of another generation. The conditions, the feeling, the atmosphere (mental, not physical) are changed. Buildings that come down to us out of the past, if ever worth anything, are worth preserving, — keeping, just as they are, as a valuable heirloom *that is not ours* except to look at, use, and pass on to our posterity. Our science is daily broadening. The theory of evolution has materially enlarged our horizon. It opened a new door, leading into vast new fields for thought; and in one of these fields we found that all work that man has done helps the workers of to-day better to understand their own work. Therefore we have awakened senses as to our duty to the historic remains of the past and the rights and claims of those who will come after us to them.

The first serious attempt to do anything towards the preservation of the California Missions was made by Miss Tessa L. Kelso, the librarian of the Los Angeles City Library, in about 1888. She organized an " Association for the Preservation of the Missions," and by stereopticon exhibitions showing the direful condition of the buildings, excursions to them, exhibitions of photographs at the library and elsewhere, the writing of articles, etc., paved the way for the later more successful work of the Landmarks Club. Nearly $100 was handed over to the younger by the older association.

In December, 1895, Charles F. Lummis, the editor of "The Land of Sunshine" (now "Out West"), published, in his magazine, a forceful appeal for the preservation of the Missions. Among other things, he said:

"There are in this State twenty-one of the old Spanish Missions, besides their several branch chapels. Seven missions and a few chapels are in Southern California; and these are not only the oldest, but historically and architecturally the most interesting. A few are re-occupied and utilized for places of worship. The others have been of necessity practically abandoned since the secularization. They are not vital to the Catholic church, now; but they are everything to us, whether we have souls or pockets. They are all falling to decay; partly by age, partly through vandalism and neglect. When the roof goes, our swift winter rains do the rest. In ten years from now — unless our intelligence shall awaken at once — there will remain of these noble piles nothing but a few indeterminable heaps of adobe.

"Now there is not in the civilized world another country so barbarous that this would be permitted. In poor old Spain the very stables of these deserted churches would be scrupulously preserved. In despised Italy they would be guarded as we guard our fortunes. In hateful England, heaven pity the vandal that should move one stone from another in them. In immoral France, there is at least morality enough to hold sacred the artistic and the venerable. It is only in the Only Country in the World that such precious things are despised and neglected and left to be looted by the storm and the tourist.

"This is a new community, and many things are thus far forgiven its youth; but there will never be pardon if we let this sin go further. We shall deserve and shall have the contempt of all thoughtful people if we suffer our noble missions to fall."

In the following January it was announced that the Landmarks Club was incorporated, and that, briefly stated, its objects were:

"The immediate and permanent preservation from decay and vandalism, of the venerable Missions of Southern California; the safeguard and conservation of any other historic monuments, relics, or landmarks in this section; and a general promotion of proper care of all such matters. It will be a function of the club to secure a permanent fund to be applied exclusively to these objects."

The president of the club is Charles F. Lummis; vice-president, Margaret Collier Graham; secretary, Arthur B. Benton, 114 N. Spring St., Los Angeles; treasurer, J. G. Mossin; corresponding secretary, Mrs. M. E. Stilson, 812 Kensington Rd., Los Angeles. The annual membership fee is $1.00.

In February it was announced that a lease had been secured of San Juan Capistrano, and work undertaken under the direction of Mr. R. Egan, who for many years had made many personal efforts towards its preservation. "The lease covers all the buildings which are in need of care, with the necessary ground and rights of way, and a preference to the club as purchaser in case the property should ever be for sale."

In November the club reported that it had replaced the broken roof of sycamore poles on the old adobe church, built by Serra, at San Juan Capistrano, with Oregon pine and the original tiles, so that it is now likely to be saved for many years. Asphaltum was also placed on the roof of the four hundred feet of cloisters. Excellent work had also been done on the kitchen, — its stone vault secured with iron tie rods, and re-roofed. "Through it was the main entrance to the *patio*, or inner court. This was broken down, but has been substantially repaired."

Further work has been done, as funds have come in, and now San Juan is reasonably well preserved against the ravages of the weather.

San Fernando was next attacked; and on September 9, 1897, the Landmarks Club and its friends enjoyed an excursion thither, not only to commemorate the centennial of the founding of the Mission, but also to personally inspect the method followed by the club in restoring these historic memorials; and its president, writing afterwards, called attention to an important fact. He said:

"One of the features of the outing (and significant as showing what sort of a valley the Franciscan frailes picked out a hundred years ago) was the fact that many of the excursionists sat down to lunch on the enormous pile of sacked wheat, covered with straw, which is now in front of the Mission — a pile worth $57,000, from the harvest of the Porter Land and Water Co. It is not everywhere that one finds such a table."

In November a temporary and protecting shake roof was placed over the adobe church, but a severe storm wrecked it, and it had to be replaced. The exterior of the old monastery has been put in excellent condition, and further work is being projected.

In 1899 brick foundations were put under some of the ruined walls at San Diego, and cement cappings on the wasting ones. About $500 was expended; and it is safe to say that had not this been done, nothing but a pile of melting adobe would now remain of this, the most interesting, historically, of all the Missions, on account of its priority.

At San Luis Rey the club has given some aid to Father O'Keefe in his heroic efforts.

At Pala the chapel, sacristy, and priest's room have been re-roofed, the rafters being pine poles hauled from the slopes and summit of Mount Palomar. Of the tiles used, eight hundred were donated by two ladies of the Agua Tibia Ranch, which once protected the buildings at San Luis Rey, and which were hauled away by the Indian founder of the ranch, Manuel Cota, some sixty years before, when the secularization decree led to the abandonment

PLATE LXVI

b. IN THE GARDEN OF THE LOS ANGELES CHAPEL

a. SIDE OF SAN LUIS REY MISSION

of that glorious Mission. Others were purchased from scattered ranches, whither they were brought at the same time of spoliation.

The interior of the chapel was also " cleaned and rehabilitated," to use the words of the president of the Landmarks Club, " with great care not to disturb any of the old Indian frescos."

It was, therefore, all the more unfortunate that an alien and unsympathetic priest should not have been warned that any attempt to interfere with them on his part would be resented. Knowing nothing of their history, he presumptuously swept them out of existence, without consulting any one, by covering them with whitewash.

It should not be forgotten that there are no salaries in the Landmarks Club. All the work is done for love, and to preserve these memorials for the future. While there may be criticism as to the work done, and the methods followed, — such criticism is to be expected in the very nature of things, — there can be no question as to the great value of the work accomplished as a whole; and Mr. Lummis is deserving of, and should receive, the grateful thanks of the whole nation for the work that has been accomplished under his direction.

In the fall of 1902 the California Historical Landmarks League was organized in San Francisco with the following officers: president, Joseph R. Knowland; vice-presidents, S. W. Holladay, Mrs. Geo. Law Smith; corresponding secretary, Mrs. Laura Bride Powers, 421 Larkin St., San Francisco; assistant secretary, Mrs. J. J. Donnelly; financial secretary, James A. Devoto; treasurer, Henry S. Martin.

The " Native Sons of the Golden West " contributed $1100 to the treasury of the new organization, and the " Native Daughters of the Golden West " have also given material aid. Mr. W. R. Hearst, of the San Francisco " Examiner," has thrown the influence of his paper towards the movement, and as a result of these united efforts the old Mission building of San Francisco Solano, at Sonoma, has been purchased, and work has already been commenced for the preservation of what remains at San Antonio de Padua.

CHAPTER XXXVII

HOW TO REACH THE MISSIONS

SAN DIEGO. From Los Angeles to San Diego, Santa Fé Railway, 126 miles, fare $3.85; round trip $6.00, good four days, or $7.50, good 30 days, with stop-over privileges, which allows a visit to San Luis Rey and Pala (via Oceanside) and San Juan Capistrano. Or steamship, $3.00 and $2.25; round trip, first class, $5.25. The Mission is six miles from San Diego, and a carriage must be taken all the way, or the electric car to the bluff, fare five cents; thence by Bluff Road, on burro, two miles, fare fifty cents. The better way is to drive by Old Town and return by the Bluff Road.

SAN LUIS REY. From Los Angeles to Oceanside, Santa Fé Railway, 85 miles, fare $3.15; round trip, Saturday to Monday, $4.50. Take carriage from livery, or walk to Mission, 4 miles. The trip to Pala may be taken at the same time, though there are no sleeping accommodations to be had at Pala. Meals may be had at one or two of the Indian houses, as a rule.

SAN JUAN CAPISTRANO. From Los Angeles to Capistrano, Santa Fé Railway, 58 miles, fare $1.80. The Mission is close to the station. Hotel accommodations are poor.

SAN GABRIEL. From Los Angeles to San Gabriel, Southern Pacific Railway, 8 miles, fare 25 cents. Or electric car from Los Angeles, 25 cents.

SAN FERNANDO. From Los Angeles to San Fernando, Southern Pacific Railway, 22 miles, fare 65 cents. Thence by carriage or on foot or horseback to the Mission, 1½ miles. Livery and hotel at San Fernando.

SAN BUENAVENTURA. From Los Angeles to San Buenaventura, Southern Pacific Railway, 83 miles, fare $2.50. Or steamship, $2.35, special, Saturday to Monday, $3.00 round trip. Electric cars from Southern Pacific Station pass the Mission.

SANTA BARBARA. From Los Angeles to Santa Barbara, Southern Pacific Railway, fare $3.35, special round trip, Saturday to Monday, $3.50. From San Francisco to Santa Barbara, 370 miles, Southern Pacific Railway, fare $13.40 and $11.65. Street car passes the Mission.

SANTA INÉS. This is not on the line of any railway. It can be reached from Santa Barbara, 25 miles, by carriage, or from Los Olivos, four miles, by stage. Los Olivos is on the line of the Pacific Coast Railway. To reach it take Southern Pacific Railway to San Luis Obispo, change cars. It is then 66 miles to Los Olivos, fare $3.00. The better way is to go by Southern Pacific to Lompoc, take carriage and visit the site of Old La Purísima, then Purísima, then drive to Santa Inés and return. With a good team this can be done in a day. Distance 25 miles.

LA PURÍSIMA CONCEPCIÓN. Go to Lompoc on the coast line of the Southern Pacific either from Los Angeles (187 miles, $7.05) or San Francisco (313 miles, $10.70). Carriage from livery to the ruins of Old Purísima, thence to the later one, five miles.

SAN LUIS OBISPO. Southern Pacific Railway from either Los Angeles (230 miles, $9.10) or San Francisco (253 miles, $7.65), or steamship to Port Hartford and the Pacific Coast Railway, 211 miles, $6.50. The Mission is in the town.

SAN MIGUEL. The Mission is but a few rods from the Southern Pacific Station, reached either from Los Angeles (273 miles, $10.85) or San Francisco (208 miles, $5.95). By far the better way, however, is to go to Paso Robles, where one can bathe in the hot springs so noted even in Indian days, while enjoying the hospitalities of one of the best hotels on the Pacific Coast. Carriages may be secured from one of the livery stables. From here visit Santa Isabel Ranch and Hot Springs (which used to belong to San Miguel), then drive 16 miles to San Miguel. On account of the completeness of its interior decorations, this is, in many respects, especially to the student, the most interesting Mission of the whole chain.

SAN ANTONIO DE PADUA. It is a twenty-mile stage ride from King's City, on the line of the Southern Pacific (216 miles from Los Angeles, $12.00) to Jolon (fare $2.00), the quaintest little village now remaining in California, which is practically the gateway to Mission San Antonio de Padua. At Jolon one secures a team, and, after a six-mile drive through a beautiful park, dotted on every hand with majestic live oaks, — ancient monarchs that have accumulated moss and majesty with their years, — the ruins of the old Mission come into view. From San Francisco to King's City is 164 miles, fare $4.65.

LA SOLEDAD. The Mission is four miles from the town of Soledad on the Southern Pacific Railway. From Los Angeles, 337 miles, fare $12.00. From San Francisco, 144 miles, fare $4.50. Round trip, six months' limit, $8.00. Livery from Soledad to the Mission.

SAN JUAN BAUTISTA is six miles from Sargent's Station on the Southern Pacific. Two stages run daily, fare $1.00 for the round trip. Visitors may be accommodated at the Plaza Hotel, conducted by William Haydon. From Los Angeles to Sargent's, 394 miles, fare $14.45. From San Francisco 87 miles, fare $2.35.

SAN CARLOS CARMELO, MONTEREY. The old presidio church is in the town of Monterey, and reached by car-line from Hotel del Monte or the town. San Carlos Carmelo is about six miles from Monterey, and must be reached on horseback or by carriage. By far the best way is to stop at either Hotel del Monte or Hotel Carmelo, Pacific Grove, and then on taking the seventeen-mile drive, make the side trip to San Carlos. To Monterey from San Francisco, on Southern Pacific Railway, is 126 miles, fare $3.00. Friday to Tuesday excursion, round trip, $4.50. From Los Angeles to Monterey, Southern Pacific Railway, 398 miles, fare $14.25.

SANTA CRUZ. It is well to go from San Francisco on the narrow gauge, 80 miles, Southern Pacific, and return on the broad gauge, 121 miles. Fare on either line $3.80. On the narrow gauge are the Big Trees, at which an interesting stop over can be enjoyed.

SANTA CLARA. While there is a city of Santa Clara it is better to go to San José (the first town established in California), and stay at Hotel Vendome, and then drive or go by electric car, down the old Alameda to Santa Clara Mission, $3\frac{1}{2}$ miles.

MISSION SAN JOSÉ. So called to distinguish it from the city of San José. By Southern Pacific Railway from San Francisco to Irvington, 34 miles, fare 85 cents. Or from the city of San José, 14 miles by Southern Pacific, or a pleasant carriage drive. From Irvington to the Mission three miles, stage twice daily, fare 25 cents.

SAN FRANCISCO DE ASÍS. Is on Sixteenth and Dolores St., three miles from Palace Hotel. Take Valencia or Howard St. electric cars.

SAN RAFAEL. There is nothing left at San Rafael of the old Mission. The town is reached by North Pacific Coast Railway, 18 miles, or California Northwestern, 15 miles, fare 35 cents.

SAN FRANCISCO SOLANO. In the town of Sonoma. Reached by North Pacific Coast Railway, 43 miles, fare $1.00.